# THE NEXT STEP

## Marcelo Cezar

Dictated by the Spirit
### Marco Aurélio

Translated to English by:
Rodolfo Avedaño
Lima, Peru, October 2023

Original title in Portuguese:
"O Próximo Passo"

© Marcelo Cezar, 2021

Translated to English from the 2nd Portuguese Edition.

World Spiritist Institute
Houston, Texas, USA
E-mail: contact@worldspiritistinstitute.org

# About the Author

Born in the city of São Paulo, Marcelo Cezar published his first novel in the late 1990s. Years later, he re-launched "Life always wins" in a revised and expanded version.

In an interview with the newspaper Folha de S. Paulo, the author says: "It's not like that, from one day to the next, that you start publishing books and get on the bestseller list. The process began in the 1980s. Then, more than twenty years later, the first book came out. To see how hard the training was and still is. Love is not enough; you have to have discipline to write".

His novel "Thirteen Souls", related to the 1974 Joelma Building fire, became a best-seller and surpassed the mark of one hundred thousand copies sold.

Through his work, Marcelo Cezar spreads the ideas of Allan Kardec and Louise L. Hay, one of his main mentors. It was with her that Marcelo Cezar learned the basics of spirituality, including love and respect for oneself and, consequently, for the people around him. His novels seek to portray precisely this: "when we learn to love and accept ourselves, we are able to understand and accept others. This is how respect for differences is generated".

In January 2014, the book "Love is for the Strong", one of the successes of the writer's career, with more than 350 thousand copies sold and 20 weeks on the bestseller lists, was mentioned in the TV Globo soap opera Amor à Vida. In an interview with Publishnews, the author of the novel, Walcyr Carrasco, says that he personally chooses books that fit the context of the plot.

In 2018, after eighteen years at Editora Vida & Consciência, Marcelo Cezar published the novel "Ajuste de Cuentas", under the Academia imprint of Editora Planeta. In 2020, the author signed a partnership with Editora Boa Nova to launch his novels and relaunch out-of-print works.

He participates in many events throughout the country, promoting his works in book fairs, talk shows, among others. In 2007, he was invited by the then Livraria Siciliano to sponsor its shop in the Metrópole Shopping Mall, located in the city of São Bernardo do Campo. With the current mark of two million two hundred thousand copies sold, Marcelo Cezar is the author of more than 20 books and admits that he has a lot to study and write about these topics.

The books are supposed to be inspired by the spirit Marcos Aurélio[1]

---

[1] Source: Wikipedia, la enciclopedia libre.
https://marcelocezar.com.br/o-autor/

# Prologue

The evening began to bid farewell to the astral colony. The sun coloured the sky, forming a rare beautiful orange canvas. A pretty young woman, with silky brown hair, the ends of which swayed gently over her shoulders, smiled for the first time in years. Her greenish eyes gazed at the horizon, and she thanked the Creator for being alive and filled with the desire to start anew. Immediately, she felt a little flutter in her stomach.

Recommend? she asked herself, in an almost inaudible voice. Am I ready?

She continued walking. She stopped near a beautiful flower garden and saw some benches. She decided to sit down, because she still felt tired. She settled her slender body on the wooden bench, closed her eyes, and breathed in the scent of the flowers. In front of her was a fountain carved in marble, from whose half-open lips little angels were pouring crystal clear, energizing water.

The young woman stretched, raising her hands in the air and yawned. She stood up, walked slowly to the fountain and bent down until her hands touched the clear, cool water. She pressed her hands together, forming a shell. She brought the crystalline liquid to her lips and savoured with pleasure.

She wiped her lips with the back of her hands. She closed her eyes again and smiled.

– How blessed to be alive! she exclaimed.

– Talking to yourself? a familiar voice asked, behind her.

– The young woman turned his face and broke into a wide smile.

– Lola!

– How are you?

– Very well! he replied with a smile. The water is delicious. don't you want to try?

Lola was a spirit whose luminosity made her even more beautiful. She had an angelic face, but her green, crystalline eyes conveyed impressive strength. She approached the fountain, took some fresh water and drank

– Mmm. I agree with you. It's really good.

– I was tired of staying in the room. One of the nurses let me walk to the garden.

– That's good. Your spirit needs movement. It's been so long.

– The treatment has been helping me a lot to remember my last life on Earth. I've started to see everything more clearly.

– Are you sure?

– Yes, she replied, determined. I found out who killed me.

– Really? You were killed?

– Yes, Lola. It's difficult to forgive someone who took away your physical life, but in the face of eternity and understanding the cycle of reincarnation, I realize it was what had to happen.

– You attracted the kind of death that was most aligned with your way of being. You allowed yourself to be suffocated by the negativity of others. You didn't listen to yourself.

– I know that. I was reckless, had a fiery temper. I've always been very manipulative and controlling. I was nervous and couldn't stand being contradicted. I never wanted to see the truth.

– Getting caught in an illusion and not wanting to see can lead to eye problems. It's better to learn not to fear what we see, even if it might hurt us.

– My eyes have been a bit cloudy – she put her hand to her mouth and asked, bewildered, Am I going to return blind?

– No. Your perispirit didn't get to the point of impairing your vision. Maybe you'll be born with a little issue, a small remnant that your spirit needs to expel.

– What else can you tell me?

– I believe you have the means to see him again. The young woman felt another flutter in her stomach.

– Meet him? Why?

– You yourself said you understood everything that happened to you in your last existence. You even stated that it was tough, but you forgave. Are you sure you really know how everything happened? Did you see the facts with the eyes of your soul?

– Affirmative – she nodded. – The technicians from the Reincarnation Department showed me everything I asked to see. No detail was missing.

– Then I don't see a reason to avoid meeting him again.

– I know what happened, I'm aware, and I've forgiven everyone. So, I ask you: meet him for what?

Lola smiled and accompanied her back to the bench. They sat down. She took the young woman's hands and looked into her eyes.

– I know it would be too much to ask for you to find it again at this time. I also know that you spent many years in the nether regions accusing each other. The dark period has passed, and both were granted the right to return to the planet.

– Are we going back together? asked the young woman, surprised.

– He is getting ready. He is set to be reborn next year.

The young woman opened and closed her mouth. Then she nibbled her lips, thoughtful. She inquired, curious:

– And the others?

– Some have already reincarnated. Others will do so at an opportune moment. What matters is that you will be able to return; however, given the past, you will need to focus on overcoming rejection.

– Are you telling me that my mother will be there too?

- You both need to reconcile. Forgiveness here in the astral world is of no use if the same doesn't occur in the next reincarnation stage, with the veil of forgetfulness over past memories.

You will go through some experiences for your spirit to learn this feeling. The young woman lowered her head. She knew that overcoming rejection would be a significant step in her evolutionary journey. She felt that she needed to face situations that would make her confront this monster that had hurt her so much in some lifetimes. She took a deep breath and looked directly at Lola.

- I'm ready. I know I'm strong, and I have friends here in the astral who will inspire positive thoughts in me. I will win.

- I'm glad you think that way. Tomorrow we'll go to the Reincarnation Department to finalize details for your next life on Earth.

- Should I go back soon?

- If all goes well, you should reincarnate in four or five years.

- Will it really take that long, Lola?

- Be grateful and seize this opportunity. Not everyone has the privilege of planning their return to Earth. Time passes by too quickly here. Before you know it, you'll be back.

- I was born, died in 1915. According to my calculations, after spending those dreadful years in that zone, I think it's been about twenty years. Am I correct?

– You have a talent for organization, but you're not so good with calculations, Lola replied with a broad smile. Your spirit has a knack for administration and the arts. Your sense of time is quite mistaken.

– Why is that?

– Earth has just reached the mid-1970s.

– The young woman put her hand to her mouth to stifle a gasp of astonishment.

– I'm dead, she did a quick calculation with her fingers – which means I've been living here in the astral for at least sixty years? All of this?

– Let's be realistic, it's not such a long time. It's the average time a spirit spends between one incarnation and another, also known as the period of errancy. You see, dear, it all depends on the level of awareness of the spirit. Some stay here for a very short time. Others, according to need, stay a bit longer. I've been here for quite a while and still have no plans to return. But you still have a few more courses to take and need to prepare for your new reincarnation. If all goes as planned, Lola made a graceful gesture with her head, you should be reborn in four or five years, around 1980.

– 1980! I can't even believe it. The world must be very different from the one I knew.

– In some respect, yes. Technology has advanced significantly, but individuals continue to face and overcome the same fears, traumas, and prejudices. The human mind still advances at a slow pace. In the face of eternity, what's the rush?

They both smiled, and the beautiful young woman rested her hands on her spiritual friend's.

- I will come back and I will conquer.

- I will root for you. Now it's time to go back to your room. Shall we?

The young woman nodded. They held their friend's hand and walked back through the courtyard to the building. She said goodbye to Lola, entered the room, and looked around. She smiled. She made a small prayer of thanks and lay back down. She would return to Earth soon. She felt ready to overcome the rejection that had been bothering her, taking the next step in the progress of her spirit.

# Part I

**The story of the parents**

# Chapter 1

That afternoon a thunderstorm had just blown in, relieving the strong heat that had persisted in the city for a few days. The rain drove people away from the funeral procession. Many lefts without saying goodbye to the family. The sisters Alzira and Arlete, aged seventeen and eighteen respectively, were inconsolable. Tears rolled down incessantly, and it was with great effort that Alzira controlled her sobbing. He blew his nose and opened the raft. Quickly picking up the book that was crumpled and the cover worn.

– I need to get better, she said to herself.

Arlete squeezed her sister's hand and tried to smile:

– This book that we've read and reread so many times... is it a coincidence?

Alzira opened it to a marked and well-worn page of *"Odes of the Countryside."* She read a few lines with great emotion: the letter that the character Olivia left for her beloved before she died. A new tear rolled down her flushed face.

– I don't know if it's a coincidence, Arlete. But Mom's death on the exact same day as the writer Erice Veríssimo makes me feel closer to him and his characters. It's as if this cry is for Mom and for him.

They heard a voice behind them, scolding them:

– But could it be the devil? Don't you even respect while the priest is talking? Where is the respect for your mother?

Alzira needed to breathe and let out the air a few times. Arlete squeezed her hand in a gesture of solidarity.

– Look who's talking! He barely helped take care of her, he's eyeing that hussy Gisele, and on top of that, he's trying to scold us?

– What will become of our lives when we return home? – Alzira asked, nervously.

– I don't know...

Arlete was about to speak, but the priest raised his voice and asked the few present to join hands and recite the Lord's Prayer while Josefa's coffin was lowered to the bottom of the tomb...

The girls took a white rose that was attached to the only wreath they had sent to the wake and gently placed it on the coffin.

– Go with God, Mommy – Arlete said.

– We'll pray for your soul – Alzira added.

Olair said nothing. He muttered something and hurried away. Gisele appeared out of nowhere, from behind a tree, and approached Olair. She was dressed in black, as protocol demanded, but it was extremely tight, accentuating her well-shaped curves. Olair smiled and approached the young woman. She whispered something in his ear, he shook his head from side to side, and smiled again. Then he offered his arm to her, and they harvested.

Alzira looked at her sister and spoke in a tone of complete disapproval:

– That snake is leaving the cemetery arm in arm with Dad. Can you believe that?

– If someone told me, I'd have a hard time believing it – Arlete replied. – Gisele has been watching her father since her mother got sick... I bet she's making her move now.

– Dad can do whatever he wants with his life, as long as he respects Mom's memory.

A lady approached and bid farewell to the girls. Then another woman, in her forties, exuding sympathy and compassion, greeted them.

– My name is Celia, and I liked your mom very much – she said to Alzira.

– We've never seen you at our house – Arlete replied.

– Olair wouldn't allow me to visit Josefa. I prayed for your mother in my home, wishing for a peaceful passing.

The girls didn't understand what Celia was talking about. She smiled and, before saying goodbye, spoke in a tone that exuded serenity:

– Death isn't the end.

Alzira and Arlete nodded.

– Is it? – Arlete asked.

– When you want, come visit me. We can talk about anything – Celia took out a notepad and a pen from her bag.

She wrote down her address and handed the piece of paper to Arlete.

– This is your Ariovaldo's address, the school guard.

– And my husband – Celia replied.

– We like your Ariovaldo – Alzira responded. – He has always been very nice to us.

– We'll visit them – Arlete said.

– You'll be welcome.

Celia bid farewell and left. A handful of more people said their goodbyes, and in the early evening, Arlete and Alzira held hands and left the cemetery towards their home.

Upon arriving home, after walking a few blocks, they didn't find Olair.

– He probably went to cry in the arms of that tramp – Arlete muttered.

– Don't speak that way. We're in mourning.

– Why do you say that? We're in mourning, but what about Dad? Is Gisele really evil?

– Alzira, you always see the good side of people.

– Mom raised us this way.

– Reality is different. Some people are good, others more or less, some are good and not so good and there are those who were born crooked, naturally bad. Gisele is part of the last group.

– You're different from me – Alzira sighed as she started preparing chicken soup. – Is she really as bad as we imagine? Or are we jealous because daddy is interested in her?

Arlete laughed and threw her head back.

– Imagine us being jealous! Dad hardly talks to us. I'm sure he'll soon fall for her, and he might even marry this harlot.

– Mom just died.

– I know, Alzira, but Dad is a man and doesn't think with his head. He's always had a weakness for women. We know he cheated on Mom. He was always unfaithful.

– Will he remarry? If he does, we'll be out on the street.

– Not at all. This house is as much ours as it is his. Half of it belongs to me and you.

– I know, Arlete, but don't forget that Dad always used to throw in our face that he had to wake up early, work to support three women.

– I'm a good person, but I have limits. Dad, I'm not going to get this sacrificial talk. If he put me in the world, patience...

The girls talked, cried a bit more, and didn't even watch the soap opera that night. They were very sad and, in the last year, had devoted themselves entirely to taking care of their mother's fragile health. It was a Saturday night, and they wanted and needed to rest. They needed to sleep and relax their bodies, minds, and spirits.

Both of them were physically and emotionally exhausted. It had been over a year since Josefa had been suffering from cancer that had taken over her entire body.

Olair didn't have health insurance, and Josefa had to be admitted to a public hospital. At that time, the healthcare wasn't as poor as it is today. The doctors did everything they could. When they realized that Josefa's condition was only getting worse and that the cancer would overcome her, they fulfilled her request and allowed her to return home to die.

The girls took care of Josefa with great affection. They gave her baths, changed her clothes, administered treatments, and medications, and cared for their mother with diligence and love. Olair was rarely at home and showed little interest in his wife's illness. He had bought a cot and preferred to sleep in his tailor shop. He felt nauseated by the smell of morphine and, using this as an excuse, avoided participating in his wife's care. Olair was a tailor and practiced his trade in a small rented shop on the corner, a few blocks from their house.

Alzira and Arlete attended a public school and didn't work because Olair claimed he couldn't afford a domestic worker. He would often remind his daughters that they had come into the world and were expensive. If they had a bed to sleep in and food on the table, that wasn't all.; such privileges didn't fall from the sky.

Therefore, the girls had to give something in return. They woke up early, made their beds, prepared breakfast, and tended to their mother's needs. They went to school, returned, and prepared lunch. In the afternoon, they took care of the house, the laundry, dinner, and Josefa. It was a tough life. The girls had little time to watch TV or even go out with friends. Olair wouldn't let them.

Meanwhile, Arlete had taken a typing course because she had won a magazine contest and received a full scholarship. She was a diligent young woman, and in six months, she completed the course.

Alzira gave Portuguese tutoring lessons, and the little money she earned was used to buy medication to alleviate her mother's pain caused by the illness.

Arlete had repeated the first grade, so she and Alzira always studied together and had just finished high school, equivalent to today's high school education. Alzira loved literature and devoured books from the school library. She was a fan of Orígenes Lessa and Erico Veríssimo. She had read *"The bean and the dream"* by Lessa and classics like *"Clarissa"* and *"Look at the lilies of the field"* by Veríssimo multiple times. She had a penchant for studying languages and was very skilled in the kitchen. Alzira was an excellent cook. With her mother's passing, she didn't know what her future held. Perhaps she and Arlete would seek employment and take care of their own lives. They felt that they couldn't rely on their father from then on.

The days passed quickly, and the first of several checks arrived on Christmas Eve. Alzira and Arlete didn't want to do anything. They had no desire to celebrate the holiday that year. They were still in mourning. Josefa had passed away less than a month ago, and they couldn't wait for the holiday season to be over. They wanted to quickly move into the next year and forget that difficult year.

Olair arrived at the house shortly after six in the evening. He was carrying a Christmas basket in one hand and a giant turkey in the other.

Arlete shook her head from side to side several times.

– What's that?!

– I got it from a wealthy client in Jardim França. He gave me the basket and the turkey.

– We've explained to you several times that we don't want to celebrate anything. Mom passed away recently, and...

Olair abruptly interrupted.

– Enough whining! I am the owner of this house, and you should respect me. I'm tired of seeing you crying in corners, kissing and crying over your mother's picture.

– Of course, we cry. We miss Mom – Alzira said.

– It's natural – added Arlete.

– Natural is to put all this aside, for heaven's sake! Josefa is dead, and she won't come back. Can't you accept reality? You're a grown woman. You should be working and taking better care of this house instead of crying – Olair ran his finger across the top of the refrigerator and showed his dusty finger – See? That's what I'm talking about. You can't even clean the house properly.

– You don't have the right to speak to us like that – Alzira argued. – Respect our grief.

Olair put the turkey on the table and smiled disdainfully.

– Well, well. I'm the father, and if another tear falls because of your mother, I'll use the belt.

Arlete knew the conversation was about to heat up. She asked mockingly:

– What are you going to do with this turkey and the basket?

– Our Christmas dinner. You'll put this bird in the oven right now.

– Impossible – Alzira replied. – A turkey this size takes hours to roast. Besides, it needs to be seasoned and left to marinate in the sauce for a day.

– Aren't you the smart one who knows how to cook? Well, turn this thing into something edible. Today.

– But it needs to be seasoned, as I said. Only if it's for tomorrow – Alzira replied, with all the patience in the world.

Olair shrugged his shoulders.

– No problem. There's plenty in this basket – he pointed – I'll go to the bakery on the corner and get some mayonnaise, stuffing, and a pork loin. We'll have our Christmas dinner.

– But... – Alzira tried to argue again.

Olair replied curtly:

– Gisele is coming to have dinner with us.

– Ah, now I get it – Arlete intervened with a mocking laugh. – So, we don't need turkey. We'll have chicken for dinner.

Alzira laughed and barely noticed when Olair's arm swung, and his large, open hand hit Arlete's face square. Slap! The slap was strong. She felt dizzy for a moment.

– Never speak of Gisele that way again – Olair warned in a threatening tone. – If you ever speak ill of the girl again, besides receiving more severe slaps, I'll give you a beating that will ruin your race, besides marking you for the rest of your life, you wretch. Why did I have children? Why?

Olair spoke with anger, spun on his heels, and left. He slammed the living room door hard. Alzira ran to her sister.

– Are you okay, Arlete?

– Mm-hmm.

– Did it hurt?

– Aren't you used to this slapping? Remember when we were little? We were always getting slapped without knowing why.

– We grew up being slapped. Mom tried to help, but the poor thing got even more.

– Dad is rude, a brute. He doesn't know how to deal with people. He didn't like Mom, and he doesn't like us, Alzira.

– He never gave us a kiss or a hug.

– I hope he suffers a lot.

– Don't call me like that – Alzira said, while helping Arlete regain her composure. – Dad doesn't know what he's saying.

– But he knows what he does. He loves hitting us. I'm tired of all of this.

– Our life is so dull. Now that Mom is dead, I feel like getting out of here.

Arlete had an idea.

– Why don't we pack our bags and leave?

– Leave?

– Yes.

– How? Where?

– We can look for a boarding house for young ladies. Marivaldo's daughter from the butcher shop, after getting pregnant, went to live in a boarding house near the convent.

– That boarding house only accepts pregnant girls. That's not our situation – Alzira justified.

– Or we can try to find Aunt Lurdes.

– Aunt Lurdes? If Dad hears us mention her name...

– She's our only living close relative. She's Dad's sister. Mom always spoke of Aunt Lurdes with affection.

– We can think about looking for her. However, we don't have a photo, address, or anything.

– We'll find her, Alzira.

– Well, let's think about it tonight. We don't want to stay here.

– He can't do this to us – Arlete said, shaking her head from side to side. It's terrible. He's suffering from the memory of our mother. Worse, he's not respecting our grief.

– I don't think it's fair either.

– How about we bail? – Arlete suggested, in a defiant manner.

– Spend Christmas night where? On the street?

– We can go to school. Your Ariovaldo, the janitor, is our friend. His wife was very kind to us.

– I liked Mrs. Celia. There was so much warmth in her voice when she came to greet us at the cemetery – Alzira said, smiling. – But thinking about going to someone else's house without an invitation? Isn't that rude?

– It's Christmas night, Alzira. We'll only stay a little while so we don't have to have dinner with that harlot Gisele.

– I don't know...

– Alzira, stop being so timid. Do you want to stay here and put up with that tramp?

– I couldn't bear it.

– We don't have any other choice. Let's go.

– Dad will be furious.

– Nothing will. He might get a little mad at first, but then he'll thank God for being alone with the snake. He's more in the mood to go out with that ordinary girl than to celebrate Christmas with his family.

Alzira agreed. It was better to be out of the house. She couldn't bear to see her father holding Gisele and celebrating a night when she'd rather be locked in her room, reading Erico Verissimo, trying to absorb the sweetness and understanding of Olivia, the classic character from the book.

– Let's get ready.

– For what? – added Arlete. – Dad will be back soon. I don't want to see his face until tomorrow.

– You're right. Let's go.

The two of them left, rounded the corner, and headed to the school. The building was dark, and there was no sign of the janitor.

– It's Christmas night – said Alzira. – The streets are empty.

– They must be at home. Here's the address that Mrs. Celia gave us – Arlete said. – We'll ring the doorbell, and...

Ariovaldo, the janitor, appeared and greeted them:

– What are you doing here? It's getting dark.

They exchanged glances, and Arlete said:

– Mr. Ariovaldo, for God's sake! We came here looking for you.

– Really?

– Yes. We'd like to go to your house, and...

Alzira protested:

– It's not that we want to go to your house, but...

Arlete interrupted:

– We don't want to spend Christmas at home.

He nodded.

– I understand. That house has become very sad since Josefa passed away.

– That's right. Our father wants to have dinner, and we don't want to. We're not in the mood to celebrate anything.

– Why not celebrate? I understand your pain. Losing a loved one always causes us great inner suffering. However, everything is temporary, and soon we will all be reunited.

– We buried our mother – Arlete said sadly. – It's all over.

Ariovaldo gently placed his hand on the young woman's.

– Death is not the end.

– Your wife told us the same thing at the funeral – Arlete noted.

– Celia and I have a different view of life and death – Ariovaldo replied with a smile.

– There was a time – Alzira added – when our mother told us she believed in the continuation of life after the body's death. She was sick, bedridden, and one day she said that her mother had come to visit her in the room.

Arlete was surprised:

– I never knew that!

Alzira smiled.

– Mom liked to talk to me about these things. Remember my nightmares?

– Of course!

– Mom took me to Mrs. Augusta, and I was blessed. After a few prayers, I never had those nightmares again. When Mom was given up by the doctors and came back home, she confided in me that she saw her mother in the room from time to time.

– That's impossible. Grandma died before we were born. Mom must have been hallucinating – Arlete changed her tone of voice and stood up straight, posing as an adult know-it-all.

– The doctors said she could lose her mind – Ariovaldo intervened in the conversation.

Alzira shivered and clung to her sister's arms.

– I'm afraid of ghosts.

– I'm not – Arlete replied. – You can talk about these things with me. I'm grown up and not scared.

Alzira was about to protest, but Ariovaldo, realizing that the conversation wouldn't end, invited them:

– Come and have dinner with us. It would be a pleasure to have you. Celia will love it, but, I must warn you, it's a very simple house.

– We also live in a very simple house – added Alzira. – Are you sure we won't be a bother to your wife? We don't want to gatecrash your dinner.

Ariovaldo laughed.

– You two won't be gate crashers. Celia and I don't have any relatives in São Paulo. Our only daughter got married early, and her husband was transferred to Argentina.

– I'd love to visit Argentina – Alzira sighed. – We've never left São Paulo.

– Once, many years ago, Dad took us, very reluctantly, to spend a few days in Praia Grande – Arlete added.

– Iara sent us some pictures of her and her husband in Buenos Aires. I'll show them to you, Alzira.

– Oh, I'd love to see them, Ariovaldo. One day I'll go there.

– Of course, you will – he checked his watch and continued:

– We usually have dinner around eight o'clock. We're almost on schedule.

The two sisters exchanged glances and nodded.

Ariovaldo smiled and concluded:

– It will be a very pleasant evening. You'll love it.

# Chapter 2

In another part of the city, in the Morumbi region, the staff was busy with the final preparations for the grand dinner. Gradually, numerous guests started arriving at the elegant mansion of the businessman America Gumercindo Calini. An invitation to any event at his house was highly sought after. Artists, businessmen, politicians, and the cream of São Paulo's society all adored him.

America was very friendly and had a strong charisma. He was tall and elegant with bright green eyes, and his features reflected European heritage. He had a head of thick, slightly silver hair, combed back neatly. His clothes always fit him impeccably. He had an athletic build and was highly sought after. He came from a humble family of Italian immigrants who had arrived in São Paulo in the early 20th century. After years of hard work, his grandfather had established a grocery store that sold various goods. The small shop expanded, eventually branching into three large markets, and a few years later, America's father established one of the first supermarket chains in the country.

America had one more brother, Adamo, who had a passion for architecture. He chose to finish his studies in Italy and visited Brazil from time to time, maintaining a strong relationship with America, exchanging letters regularly. America and his daughter visited Adamo frequently.

Américo now managed the network, which had grown significantly, reaching the interior and also other capitals of the country.

In his youth, America had a girlfriend with whom he was deeply in love. They were very much in love and made plans for a wedding; however, at a party filled with a lot of drinking, the boy had an affair with a young woman and got her pregnant.

Aware of his slip, America reluctantly ended his relationship and entered into an arranged marriage with Amelia Vaz, a woman from a prestigious São Paulo family.

Their marriage was a notable event, covered in the magazines of the time because it involved a *nouveau-riche* man marrying into the São Paulo elite, descendants of the coffee barons.

A few months after their marriage, Amelia gave birth to a beautiful daughter, Valeria. Unfortunately, Amelia died due to severe haemorrhaging just days after giving birth. In the face of such a tragic event, America became the most beloved, celebrated, and sought-after widower of his time. He tried to find his former girlfriend, his one true love, but she had disappeared without a trace. He even hired a detective, but to no avail. The woman had vanished. Disillusioned and heartbroken, he decided to stay single and dedicated himself entirely to his work. His business thrived, and he raised his daughter on his own.

Valeria had just turned eighteen, and America, who fulfilled her every wish, had bought her a brand-new car as her Christmas gift. The car was hidden in the garage and would be her surprise present.

The young woman was beautiful, taking after her father. She had a slim figure with well-defined curves. Valeria also had green eyes that perfectly complemented her naturally wavy auburn hair. The freckles on her face gave her the appearance of a mischievous girl.

Usually the spoiled side? It showed up when she wanted her father to do what she wanted. With her friends and even with her employees she was cordial and very friendly and, perhaps from past experience, she was terrified of children. She fled from a child, or from contact with him, as the devil flees from the cross.

Valeria had a deep affection for America. When she was around ten years old, he had tried dating a few women, but those relationships never went far. Valeria always found a way to disrupt her father's romantic involvements. Then, when she entered adolescence and began to feel attracted to boys, she became more malleable, to the point of changing her attitude and starting to think about finding someone for her father.

– Even more now – she said to herself as she adjusted her appearance in front of the bathroom mirror.

– Now what? – asked Natalia, her friend since childhood.

Natalia was the only person on the face of the Earth, excluding Americo, for whom Valeria was very fond of and trusted. Valeria told her friend absolutely everything about her life. Natalia, in turn, was very attached to Valeria, because she had a heart of butter and often got into a bad mood because she didn't know how to say no. She thought she needed to resign herself and accept her life. She believed that she needed to resign herself and accept situations without forcing herself to change them. If something adverse happened to her, it was because it had to do with some wrong action in a past life.

Natalia was deeply involved in spiritualism and often tried to convert people to accept the world of spirits. Valeria didn't pay much attention to that side of Natalia. She liked her friend just the way she was. When Natalia started talking about accepting negative astral influences without question, Valeria would counter with, "I'm in control of my own thoughts. Nobody has power over me".

Valeria tossed her hair and applied a little perfume on her chest and neck.

– My father has never looked more handsome, and we've never had this much money. He was named Businessman of the Year, and there will be women flocking to him.

– There have always been women falling at the feet of your father, Natalia added, while fixing her bun.

– I know that.

– You're not telling me you're jealous of your father? I thought that phase was behind you.

– It is. I don't play the daughter who tries to sabotage her father's relationships anymore. I've moved on. I would really like my father to find a girlfriend, a woman who genuinely cares for him. Most of them are after his money.

– That's a fact.

– I won't allow any woman to get close to him for financial gain. My father is good and deserves a loving companion in his old age. He should have a woman who truly loves him, not this horde of fake women who want jewellery and a life of luxury. My father is not a financial institution; he's a man with feelings.

– I agree. Don't forget that your dad can spot a gold-digger from a mile away. He knows how to handle it.

Despite her peculiar views on spirituality, Natalia was an enchanting girl. Daughter of parents who had once been wealthy, she got along well with Valeria. Natalia's family had lost their fortune. Her father was fond of card games, and over the years, they had lost everything to pay off debts that kept piling up. Her parents separated, and she and her mother moved to a more modest neighbourhood to start over.

Natalia's mother, Elenice, studied and passed a civil service exam to become a public-school teacher. She was a woman with a balanced temperament and paid no attention to the judgement of friends who criticised her for being a divorced woman. In those days, a divorced woman was often ostracised by society, with friends distancing themselves, fearing that she might pursue their husbands. This social torment would only subside with the approval of the divorce law.

Elenice was unfazed by societal expectations. She was a woman of strong convictions who knew her worth. She met

Milton, a man in his forties who was retired from the local municipality and lived a few blocks away. They married in Uruguay and lived in a modest but tastefully decorated home due to the refined education and luxurious life Elenice had experienced in the past.

Natalia had just taken her entrance exams for architecture. Of average height with a well-proportioned figure, she caught the attention of young men more for her gentle and sweet demeanour than for her physical appearance.

She smiled at her reflection in the mirror.

- We look beautiful.

- We don't just look beautiful, - Valeria concluded. - We are beautiful.

- Mom must be worried. We've been in this room for a long time.

- You're right, - Valeria agreed. - And, to be honest, I need to act surprised. Daddy thinks I don't know, but that Maverick in the garage is going to be my Christmas present."

- Wow! - Natalia exclaimed. - It's a very nice car. By the way, has your driver's licence been issued?"

- Not yet, - Valeria replied. - The unlucky clerk decided to go on vacation and won't be back until after the holidays.

- Better not use the car until...

Valeria interrupted her friend. - Hey, are you crazy? Do you think I'm not going to drive my brand-new car?

– Do you know how to drive, but you don't have a licence? Don't get into trouble.

– Dario can drive.

Natalia frowned. Valeria noticed and, while adjusting hoop earrings in her ears, said, – You really don't like him, do you?

– I've been your friend forever. You know what I think of Dario. You've always been spoiled.

Valeria interrupted her – Don't exaggerate.

– My friend, you always wanted your father to do everything you wanted. I remember you were less reckless, you started getting into trouble after Taviño's death and you started going out with Darío.

– What trouble? Going out to dance at a nightclub and having fun is getting into trouble? I like to have fun.

– Bearing the energetic burden of the environment. If I go into a disco, I hear about all the bad stuff that's in there

– Why not pick up the good stuff?

– Because there's nothing good in a nightclub?

– Don't be a killjoy. There are plenty of people who go out at night to dance, relax, chill out, meet someone, hook up... The night can be very good, or very bad, it depends on your head and not on the "energy" of the place.

– We think differently. I prefer to stay home and read.

– Each one does what they think is best. I prefer going out.

– Back to Dario. Even if I'm the quirky friend who feels things, I don't like him.

– He's good for me. Dario helped me get through it when I lost my ex-boyfriend.

– You weren't in love with Taviño. It was a high school romance, a passing thing. I know you well, and I know you never loved him. Besides, you were fifteen at the time; you didn't even know what love was.

– You're right. But Dario is a good guy.

– He might be a decent person, Valeria, but he likes drinking and drugs. What kind of future do you expect next to a guy who enjoys drugs?"

– It's just a phase. Who said I'm going to marry Dario?

– But you… – Natalia blushed, – you… have an intimate relationship with him!"

– So what? It doesn't mean I'm going to marry him. Wake up, Natalia. I'm just enjoying life. That's all.

Natalia turned her head from side to side in disbelief. – You're so beautiful! There are so many more interesting guys at your feet. What do you think of Lauro Vasconcellos? He's the son of that Supreme Court justice, Robertinho.

– They're not for me.

– Dario isn't for you either. Think and reflect, dear. Natalia reflected –. Re-evaluate your feelings. Don't waste your time on things that don't make you happy.

– I'll think about it. You're capable of saying things that make me think sometimes.

– It stirs in a good way. I genuinely like you.

Natalia hugged Valeria and kissed her on the cheek.

– Know that I'll always be by your side, no matter what happens.

Valeria got emotional and stepped back, wiping her eyes with the back of her hand.

– Stop talking like that. This way, we'll spend hours redoing all the makeup.

They laughed, and as they left the room and walked down the hallway, Natalia noticed a different picture frame on a dresser.

– I don't remember this picture frame, – she pointed. – Who's this man? – Natalia spoke and felt a warmth spreading through her body. Valeria laughed.

– Do you like it?

– Wow, I liked him. Do I want him?

– My uncle Adamo.

– He looks so different. I only knew him from this old photo, – she pointed to an old, weathered photo in which there was a young man whose face was turned to the side.

– Ah, you were used to that old photo of my uncle. This black and white photo is as old as us. It must have been taken when he moved to Italy.

Natalia was impressed. And she wasn't exaggerating. If Americo was a handsome man, Adamo was a Greek god. He looked like a movie star. He reminded me a bit of the actor Robert Redford in his youth. Adamo had wheat blond hair, green eyes, big and expressive. His mouth was formed by full lips and his smile was impressive.

Valeria smiled

– You're smitten with my uncle.

Natalia blushed.

– Is he married?

– A confirmed bachelor. As far as I know, he's never had a serious relationship.

Natalia felt a new surge of emotion. She changed the subject.

– Let's go downstairs. We're running late.

– You know, I don't know what makes me such good friends with you and like you so much – We don't have common tastes – said Valeria.

– I'd never be interested in someone like my uncle. I prefer dark-haired men with a tough look. Men who look like angels don't attract me.

– Thank goodness we don't like the same type. Imagine the confusion it would be?

– That's why I'm attracted to Dario, Natalia. He has a big build, a muscular body and a sleazy face. That's why I'm attracted to him.

– Why don't you respond to Thomas's advances? He has a tough look, a face marked like a gangster.

Valeria closed her eyes and sighed.

– Thomas is the man I dreamt of having for the rest of my life.

– I don't understand – Natalia was surprised. – Thomas is crazy about you. Why don't you date him?

– Are you crazy, Natalia? Marion is obsessed with Thomas.

– So what?

– That's why I don't want any trouble on my side. Thomas is a very interesting guy, even more so than Dario. However, I'd rather endure unfulfilled desires and forget about him than deal with Marion. Do you remember when Thomas kissed Laura at my fifteenth birthday party?

Natalia felt a shiver run down her spine.

– How I remember! Marion nearly ruined your party. It turned into a shouting match, a big commotion.

– That's nothing – Valeria continued. – The most frightening part is that Laura got run over the day after the party and almost died. The poor thing was crippled.

– Do you believe that Marion... – Natalia didn't finish her sentence.

– Surely. One of the witnesses to the accident claimed that the car was a red Corcel GT with black stripes, and the licence plate had the letters BT. Who has a car that matches that description?

Natalia brought her hand to her mouth, feeling stunned.

– I never knew about this.

– My dad told me. Marion's family paid that witness, and they went back to the police station and retracted everything. They said the car was yellow. You know what? Deep down, I'm in love with Thomas, but I won't take the risk. I don't want to be Marion's next victim.

- If you talk to Thomas, maybe...

- What's the point? I know if I open my heart, he'll break up with her. But I'm going to make an enemy for the rest of my life. I don't want that for myself. I'm too young and I have yet to find a man who will attract me in the same way I loved Thomas

- You're right - Natalia agreed. - I still prefer your uncle.

The two of them laughed heartily. Valeria placed her hands on her friend's.

- Let's put our preferences for men aside. What's important is that we genuinely like each other.

- That's true.

- Maybe it's a past life thing - Valeria added.

Natalia smiled.

- Are you saying that to tease me, or because I'm interested in the subject?

Valeria gently ran her hand across her friend's forehead.

- I don't know. Sometimes I believe in something beyond, but there are also times when I believe that everything ends with death. It's the end. Maybe we're afraid to admit that life is just one. That's one of the reasons I enjoy life.

- You need a little more balance.

- I try, even though it's not easy.

– If you read a little from the spiritual books I'm trying to get you to read...

– That's the problem: you want to impose something on me that I'm not ready to understand yet.

The two continued their conversation as they walked down the corridor. They descended the white marble spiral staircase, holding onto the beautiful bronze railing, and soon the noise and excitement of the guests outside the mansion could be heard. They were already seated at round tables along the extensive garden by the pool.

America was in conversation with a banker and his wife when he was embraced by his daughter.

– I missed you – Valeria said, planting a kiss on his cheek.

He kissed his daughter back and introduced her to the couple. Valeria greeted them briefly and then guided her father to their table. There were Elenice, Milton, and, of course, Natalia.

Americo greeted them and sat down. As the waiter poured him a glass of ice, he commented:

– Beautiful evening! I was afraid the rain would catch us by surprise.

Milton adjusted himself in his chair and said:

– Your house is very beautiful. Congratulations!

– I deserve the congratulations – Valeria replied.

– Oh, why?

– I take care of the house's decoration. I enjoy changing and arranging the furniture, I'm interested in coordinating colours...

Americo smiled contentedly:

– This girl has excellent taste. Since she was a child, she used to scribble the rooms in notebooks, using coloured markers for each wing of the house. Then she'd draw the furniture, cut them out, and arrange them on a sheet of paper.

Elenice interjected:

– I remember when we moved, and Valeria spent two days arranging the furniture.

– You were living in a big house and suddenly you moved into a very modest house. If it weren't for my insight and spatial sense, how would those enormous pieces of furniture fit in the small house? I was a genius!

Everyone laughed, and Elenice continued:

– You have a sense for decorating, Valeria. You hit the nail on the head when you took the architecture entrance exam.

The young girl shrugged, tossed her hair back, and said:

– I'm not as dedicated to studying as Natalia. I won't pass the entrance exam.

– Oh, come on, girl! Giving up even before taking the test?

– The entrance exam is serious stuff, it's only good for people who are all in, who are truly dedicated. I'm not into studying for hours like Natalia. Maybe later on, I'll take a course in Italy, and when I return, Dad will give me a decorating studio as a gift.

- I insist on giving you the best location in town. I'm thinking of the Jardins neighbourhood.

Elenice exclaimed:

- Perfect! I lived in Jardim America for many years. There are wonderful mansions there, perfect for housing a beautiful decorating studio.

Valeria sighed:

- I'm not sure, though.

- Why?

- Sometimes I feel like leaving this place. São Paulo's traffic is becoming more unbearable every day.

- That's progress - Milton said. - Nowadays, we have a metro line, and we're catching up with the major cities in the world.

Valeria laughed dismissively.

- Milton, don't compare this haphazardly growing city to New York, London, or Paris. Our subway connects nothing to anywhere.

- It goes from the Jabaquara neighbourhood to Santana.

- And there's still no date for the inauguration of Se Station, which is the main one. This is a third-rate country.

- I'll say it again, it's progress.

– I get so irritated with society's negligence. Milton, did you see how many buildings were demolished to build this so-called Se Square station? – Valeria asked, concerned.

– Valeria is concerned about the deterioration of public heritage. She's always been like that, ever since she was a child – America admitted.

She was excited. She took a sip of champagne and asked Milton:

– What do you think of the Santa Helena Mansion?

He whistled.

– One of the most beautiful buildings ever constructed in the city!

– Exactly – Valeria added. – A mansion with a façade full of sculptures, designed by the Italian architect Corberi. It was located in Se Square and inaugurated in 1922. Inside, apart from shops and offices, there was also a cinema as luxurious as the Municipal Theater, the Cinetheather Santa Helena. The mansion was demolished to build the central metro station, which was going to be called Clovis Bevilaqua. Now, it's going to be named Se Station. The destruction of the mansion – Valeria took a sip of her champagne and continued, –It was entirely unnecessary, dispensable. It's a significant architectural loss for the city.

– My goodness! This girl is an architecture encyclopaedia, – America said proudly.

– And she's my daughter! – Valeria smiled and concluded, –Besides, they decided to remove the Mendes Caldeira Building from the scene with the same justification, which was the need to demolish it for the metro's construction. Bringing down one of the city's tallest buildings? It's madness. Do you understand why I feel sad and angry? Our heritage, our memory in a general sense, is being destroyed every passing day.

The conversation was lively and interesting, but a deep voice greeted them, saying, – Valeria is right. This city's a mess. – They all turned to see Dario, Valeria's boyfriend, who they had been dating for a few years. At first, America hadn't allowed the relationship. However, since Dario was the son of a famous banker from São Paulo, and America had contracted some loans from that banker's institutions, he played dead and let the relationship continue to avoid personal issues interfering with business. America knew that sooner or later, his daughter might marry Thomas. The young man came from a good family and had a promising future. America dreamed of that union.

Natalia greeted him with a cold – Hello. – Dario responded to everyone with a "How are you?" and pulled up a chair. He joined the group. The conversation took a different turn. Natalia and her mother got up to take a stroll around the garden. Milton and Americo began discussing economic forecasts for the upcoming year. Dario pulled Valeria close to his chest.

– What's the matter, honey, shall we stop this silly party and have some real fun?

Valeria smiled but didn't say anything. She remembered her conversation with Natalia. Why, after all, was it so difficult for her to part ways with Dario?

He was an attractive and charming young man. Tall, handsome, and tanned, Dario was the object of many women's attention. However, he had a rather empty life. He had repeated the third year of high school twice and didn't seem interested in anything. Coming from a wealthy and well-bred family, Dario was a troublemaker. He engaged in silly and senseless pranks, got into fights wherever he went, and had many enemies. His misbehaviour had escalated over the past three years. Dario had become more violent and reckless, sometimes not even aware of his actions.

As an example, he once got into a fight with another guy over a trivial matter. Darius was born out of the fight; he had practiced judo for many years. However, in that particular case, he beat the guy senseless. The guy almost died. Dario swore he didn't remember hitting the guy. He only remembered feeling intense anger, being consumed by rage, and then blacking out. When he regained consciousness, he had no recollection of what he had done.

His parents took him to a renowned psychiatrist who only identified a certain pattern of behaviour deviation. Later, his parents divorced. His mother went to live in the United States, and his father remarried and had another child. He wasn't even happy with Dario's behaviour. He didn't care about his son.

Valeria felt a strong physical attraction to him. She had never loved him. It was purely physical attraction, nothing more. They had met in school. Dario was now twenty-one years old and lived off the generous allowances his father deposited into his bank account. Alone and without prospects of building a stable and dignified life, he allowed himself to be carried away by parties fuelled by plenty of alcohol and drugs.

Cocaine was beginning to gain popularity among the more privileged classes of society, becoming an indispensable item at the parties of the chic and famous, known at the time as "*gra-fines.*" Dario was a regular marijuana user. Strangely, over the past three years, he had become addicted to cocaine.

Natalia had caught him snorting lines of cocaine before. She had warned Valeria, but her friend argued that Dario was an adult and responsible for himself. If he wanted to snort or smoke whatever he pleased, that was his business. As long as he remained a good lover, Valeria didn't care about this dark side of her boyfriend. She would have loved to pursue Thomas, but he was dating Marion, and Valeria didn't want to face Marion's malice.

After the dinner was served and the guests had gone, the early hours of the morning were passing. Natalia said goodbye to her friend and they ended up meeting after Christmas Day.

In the car, she shared with her mother and stepfather:

– I get chills when Dario is around.

– I've seen some dark shadows around him – Elenice said. – This boy needs spiritual treatment.

– I feel uneasy around him. I was born like this, a sponge. I pick up everything from others.

– You need to pay more attention to your thoughts and better filter what you absorb, my daughter. We own our minds and can't allow any thought to invade us.

– Here comes you telling me that I'm wrong in the way I think. I'm very sensitive, patient.

The conversation continued in the same vein, with Elenice advising her daughter to be a firmer and less susceptible person to the energies of others, and Natalia excusing her extreme sensitivity, claiming that she was born this way and couldn't change.

Milton knew the direction the conversation was heading and added:

– This boy needs, above all, support and attention from his parents. Dario has no boundaries and may pay a high price for the excesses he commits.

Natalia closed her eyes and offered a silent prayer for her friend. Despite believing that her friend was a bit of a scatterbrain, she genuinely cared for Valeria.

– I ask God to protect my friend. May nothing bad happen to her!

# Chapter 3

It was past ten when Alzira and Arlete woke up.

– Good morning – said Alzira.

– Merry Christmas, my sister – Arlete replied and got up. She approached her sister's bed and kissed her on the cheek.

– Last night was so pleasant. Your Ariovaldo and Mrs. Celia are lovely people.

– I felt immense peace there. Even with Mama's death, I felt well received by these simple and kind-hearted people.

– Me too – agreed Alzira.

– You know, I sensed a presence during dinner.

– A presence? What do you mean? – asked Alzira.

– As if someone invisible was there. Didn't you notice the atmosphere of harmony that prevailed in that blessed home?

– Arlete, you're imagining things. The night was great, but it was just us, you, Ariovaldo, and his wife. Maybe you were just impressed by that conversation about spirits.

– Mrs. Celia is a simple woman but very intelligent. She talked about spiritualism in such a... natural way, that's the word!

– In fact, I agree with you. I even got interested in the subject myself. Did you like that we received this novel, *"Between Love and War"*?

– I've never read a spiritualist novel, Alzira. I've heard positive comments about this writer – she picked up the book and read the name: "Zibia Gasparetto".

– Mrs. Celia said that the book has just been released and is gaining great success among the public.

Alzira opened the book and read a random excerpt from the prologue aloud:

– The unchanging laws of divine justice give to each one according to their deeds. And time, the constant friend, takes care to restore the truth in the intimacy of the being.

– If God gives to each one according to their deeds, why do we have to live like this, motherless and with a father who despises us? Could it be that we were bad people in past lives?

– I don't know. The topic is new and it piques my interest. After we read the book, maybe we can reflect better on everything that Mrs. Celia told us.

– You're right.

They stretched out and Arlete asked:

– When we arrived, it was past midnight, and Father wasn't at home. Where could he have gone?

– He must have ended the night in the arms of that harmonious crab. I bet you.

Arlete bit her lips.

– I'm worried, Alzira.

– What happened?

– I'm sure Father is really going to get involved with that floozy. I have a feeling that our life will turn into a nightmare. Gisele isn't a good person.

– I have the same feeling too. What if we talk to her? Could the coexistence be more harmonious?

Arlete shrugged and shook her head from side to side.

– Never! Gisele wants Father all to herself and doesn't want us around.

– Father could kick us out of the house. He has always threatened us. Mother was the one who didn't allow it. Now that she's gone, I don't know if...

– What nothing! Half of this house is ours. I'm not leaving. Unless Father sells it and gives us our share.

– Arlete, why are you so attached to this house? Can't you see we have a whole life ahead of us? Don't you see that we can have our own house without depending on our father?

Arlete didn't respond. She thought for a moment.

Alzira continued lovingly:

– We've finished high school, and you've completed your typing course as well. I'm turning eighteen, and you'll be nineteen. We can get jobs and go live in a boarding house. There are still good boarding houses for young ladies in the city.

– I've told you I only know the one for pregnant women, where the butcher's daughter ended up.

– Yesterday, while you were clearing the table, Mrs. Celia told me that Mr. Tenorio's daughter, after he passed away, had to give up their house and went to live in a boarding house just for young ladies near Ponte Pequena.

– Alzira, with you by my side, supporting me, I'm capable of anything to maintain our happiness.

– Let's talk to Father. We need to know his feelings about Gisele. It could be something temporary – said Alzira, naively.

– Well, nothing! I've known our father since he used to stay late at the tailor's shop. How many times have I seen him in intimate situations with other women? He has a difficult fire to put out. He's the match and Gisele is pure gasoline. Together they burn. And what's more, we have no close relatives.

– We have aunt Lurdes – Alzira added –. I noticed that Miss Celia was going to say something about her aunt.

– What could she say? As far as I know, nobody here knew Aunt Lourdes.

– You're right.

Arlete shook her head to one side.

– Dad can't bear to hear her name. We know that Cronica is his living sister and relative here. The rest of the family lives in Jutaf, in the Amazonas. He did not allow us to try to locate her and inform her of her sister-in-law's death.

– We don't know where she lives – Alzira said –. I only remember that my mother spoke very well of Aunt Lurdes and, sometimes, she would take out an old photo, yellowed by time, in which she and another girl who looked a little older appeared. I'm sure it was Aunt Lourdes in that photo.

– We can go through mom's belongings. Maybe we haven't found any documents that inform us about the aunt's whereabouts?

– We might have.

– I'll see if Dad's up.

– He wasn't home when we arrived. He really must have spent the night out – Alzira said.

– He must have taken her to the slaughterhouse, at the back of the tailor's shop.

Arlete said this in an ironic tone. He put on his shirt, slippers, opened the bedroom door and looked around. The house was silent.

– Let's go to the kitchen.

On the way, down the hallway, he found a woman's private parts. She was horrified. She went to her father's room. and pushed the door. There was no one there, although the bed was unmade and liquor bottles were strewn beside the bed. The young woman shook her head negatively sideways.

The young woman shook her head disapprovingly.

– My God! Father has no limits!

She then went to the kitchen and made some coffee. She heated a little milk and opened a glass jar of plain biscuits. The sink was filled with dirty dishes, and the table still had the remains of the "dinner" Olair had improvised.

Alzira arrived shortly after.

- Did you see that pair of panties and a bra on the hallway floor? We didn't notice anything when we arrived.

- We didn't pay attention. But they can only belong to the prostitute.

- Are you sure, Arlete?

- I'm certain. Look at this filthy kitchen around us, she pointed out. - They must have had a great time and then went to sleep in the back of the tailor shop.

- Dad doesn't have a hint of shame on his face. If he wants to date, fine, but he could at least respect his wife's memory. We are in mourning.

- He never respected us, Alzira. He has always treated us with coldness and distance. We only get slapped in the face. Do you remember the last time he kissed us? Or gave us a hug?

Alzira looked up, thinking for a moment. Then she replied:

- I can't remember Father ever giving us a kiss.

- Because he never showed any affection towards us - added Arlete.

- You don't remember because there is nothing to remember. There has never been any affection between us and him. He never showed any affection to Mom either.

- I also can't remember him kissing her or hugging her. Mom was always very obedient; she didn't complain.

- But with Gisele, it's different. He's always hugging that low-class woman.

Alzira opened the refrigerator and took out the margarine tub. They put away the leftover food from dinner, storing it in the oven, and set the table. They served themselves coffee with milk and had some salty biscuits with margarine.

As they were finishing their breakfast, the doorbell rang. Arlete put on her robe and went to answer it.

A young man with handsome features and an athletic build opened a wide smile, displaying his white and aligned teeth. Arlete smiled without realizing it.

- Hello, how can I help you?

- I'm looking for Miss Gisele Correia.

- No woman with that name lives here! she exclaimed vehemently. And she changed her tone. - Is there anything else?

The young man felt embarrassed. He bit his lip and smiled.

- Forgive me. It's just that I'm after this lady.

- I'm sorry. I've been looking for this lady for days, and she's never at home. I'm discreet, and I don't want to have an official notice waiting for her. I know today is Christmas. I came to wish a friend of mine and his family who live nearby happy holidays. I apologize for not introducing myself. He took a card out of his pocket and handed it to her.

Arlete took the card and read it: Osvaldo Pimentel - Lawyer.

- A lawyer looking for Gisele on Christmas Day? This must be trouble.

Osvaldo nodded his head up and down, making an affirmative gesture.

– Yes, I'm a lawyer and also a judicial officer.

– Important people. What do I owe the honour?

The young man smiled and said:

– A neighbour of yours – he pointed to the house next door – informed me that Miss Gisele usually visits this house. I have a summons that needs to be delivered in person.

Arlete felt her face turn red, and sudden anger overcame her.

– She's at home! – she said in a dry tone.

– I rang the doorbell and knocked on the door. Nothing. She's there. I'm sure. Can you give me a minute?

– Of course.

Arlete closed the door and rushed to her room. Alzira left the dishes on the crowded sink and followed her. She asked – Has something happened?

– There's a judicial officer outside looking for Gisele. How is that possible? Today is Christmas! – exclaimed Alzira.

– Yeah. Something is definitely wrong.

– Are you sure it's a process server?

– He's also a lawyer.

Arlete spoke and showed the card to her sister while putting on a floral dress with spaghetti straps and tying her long hair into a ponytail.

– He's a lawyer indeed – confirmed Alzira.

– The young man is very handsome.

Alzira rushed to the living room window, pulled back the curtain, and peered out.

– You're right. The guy is handsome. He dresses well. It's so rare to see a good-looking, well-dressed guy around these parts!

– I'll go with him to the lady's house. Our father must be there too. I want to see if this circus is going to catch fire. Plus, I might learn a bit more about the good-looking vigilante lawyer.

The two of them burst into laughter.

– Arlete, you're impossible!

– I'm not at all. I want to combine business with pleasure, get to know this doctor better, and find out what this vixen wants with our father. Do you think she fell head over heels for him just like that – she snapped her fingers – from one moment to the next?

– She's always been notorious in the neighbourhood. She used to hang around Rodinei, the owner of the corner bar.

– Afterwards.

Arlete sprayed a little Mistral deodorant under her arms and applied a delicate lipstick to her lips. Then, she took a bottle of Leite de Rosas and spread a few drops on her neck and collarbone. She walked out. Osvaldo complimented her:

– You look beautiful... and you managed that in record time.

Arlete shrugged.

- I'm practical, I don't waste hours in front of a vanity table. Shall we go, doctor?

They walked a few steps and turned the corner without talking. Arlete stopped in front of the side gate of Gisele's house and knocked on it. Nothing.

- We'll have to go in.

- No! We can't break into the house. I'm a lawyer, and I know that if we enter the house without consent...

Arlete cut him off gently:

- I know the type. She's in there with my father. I guarantee you won't be sued by anyone.

Osvaldo said nothing, just nodded. Arlete opened the gate. It was rusty and made noise as she pushed it open and entered the area that led to the front door.

- Well, we're almost there.

- I'm not sure if we should... - Osvaldo hesitated.

- I've already said it. If anything, I'll tell them I came to look for my father. Don't worry.

Arlete turned the doorknob, and the door was unlocked. They entered, and the house was eerily quiet. They walked through a foul-smelling corridor - Gisele wasn't fond of cleanliness - and stopped at the door of the room. Arlete put her hand on the doorknob and pushed.

The scene was worthy of a fifth-rate adult movie. Gisele was lying, or rather, sprawled over Olair's body. She was naked, and Arlete's father was wearing a far from enticing pair of boxers. They had an undefined colour, were loose, and worn out. Olair also wore black socks. They both snored loudly. There were bottles of cheap champagne on the nightstand and beer bottles scattered on the floor.

Arlete began clapping and shouting:

– Come on, gang. It's time for Christmas lunch. Get up.

Osvaldo stood behind her, silent, without action. In reality, he had a strong urge to laugh. The scene was, indeed, hilarious. Olair moved his mouth, swallowing saliva, running his tongue over his lips. He mumbled something. Gisele opened her eyes, let out a belch, and, with swollen eyes, turned her face towards the source of that loud voice. After a few seconds, when she realized it was Arlete in front of her, she jumped followed by a scream.

– What are you doing in my house, you brat?

– I came to get my father. That's all – Arlete replied in an ironic tone.

That's when Gisele noticed she was naked. She shook her head from side to side, pushed Olair to the edge of the bed, and covered herself with the greasy sheet that hadn't seen a wash in a long time.

– If you stay here, I'll call the police. – Arlete laughed out loud.

– Call the police? You? Don't make me laugh, for God's sake. You're as afraid of the police as a vampire is of light. Spare me, Gisele.

The girl was left without anything to say. With one hand, she held the handkerchief over her body. With the other, she rubbed her eyes. Recognizing the young man behind Arlete, she gave another scream:

– What are you doing inside my house? This is an invasion of privacy.

Arlete looked at him and then at Gisele:

– Do you know each other?

– Mm–hmm – he affirmed. – Then, he took a step forward and greeted – How are you, Miss Gisele Correia?

– I can't believe you know each other. I thought you were such a distinguished, elegant young man. You don't seem to fit with her.

– Miss Gisele has been avoiding me for a long time. Given the circumstances – Osvaldo placed an envelope on the nightstand – I can now confirm that the citation has been delivered. The owner is an upright man and doesn't want any scandals. I was supposed to be accompanied by a police car at the door. I want to handle everything discreetly, of course, if Miss doesn't object.

Osvaldo handed the document to Gisele. She made a face. Then he took a copy of the document, took a pen from the inside of his jacket, checked the time, and wrote on the back. Then he said, serious:

– Execution of eviction sentence issued on December 25, 1975, at eleven thirty-two minutes past eleven.

Arlete opened and closed her mouth to avoid astonishment:

– Eviction demand? Does this mean that the lady, besides being a good cook, is also a bad payer? Trap with letters?

Gisele swallowed hard. She didn't know what to say. She had been avoiding Osvaldo for months. She knew that sooner or later she would have to surrender the property.

She puffed up her chest and tried to give her voice a firm and threatening tone:

– I'm not going to read the sentence.

– Why? – Osvaldo inquired.

– Because I talked to my lawyer...

He interrupted her gently:

– When was that?

Gisele thought and said:

– In April, I think. He assured me that upon receiving the judge's sentence, I still have at least three months to leave here.

Osvaldo shook his head negatively sideways.

– If more than six months have passed between the date of the first instance sentence and its execution, which is your case, miss, the deadline for vacating the property will be thirty days. The judge set the deadline for thirty days from December 13th. Since I only managed to deliver the citation today, the thirty days start counting from the subsequent business day after the delivery. You have until January 26th to leave.

Arlete was impressed by Osvaldo's natural way of speaking. He seemed to have a good understanding of the laws.

Gisele couldn't contain herself. She was overcome with sudden anger and almost lunged at Arlete and Osvaldo. She began to curse at them with everything that was bad words. Some of them the young men did not know.

It was in this chaos and shouting that Olair woke up. He laid his body on the bed; his eyes widened and went white as wax when he saw his daughter there in the bedroom doorway. He jumped up.

– What are you doing here? How dare you?

Arlete took a step forward and pointed her finger accusingly.

– I'm the one asking. What are you doing here in this dirty and smelly house, with this equally dirty and smelly woman?

Olair wanted to slap his daughter in the face. Gisele restrained him:

– It won't help if you two fight here in my house – she changed her tone of voice, pouted, and approached Olair. – Leave the poor thing alone. She doesn't know what she's saying. We need to talk.

Osvaldo sensed the increasingly awkward atmosphere in the room. He touched Arlete's arm.

– Let's go. I've done what I needed to.

– Me too – agreed the young woman. – I don't know why the hell we're still here.

The two left the room and minutes later were outside the house. Osvaldo flashed a new smile:

– You're brave, girl. I like your style.

Arlete blushed and lowered her head. She smiled shortly after.

– I'm a bit headstrong. I mean, I'm a good person, but I'm very firm and determined. I'm not easily swayed.

– That's a shame.

– Why is that?

– Because I would love to sway you!

– Are you hitting on me? – asked Arlete, surprised.

– I am. You know my name and you know I have a profession. I'm a court officer and I also work in the legal department of a real estate agency in the city centre. I'm twenty-six years old, come from a humble family. My father died when I was eleven years old. I have a wonderful mother and two brothers I adore. They're married and I'm still single. Currently, we live in Diadema. I hope to get married someday and live in the capital.

– What else?

– I'm going on vacation now and I'll be back at the end of next month. I'm going to help my brother move. Jair lost everything in a flood, and we managed to find him a nice little house, in a high place, far from any river or stream.

The conversation went on for a long time. Osvaldo talked about his life, his difficulties, his dreams, and his desires. Arlete did the same. They felt very comfortable next to each other. At a certain point, she asked directly:

– Do you have a girlfriend?

– I've had some flings, nothing serious – Osvaldo replied, sincere.

– Never had a serious relationship?

– Not yet. It depends on you.

– What do you mean? – she was surprised.

– How old are you?

– Eighteen years old. I'm turning nineteen soon.

– I bet you don't have a boyfriend – Osvaldo continued.

– Is it that obvious? – Arlete asked, curious.

– No. It's because you were born to be with me.

Arlete swallowed her saliva and felt her legs go weak. She'd had crushes on some boys in the neighbourhood before, but she'd never felt this. It was a warmth that surged up and down inside her body, a pleasant, pleasurable sensation.

She leaned against the gate so as not to fall. Osvaldo approached and took her in his arms. He was even more handsome up close. His breath was pleasant, and she couldn't resist. She closed her eyes and pressed her lips against his. That was the first love kiss Arlete had ever given in her life. She felt like the happiest girl in the world.

# Chapter 4

Valeria and Dario went to spend their January vacation in Guaruja. America owned a mansion on Enseada beach, built right on the sand, just a few steps from the sea. The plot of land had a beak-like shape, making it difficult for beachgoers to access the area. So, he had a piece of sea all to himself. A private little beach, indeed.

The morning had started muggy. The sky was overcast but no sign of rain. Valeria adjusted her bikini and plunged into the warm, crystal-clear water.

– Come on, Dario.

The boy was a little dazed by the excessive consumption of alcohol and marijuana. He walked slowly to the sea. He entered the water, and Valeria pressed her body against his.

– Come on, handsome. Let's play.

– I'm feeling a bit queasy.

She pushed him playfully with force.

– What the hell is this? Are you stoned all the time? It's getting hard for you to pleasure me this way.

– I'm sorry, babe. I need to control myself. There are times when I don't want to smoke or snort, but it's like there's a crowd around me. I hear voices. They ask for more. Always more.

Valeria shook her body and lunged. She returned to the surface and shook out her long red hair.

– It's just you and me here, Dario. What's with this talk of a crowd and voices? Are you going crazy?

– It's true. This morning, while you were sleeping, I went to the balcony and a man asked me for a cigarette. I gave him one. Then he asked for a glass of vodka. And then he vanished. Disappeared right in front of me.

– I'm telling you... you're smoking and snorting too much. Can't you stop for a while? I read in a magazine that drugs can destroy neurons and...

Dario cut her off:

– Don't say that, babe.

– But it's true. They stop functioning. You always have booze, smoke or dust in your head. There's got to be a brake, man. Can you imagine being stupid for a while?

– You're right. I'll think about it. But what do I do about the voices?

– It's in your head.

– Do you really think so?

– I do.

Valeria moved her warm body closer to his. She wanted to cuddle a bit. He backed away and dived. He resurfaced and jumped on top of her. He found it amusing to play a little rough, that graceless game of putting an arm around the opponent's neck and pretending to drown them.

– You're hurting me, Dario.

The guy didn't listen to her. He seemed to transform into a bigger fountain. He acted brutishly and aggressively. He forced Valeria's head underwater, and with great effort, she resurfaced, already pale and almost out of breath. She pushed Dario away forcefully.

– What do you think you're doing? Trying to kill me? – she spoke angrily, while coughing.

– I was just playing with you, sweetheart. A dunk...

– Idiot! Why don't you go do that with your stoned friends?

Valeria coughed again and spat out some water. Then, she started crying softly.

– You've never been this stupid, Dario.

Watching her cry, she came to her senses. It was as if she didn't realize the moment she entered the sea a moment ago.

– What did I do, babe?

– You hurt me. You almost drowned me.

– I'm sorry, Valeria, I don't know what came over me...

– I'm going home.

She started to leave the water and gestured for him to stop talking. Valeria was sad and truly getting tired of Dario. He used to be an attentive and loving guy, a good lover. He was affectionate and used to have a lot of fun around the city. But lately, the excess of alcohol and drugs was beginning to affect their relationship. She remembered Natalia's words, back on Christmas.

She walked on the sand and Thomas' face came to her mind. She felt a little flutter in her stomach. Was it worth fighting for Thomas' love and facing Marion?

Was it?, she asked herself.

There were so many doubts. Valeria thought and thought. She came to a conclusion: she wanted to disappear from that place.

I'll take a shower, grab my bag, and head to Santos. I need to confide in my friend Natalia.

She entered the house and headed to her suite. She came face to face with Marion.

– What are you doing here? – she asked, surprised.

– Daddy came to spend a few days at the beach. I knew you and Dario were here. I asked the driver to bring me. Is it okay if I stay?

– Your apartment in Pitangueiras Beach is three times bigger than this house. Why do you want to stay here?

Marion was about to respond, but Valeria interjected:

Because of Dario.

– Imagine! – the friend lied. – I'm dating Thomas. I've known you for years. I know you have a crush on Dario.

– Marion blushed.

– You're mistaken.

– Why do you string Thomas along? What do you want from him?

Marion was furious:

– It's none of your business – she laughed. – And may I ask what it has to do with my relationship? Are you interested in Thomas?

Valeria didn't answer. Marion proposed:

– Why don't we exchange boyfriends?

– How's that?

– That's right. You give me Dario, and I'll give you Thomas. Could work for a few days.

– You're insane, Marion. Do you really think I would be capable of swapping boyfriends, as if they were objects we trade at a market?

Marion let out another laugh.

– I see men as objects. All I want from them is money and pleasure, nothing else. Once I get what I want, I throw it away like garbage.

– Where's your boyfriend, may I ask?

– He's probably working at some hydroelectric plant. Engineer stuff.

Valeria shook her head.

– If you really want to know, I couldn't care less about both of you. I'm going to take a shower and go for a walk. If you want to stay here, you can. I don't have a set time to come back.

Marion smiled. She put on an angelic face, but inside, she was fuming.

Why on earth does Dario pay attention to this scrawny, pale, red-haired girl? She looks like a scarecrow! I'm much more of a woman than Valeria. I'm only dating that idiot Thomas because he's going to be the stepping stone for me to get to Hollywood. Once I become a famous star, I'll kick him to the curb and get Dario. He'll be mine. Oh, he will be.

Marion had a huge fixation on Dario. She had always been attracted to him, but Dario had never paid her any mind. Since high school, she had been after him, and nothing. She wanted to be a movie star. She had no shortage of talent, but Marion was a very beautiful woman, with stunning beauty. Some said she was born beautiful and would die beautiful.

She had a special ability to attract men and make them fulfil all her desires. She met Thomas and, knowing that her father was a wealthy banker with connections in the United States, she used all her charm on the guy, and they had been dating for a few years now. The young woman didn't have an ounce of feeling for Thomas. She treated him like a plaything and didn't allow any other woman to get close.

- Until I go to Hollywood and become a famous actress, Thomas will be mine. If any girl tries to get close to him, I'll get her out of the way, she said to herself.

Marion remembered Laura, the girl who kissed Thomas at Valeria's fifteenth birthday party. She laughed like a hysteric.

- Too bad she didn't die. But she was lame. That already made her happy. "Every time she takes a step she'll remember me."

Marion was spoiled, stupid, and arrogant. She grew up in a very rich family and, sure of her superiority over the rest of the mortals because she possessed dazzling beauty, she had a genius for dogs. Beautiful and with such perfect facial features, she had been invited to be on the cover of the Pop magazine, aimed at the teenage audience of that time, and more recently, on the cover of the *Realidade* magazine.

Marion had just turned twenty and was up to all sorts of mischief. She had fooled around with her father's married friends. She had no boundaries and seduced anyone she desired. Then she would drop them, which only increased the fascination she exerted over these men. Poor Thomas barely suspected his girlfriend's infidelity.

At the moment, Marion was preparing to pose for the famous nude magazine, Status, which was a hit all over the country. Her very conservative parents forbade her from doing the photo shoot. Marion shrugged it off. She had never, ever, in any way, followed her parents' considerations. She was going to pose naked and drive men even crazier.

– I can have any man in the palm of my hand. Now I want Dario. He'll be my new little toy, for as long as I want.

Determined, Marion pulled up her tiny thong. She took off the top of her bikini, leaving her breasts exposed. In this very uninhibited way, she went to find Dario.

– I want to see what will hold out!

Dario was still in the sea. He dived, swam, and walked to the shore. He lay on the mat, lit a cigarette, and began to think. Soon he heard the same voice that had been tormenting him for a while:

– We need to find other women. Valeria is marriage material. We need to be more careful with her.

– It was as if there was someone by his side. Dario responded, aloud:

– We need to go easy on Valeria.

– Exactly. Valeria will always be ours. But while she's crying her heart out to Natalia, why don't we take advantage and have a little fun with Marion? What do you think?

– The seed of doubt had been planted and it deeply disturbed Dario.

– I never thought about that before – he responded, aloud. – Marion is quite a woman.

– Well, you should start thinking. How about we take Marion for a little trip to Porchat Island? She's a much easier girl to satisfy our desires.

– Dario laughed and didn't respond. He rambled on for a long time... Then he saw Marion approaching. She winked at him and went into the sea. Dario was undecided about whether to join her.

– Go on, silly, enjoy yourself. Valeria just left to meet up with that fool Natalia.

– Dario saw the Maverick leave the garage and disappear down the street.

– Go get Marion. Are you going to let a woman like that slip away?

– Dario felt tempted and spoke to himself:

– I'll give it a try.

– And he began to walk towards the sea. By his side, the spirit of a guy the same age as him was having a blast. He had been in Darius' company for more than three years...

While Dario wandered and laughed, the spirit thought, resentful:

– You're going to pay for everything you did to me. Everything! – he shouted.

Since that incident on Christmas Day, Olair had barely spoken to his daughters. It was as if they were to blame for the eviction action against poor Gisele. He was even more enraged when Gisele surrendered the property and went to live in the back of Rodinei's bar.

Olair, every Tuesday and Thursday, would close the tailor shop early and anxiously await Gisele. She would arrive all perfumed and in tiny clothes. Olair would lie on the mattress and they would love each other until the wee how the morning.

One of those nights she asked me for the umpteenth time:

– Why don't you come live here?

– Here in the tailor's shop? No!

– Why not?

– Imagine what your reputation would be like. You've just become a widower. You've got the girls. It doesn't look good, he hid it.

– I've been a widower for over two months. I'm a man and I have needs. You complete me like a woman, no one's ever completed me like that before.

– What about the deceased? Weren't you two close?

Olair laughed jocularly, disdainfully.

– Josefa was a prude. The rare times we made love, she would ask us to turn off the light. Poor me, I had to look for something outside that I didn't have at home.

– And you're still looking outside the house? – She asked, pretending to be jealous.

– No way! After I found you, I stopped chasing other women.

Gisele pouted:

– Did you really stop looking for the others? Look how jealous I am!

– I give you my word.

Olair was sincerely in love with Gisele. And it was a strange feeling, because he was part of a generation that was not raised for love. As it turns out, Gisele got in with his heart in the flesh. According to the cultural heritage that had been handed down to Olair, a man had to find a good girl to be a good wife and exemplary mother. Love, affection, intimacy, none of that was taken into consideration. He had grown up believing that he had to find a good girl and "prepare" himself outside the home. After all, a married woman was decent and not used to sexually satisfying her husband. A wife was used to procreating, taking care of the home and family. Point.

Josefa was a pretty girl, from a humble family, who knew how to cook, iron, take care of the house and was a great mother. In Blair's eyes, Josefa had been a maid sleeping in her boss's bed.

Olair felt nothing when the doctor diagnosed his wife with cancer and was not moved when she died. On the contrary. On the day of Josefa's death he was grateful that he no longer had to spend money on medicine and live with that bittersweet smell of morphine all over the house.

Now he had met Gisele. Any man less blinded by passion or more experienced with women would understand from afar that Gisele was a vulgar, selfish woman; that is, a con artist. Olair shuddered with pleasure every time their bodies touched. He was approaching forty-five, but felt like a boy of just over eighteen. He had an incomparable fire.

Gisele rested her head on his chest. As she rolled her chest hair with her long, sharp red fingernails, she said:

– You're a man to marry, Olair. It's a pity I'm a widower and you probably don't ever want to marry again.

Olair felt his heart beat faster.

– Why do you say that?

– I don't know. You were married for twenty years, you had two daughters. You lived a gruelling routine, you had to work hard to support the family. I don't think it's fair that you have to tie yourself to someone again.

– The girls are grown up now.

– But they still live with you," she said, provocatively.

– I'm going to put them both to work. Do you think they'll still depend on me? Now that their mother is dead, I'm going to put that house in order.

– Or they could find a husband.

– I've thought of that. They're both too much work, too wasteful. I don't know why they use hairdryers. I spend a fortune on the electric bill.

– It's not fair. You're a worker, you deserve to enjoy your money. I would never do anything to hurt it. That's why I think we should be good friends.

– I don't just want to be your friend. I want more.

– Gisele hid her sarcasm. If she could, she would burst out laughing. But she had to stop. She spoke in a sweet voice:

– If you didn't have so many problems, I'd really go out with you.

– Are you in love with me?

– Gisele bit her lower lip and pouted.

– I could leave everything and be with you, be your wife. But I don't know... your daughters don't like me.

– Arlete and Alzira are not a problem.

– How can they not? They can't stand me. Can you imagine me living under the same roof with them? It would be hell. No, I couldn't stand it.

– Olair scratched his chin. He took Gisele's hand and kissed her fingers.

– If you'd have me, I'd do anything for our happiness.

– I don't know. Alzira is more obedient, I think. But Arlete has a bad temper. Do you remember what she did to me on Christmas day? She even called me a slut! She will never respect me.

– Of course she will – he said in a firmer tone. – They are my daughters, and they must respect me. If not, I'll use the belt on them.

– Really? Look, if they weren't a hindrance to our relationship, I would marry you right now.

– For real? You're not joking with me?

– Not at all – Gisele squeezed her eyes and tried to remember a romantic scene she had seen in the 8 o'clock soap opera. She recalled it and repeated: – I love you more than anything in this life.

– He hugged her tightly.

– Marry me, Gisele.

– Are you sure this is what you want, my dear?

– Yes. I will make you very happy. You can bet on it.

– Then I accept. Of course, I accept!

– Olair hugged her and kissed her lips several times. Then, they made love again. He felt like the most fulfilled man on the face of the Earth.

# Chapter 5

– It was on an early Sunday morning, sometime later, that the bomb dropped on Alzira and Arlete. Olair had cut his hair, applied cream to make it well-groomed, smooth, and fragrant, made adjustments to a well-tailored suit that a customer no longer wanted, and even bought a bottle of Pinho Campos do Jordão cologne, something he had never used before. He had hired a manicurist to do his nails, removed the excess cuticles, and even asked for clear nail polish. His eyes were more vibrant, shining.

– After brewing coffee and heating up milk, Arlete whispered to her sister:

– Did you notice how well-dressed and perfumed Dad is?

– I noticed. Do you think he's going to mass?

– Oh, Alzira, don't be silly. Dad has never been one to attend church.

– I did the math, and next week will mark three months since Mom passed away. Maybe Dad remembered and asked the priest to say a Mass for her.

– I doubt it, but it's possible.

– Alzira got up from the table and hugged her sister. A tear escaped from the corner of her eye.

– I miss her so much...

– Me too – Arlete agreed.

– Olair appeared in the kitchen with some packages.

– Lunch is all in these packages. The mayonnaise should go in the fridge, and the pasta and the stuffed chicken with stuffing should be heated. Alzira, see if you can add some special spice to all this and prepare dessert.

– Dessert? Me?!

– Who else would it be? You've always been good in the kitchen. I want a colourful jelly with whipped cream.

– You can't make that from scratch on the spot, Dad.

– Olair took one of the packages and removed a few boxes of gelatin from inside.

– Here are the packages. I also brought the whipped cream. Start now – he ordered in a surprisingly cordial manner.

– They looked at each other in surprise. Olair had never been friendly with his daughters. Alzira smiled and said:

– All right, Dad. Leave it to me.

– We'll have lunch at noon. I'll take another little trip and go to Rodinei's bar. You can have some soda. It's a special day. Don't forget to dress nicely.

– He said and left. Alzira started to open the packages and said:

– See, Arlete? We've been judging Dad incorrectly. He definitely remembered the anniversary of Mom's death.

– And we're going to celebrate her death? Is that it? If it were her birthday, I'd agree. But the anniversary of her death? This smells fishy to me. Your Olair is up to something.

– I don't know. In the past few months, after we became friends with Ariovaldo and his wife, I feel like Dad regrets the fights he had with Mom. He must be missing her.

– I don't believe that Dad feels remorse. Let's wait and see.

– Alzira closed the fridge and placed the chicken on a baking sheet. She took the pasta and poured it into a pan. She placed everything on the stove. She opened the cupboard and retrieved spice jars.

– I'm sure you're going to make this lunch divine – Arlete complimented.

– I love cooking. I learned so many recipes from Mom.

– I never had a knack for cooking. I'm better at cleaning the house – Arlete said.

– When it's about 11:30, we'll heat up the food and set the table.

– That's perfect

– They left the table set and washed the coffee dishes. They turned on the radio and sang along to the songs. It was a radio program that played the most requested songs of the week. At a certain moment, the announcer played the song "*Moça*" by the singer Wando. They squealed with delight and sang along loudly. After the song ended, Arlete said:

– This song reminded me of Osvaldo. You know, I miss him so much?

– Really? – Alzira asked, smiling. – Is he really coming back from vacation? It's been too long, don't you think?

– He had to help his brother move and take care of his sick niece. His boss granted him an extended leave of two months.

– Good thing you talk on the phone every Sunday. It helps ease the longing.

– I'm anxious because he should call any minute now.

– You're in love!

– Of course I am – confessed Arlete. – We've made many promises of love. Osvaldo is coming back, we'll make our relationship official, and who knows, maybe we'll get married soon?

– Alzira smiled broadly.

– You deserve all the happiness in the world. You just need to be less bossy.

– That's just the way I am, Alzira. I'm bossy, and things have to be my way.

– Poor kids!

– I'm going to be a tough mom. They always have to be in line. You'll see how I'll raise them. I hate rude kids.

– The phone rang, and Arlete let out a delighted squeal.

– It must be Osvaldo.

– She hurried to the hallway, sat on the stool, and picked up the phone.

– Hello.

– Hi, my love, how are you?

– She recognized Osvaldo's voice and felt a slight tremor in her body.

– Better now!

– I'm glad. I miss you so much.

– Me too. I can't wait to see you.

– Osvaldo cleared his throat and started to sing on the other end of the line:

– I want to wrap myself in your hair, embrace your whole body, die of love, get lost in love...

– Arlete fell silent and almost lost her senses. After a few "hey, are you still there," she mumbled:

– I can't believe it.

– What's wrong? Didn't you like it?

– Yes... – the words were escaping her mouth.

– Do I sing that badly?

– Arlete laughed.

– Not at all.

– I was here helping my mom with lunch, and they played this Wando song. I immediately thought of you and couldn't resist. I called as soon as the song ended.

– I was also listening to the same radio program.

– Another coincidence! Do you want some now?

– Give me the time of day, really?

– I've been interested in you from the very moment we met. I've never hidden the fact that I like you. And this long-distance relationship over the phone is proof that I'm in love.

– I'm in love with you too. You can believe that.

– I do!

– I called because I have an invitation to make.

– Invitation?

– Osvaldo was beaming:

– First, before I invite you, I want to tell you that I came home last night.

– Oh! – she exclaimed. – Are you in São Paulo?

– Yes. I can't wait to hug and kiss you.

– Arlete blushed and asked, curious:

– Tell me about the invitation.

– My boss had to go on vacation to the beach and gave me two tickets to see Elis Regina at the Bandeirantes Theather as a gift. Will you come with me?

– Are you inviting me to see "*False shine*"?

– Yes.

– I can't believe it! I would give anything to see Elis perform in this show!

– Then get ready because my brother lent me his car. I'll pick you up around seven, is that okay?

– Of course.

– They talked a little more and exchanged more declarations of love. Arlete hung up the phone and let out a cry of joy.

– Alzira came to the hallway, finishing drying a cup.

– Was it him? Osvaldo?

– It was. And he even sang the verses of the Wando song. Look how my heart is – Arlete took her sister's hand and placed it on her chest. – It's going to burst from so much happiness.

– Osvaldo came back from his leave?

– He came back yesterday. And he's taking me to see the Elis Regina show.

– That's great! But will Dad allow it?

– He's more interested in that floozy Gisele. He doesn't care whether we're at home or not.

– In any case, you'd better control your excitement. Don't let it show. Dad is eager to ruin our happiness.

– You're right. I'll change my attitude. Today, I'll stay quiet. If he brings that woman for lunch, we'll pretend everything is fine. Then he'll want to take her to the movies, like he does every Sunday. They'll come back late, as usual. I won't stay out so late.

– It was one in the afternoon when Olair arrived with Gisele in tow. The woman was wearing an overpowering, sickly sweet perfume. Her clothes were nothing to write home about. She had on a golden bustier and a tiny, tightly fitting skirt. Gisele might have a voluptuous figure, but her fashion sense and demeanour left much to be desired. She was vulgar from head to toe.

– She sat down at the table and, without manners, took a piece of chicken in her hand. Then he filled his glass with beer.

– So, girls, how are you doing?

– Arlete didn't respond.

– Fine – said Alzira, unenthusiastically.

– The house is well-kept.

– We learned from our mother to keep the house clean. It's harder for pests to get in that way – Alzira remarked.

– Of course, sometimes, even with a clean house, some nasty pests still manage to get in. We can't help it – Arlete quipped.

– Gisele noticed the tone and felt she was being harassed. She turned to Olair and hid it.

– Sweetie, do you have any dark beer? A Ma/zbier?

– No.

– Would you mind going to get some from Rodinei's bar? Do you want dark beer? A...

– Gisele cut him off with a playful and sweet voice:

– My God! I just love eating chicken with dark beer. But if you don't want to, it's not a problem – she said in a childish and syrupy tone.

– Olair didn't say anything. He got up and went to fetch the beer. As soon as he closed the door of the house, Gisele glared at them.

– You idiots! Do you think you can fool me?

– Hey, watch your tone! – Arlete exclaimed.

– What tone, no way! Both of you hate me.

– We don't hate you yet, but it's true that we don't like you.

– I'm going to marry Olair, and whether you like it or not, you'll have to put up with me.

– I'm not obligated to live with a bitch under the same roof.. Furthermore, we are the rightful owners of half of this house.

– Oh, really? – Gisele added, in a threatening tone. – Just because you have fifty percent of this miserable little house? Either you get into my rhythm or I'll make your life a living hell.

– Isn't it enough that my father is overbearing?. I won't tolerate a harpy giving me orders.

– Gisele laughed loudly, took another sip of her beer, gargled, and swallowed. She retorted:

– The harpy is going to give orders to both of you. You'll have your meals right here – she pointed – in the palm of my hand.

– You don't know us – Arlete added.

– Oh, but I do. I've been around the block; I know who I'm dealing with. I'm marrying Olair, and you'll do everything I want. Do you think I'll ruin my beautiful, long, red nails? I wasn't born for washing, ironing, or cooking. I only know how to love, and I'm good at it.

- If we ask the men in this neighbourhood, I bet many of them know how good you are at that - Arlete retorted.

- Gisele shrugged.

- I've slept with many, yes. So what? Your father likes me. We're all going to live together. We'll be happy forever! - she said provocatively.

- I won't allow it.

- Gisele locked eyes with Arlete.

- You and that fifth-rate lawyer took my house away from me.

- Hold on! The law took your house away. If you had paid your rent on time, it wouldn't have happened. Now you want to blame the world for the consequences of your actions? Take responsibility for your own life - Alzira responded, with a conciliatory yet firm voice.

- Don't dare to give me a lecture about morality. Now you're going to learn not to mess with me.

- It's no use threatening me. We'll make your life a living hell. Want to bet? - Arlete provoked; her voice filled with resentment.

- Gisele gave a wicked grin, finished her piece of chicken, and then refilled her beer glass.

- Alzira shook her head, and Arlete taunted:

- Aren't you going to wait for the dark beer, dear?

- You're right - Gisele agreed.

- In a split second, she grabbed the beer glass and threw it in Arlete's face.

– The young woman jumped up and couldn't believe it.

– What do you think you're doing, you crazy woman?

– Alzira grabbed a cloth and handed it to her sister. Arlete wiped her face and gave the cloth back to her sister. Then, she lunged at Gisele, and there was no power in the world that could separate them. Gisele intentionally pulled the tablecloth, and everything came crashing down: plates, glasses, and serving dishes filled with food. She also allowed Arlete to land a few slaps on her.

– Olair arrived just after the commotion had started. He was stunned by the chaos. He abandoned the beer bottles and forcefully pulled Arlete away, hurting her in the process.

– What's going on here? – he yelled.

– Gisele pretended to cry and stood up slowly. Her clothes were stained with bits of macaroni, and her hair was dishevelled, covered in tomato sauce. Her face was red and marked from the slaps.

– I don't know what happened – she whimpered. – As soon as you left, they started verbally attacking me. I tried to ignore them, but Arlete got angry. She lost control and came at me. Alzira tried to topple the table on me. They tried to kill me, Olair!

– Alzira protested:

– It's a lie, Dad! I didn't do anything. She started the fight.

– Arlete also said:

– She threw beer in my face.

– No, Olair! – Gisele pleaded. – I would never do that. You know me. Your daughters hate me.

– Gisele spoke and wiped her hands across her face, pretending to cry. The sisters exchanged glances, unable to believe the act. Olair glared at them angrily.

– You two have messed up my life quite a bit since you were born. Your mother gave you a lousy education, and she was a terrible woman. It's all come back to haunt me.

– Arlete stood tall and confronted him:

– Don't talk about our mother. You have no right.

– I do have the right. I was married to that nuisance. Look what she left me with: two ill-mannered, insolent daughters. Two freeloaders. It would have been better if you had never been born.

– He spoke and turned to Gisele. He embraced her.

– Are you okay?

– How can I be? – she said in a tearful voice. – Your daughters don't want us to be together. I better go back to my little room behind the bar.

– No way. You're not leaving here.

– That's fine – Alzira added. – Arlete and I will leave.

– It would be best if you didn't come back until tomorrow, or never again – Olair said, in an angry voice.

– Don't forget that we have the right to half of this house. You could sell it, give us our share, and everyone can go their own way. What do you think?

– Olair was about to respond, but Gisele scolded him.

– Don't say anything, dear. The girls are upset and angry with us.

– You're right. I won't listen to those two airheads. Get out of here, you brats! – he yelled.

– Arlete rushed to the bathroom and quickly cleaned herself up. She wet her hair, dabbed her face with some lavender, and returned to pull Alzira by the hands to leave the house. They walked away aimlessly, not knowing where to go.

– She poisoned our father's mind – Alzira said. – She's going to make our lives a living hell.

– Gisele calculated everything correctly. What an idiot I was! I let myself get carried away by this unfortunate woman. What are we going to do, Arlete? I'm afraid.

– Scared of what?

– I don't know. I couldn't stand living under the same roof as Gisele.

– Me neither.

– Let's pray and ask God for guidance – Alzira implored.

– I said we could leave.

– Then, let's go.

– And leave the house on a silver platter for that tramp? Never.

– Arlete, why should we fight for this house? Let's roll up our sleeves and forge our own path. We're strong and can build our lives without relying on our father.

– But it's not fair.

– Fair or not, we need to think about ourselves and our future. We are good people, and life will help us. You're in love with Osvaldo, and I'm sure you'll get married. I will go on with my life, and soon everything will pass. We'll be happy and fulfilled people.

– Arlete hesitated for a moment. – You're right. We need to think about the two of us.

– Everything has a solution in life. We have each other – Alzira added.

– They hugged each other, and at that moment, a ray of light seemed to descend from above onto their heads. The next moment, as they turned the corner, they came face to face with Ariovaldo and Celia.

– They were about to speak, but Celia was quick:

– I woke up thinking about you two. We were heading to your house to invite you to lunch with us.

– The sisters exchanged glances, embraced Celia, and started crying.

# Chapter 6

– Valeria crossed the ferry, and ten minutes later, she was at Elenice's apartment, located near the orchidarium, in the Jose Menino beach area. She and Milton were at the beach, and Natalia was alone. She received her friend with an affectionate hug and then said:

– You don't look well.

– No. In fact, I don't feel well at all.

– They settled on a sofa-bed. Natalia poured some iced mate and served it to Valeria.

– Here, I just took it out of the fridge. I added a few drops of lemon.

– Valeria took a sip of the refreshing cold drink.

– All was well at the beach house. Marion showed up and started talking about something strange. She's dating Thomas, but she's interested in Dario.

– Marion is crazy, unhinged. She only thinks about her beauty, uses men to satisfy her desires, and increases her bank account.

– She gives me the creeps, Natalia. I thought of poor Laura. Marion was cruel enough to run over someone. She's not normal.

- Let's leave her aside. Marion doesn't deserve our attention. But you didn't come from Guaruja to talk about Marion.

- Valeria nodded.

- That's true. The problem is Dario. He went mad and almost drowned me. He plays these stupid, idiotic pranks. I don't like this rough way he's treating me.

- I don't like him. I've never hidden that from you.

- I know. However, we have a very strong intimate connection, Natalia. Every time I try to break up, he wins me back. I end up giving in, and we get back together.

- A couple that really loves each other can't live with so many ups and downs. They fight a lot, argue a lot. Could this be the man you want by your side in the years to come?

- I don't know. You know I even liked Otavio. If it weren't for...

- Valeria couldn't finish the sentence. She hugged Natalia and began to cry. As she gently ran her hand through her friend's silky hair, Natalia considered:

- You really liked Otavio. It's a shame he's so reckless and into drag racing.

- I don't want to remember that night...

- Valeria didn't want to, but the image always came to her mind. She had turned fifteen and, at the end of her debutante party, some friends and her then boyfriend - Octavio, known as Taviño, had just turned eighteen - went to a deserted avenue near Interlagos to participate in a streak, a sort of clandestine car race. The boys and girls had a lot of drinks in their heads and wanted to end the night with a little more adrenaline in their blood. They went to the point where these races took place. The dispute was between Taviño and Darío. Whoever had the most powerful car and got to the other end of the avenue the fastest would win a small amount of money. Valeria and the other girls went to the place where the winner was scheduled to arrive.

- Dario and Taviño revved their cars, and the race began. The tires screeched and burned the pavement. To show off, Dario wanted to perform a stunt called a *"wooden hourse,"* a radical manoeuvre where a vehicle's direction is changed abruptly using the handbrake, causing a spin with a 180 to 360-degree turn. That's when the tragedy occurred.

- Taviño got scared, lost control, and crashed the car into a lamppost. His death was instant.

- Natalia tried to comfort her:

- I know it was terrible. Your night of celebration could have ended differently. But you chose to go out with that gang of delinquents.

- After the funeral, Dario approached, feeling somewhat guilty, and we started seeing each other. I felt very lonely and ended up getting involved.

- Do you love him?

- No, I can say that for sure. I like Dario, but I don't love him.

- You're turning nineteen, Valeria, you're not a little girl anymore. You're beautiful, you have a good life, a father who adores you. Why stay in a relationship that brings you nothing but trouble?

– I don't know. As I told you, the attraction is too great. I may not love him, but when we're together, I go crazy, I lose control, and by the time I come to my senses, the damage is already done.

– What do you tell me about your feelings for Tomás? – Valeria shrugged her shoulders.

– You know I like him. But I'm afraid of Marion.

– This fear is too strong for my liking – Natalia retorted.

– What do you mean?

– I don't know. My intuition tells me there's something that prevents her from being in a relationship with Thomas.

– Oh, Natalia, stop with the nonsense. A ghost prevents me from being with Thomas? That's a good one – Valeria replied sarcastically.

– Elenice arrived at the apartment, greeted Valeria, then covered herself with a bathing suit, adjusted her hat, beach umbrella, and mat in a corner of the balcony. She looked great, with a tan and lively, bright eyes.

– Where's Milton? – Natalia asked.

– He met two friends from the city hall, and they're having a beer on the beach. The sun is scorching, and I've already tanned a lot today.

– Your skin looks divine, Mrs. Elenice.

– Thank you – Elenice noticed Valeria's puffy eyes.

– Did something happen?

– She was remembering that tragic night. Taviño's death.

– Elenice felt a shiver run through her body. She ran her hands over her arms.

– Just talking about that boy gives me the creeps.

– I liked him, Mrs. Elenice – Valeria said tearfully.

– I know, dear. We all had teenage crushes.

– If he were alive, we could have been engaged.

– I don't think so. It was a teenage romance. You and Taviño had nothing in common.

– Really?

– Yes – observed Elenice. – Just like you and Dario have nothing in common either.

– Is that what I was telling you, mother? – Natalia intervened. – Valeria and Dario have nothing to do with each other.

– Maybe you need to meet a man who truly sparks love in you.

– I don't believe in that, Mrs. Elenice.

– Why not? Thomas has always liked you. He's a good guy.

– I don't know; I'm afraid of getting too seriously involved.

– I understand that. You don't want a serious relationship. Now I understand why you only attract problematic relationships into your life.

– My relationship with Taviño was full of fights and with Dario it's no different!

– Does love scare you?

– Valeria didn't know how to respond. She had never truly loved before. Still, getting involved with someone made her anxious. Her relationship with Dario didn't count. She knew it was a relationship with an expired expiration date. She realized that she needed to get help and overcome the sexual fascination that Dario had over her.

– As for Tomás, she really didn't know what was going on. She liked him, but something in the back of her mind always warned her to be careful with Marion. The voice was clear and threatening:

– If you get involved with Thomas, Marion will do something worse to you than what she did to Laura.

– Just thinking about that phrase that echoed in her mind gave Valeria the chills. Trapped in her fears and insecurities, she lowered her head and fell silent. Elenice gestured with her head, and Natalia got up, drawing the curtain over the window. Then she moved the fan closer and turned it on. The heat had made the room stuffy. Elenice got up, placed a cassette tape in the small device nearby, and then a classical piece of rare beauty filled the room. She sighed and said:

– Let's close our eyes and tune in to the music. Now, let's set aside all external things, forget our problems, doubts, and anxieties. Let's connect to the power of goodness, which is the only force that exists. Goodness elevates our souls and immediately connects us with God. What we can resolve, may He give us strength, courage, and clarity to make the best choice. What we still lack the strength to understand, accept, or resolve, let's leave it in His hands, so He can do what's best.

– She let out a long sigh and continued:

- May God and the good spirits protect and assist us! So be it.

- Elenice finished speaking and felt a mild sensation in her chest. She opened her eyes, and Valeria still had her eyes closed. She had fallen asleep. Elenice gestured to her daughter, and they both got up without making a sound. Elenice picked up a pillow and gently placed it behind Valeria's head. Then, they went to the balcony.

- Mom, do you think Valeria might be dealing with some spiritual disturbance? - Natalia asked.

- I feel like her emotions are quite confused. It might be related to something from her past life. She has a huge emotional block that prevents her from loving.

- I tried to talk to her about spirituality, and she always cuts me off, politely.

- We should respect her. People become interested in spirituality for two reasons: love or suffering. We need to let Valeria feel comfortable. In due time, she'll open her heart to better understand spiritual values.

- Dario and Marion are at the house in Guaruja. You know how I feel about those two.

- Valeria will need to decide for herself with whom she wants to maintain relationships of affection and friendship. We can't tell her that so-and-so are people who don't do her any good.

- Well, if we realize that Dario is not a good person, why keep him by Valeria's side? And Marion? She's a vein, self-interested, and shallow girl. I never liked her.

- What good would it do to open Valeria's eyes? Haven't we already confided our feelings to her about these friends?

- Yes.

- Did she accept our impressions?

- Natalia shook her head. Elenice continued:

- I don't know Marion. I have nothing to say about that girl. But I know Thomas. Something tells me there's some kind of spiritual disturbance preventing his closeness with Valeria.

- I feel the same way, Mom.

- As for Dario, I feel that he's lost and disturbed. He needs prayers, not accusatory fingers.

- It's difficult. I don't like him.

- There is no room for your personal taste here, my daughter. How hard is it to send him a positive vibration, directed to his heart, to change his attitude towards life and receive spiritual support?

- Do you really feel he's disturbed?

- Yes, something tells me that Taviño's spirit is connected to him.

- Natalia wasn't surprised.

- I suspected that. Dario has had some very strange behaviours since Taviño's death. If it's his spirit negatively influencing Dario, how can we warn him?

– Through prayers, positive vibrations. Let's always try to surround him in a circle of light whenever possible. Let's envision Dario always well and smiling. God will do the rest.

– You're right. It doesn't hurt to try.

The conversation flowed pleasantly. Elenice and her daughter talked animatedly about Natalia's future. She had passed the entrance exam for architecture at the university and was overjoyed. Valeria hadn't been as fortunate, but she was starting to feel the desire to study abroad.

– Maybe I'll talk to Mr. America. If he sends Valeria to study in Italy, the chances of her and Dario continuing their relationship will be very slim.

– Do that, Mom. Mr. America likes us, and he's always listened to you.

– We like Valeria, and we'll pray for the best. I was very fond of Amelia. We were school friends. If I wasn't here and you were facing the same problems, I'm sure Amelia would help you.

– Sitting on the couch, Amelia, in spirit, stroked her daughter's hair.

– Now you'll have to make a choice, my angel. May God protect you!

– The spirit got up, passed through the wall, and gave Elenice a loving hug.

– Thank you. I knew you'd be nearby and take care of my little girl. – Then, turning to Natalia, she said, – You're a true friend. May God bless your endeavours, always!

– Amelia kissed Elenice's forehead and did the same with Natalia. Then, her spirit dissipated into the air.

– Elenice and Natalia felt a pleasant sensation. Elenice remembered her friendship with Amelia and the pranks they used to pull in the school corridors, much to the dismay of the nuns. Natalia burst into laughter, and time passed.

– Two hours later, Valeria woke up in high spirits.

– Mrs. Elenice, I haven't napped so nicely in a long time. I feel light and refreshed.

– I'm glad you're feeling better.

– That little nap opened my appetite. Aren't you all hungry?

– Elenice looked at her watch and it was after two in the afternoon.

– Milton is going to spend the whole afternoon with his friends. How about the three of us going to a restaurant around the corner? They serve amazing fish. Afterward, we can have ice cream and walk in the beautiful gardens by the waterfront.

– I'm in.

– Natalia nodded too, and a few minutes later, the three of them were comfortably seated in the restaurant, chatting, gesturing, and placing their orders.

## Chapter 7

– After lunch, Celia invited the young women for some coffee in the backyard of the house. It was a simple, well-kept two-story home. Ariovaldo had insisted on maintaining the trees in the backyard. He had created some wooden benches from leftover crates, painted them dark green, and improvised a table from some iron brackets given to him by the school director. On the table, there was a pergola made of bougainvillea and red hibiscus.

While carrying a tray with a coffee pot and cups, Alzira confessed:

– Your house may be small, but it's very cozy.

– This backyard is divine. It doesn't even feel like we're in the same neighbourhood – added Arlete.

– Ariovaldo and I took many years to buy this piece of land. Then, it took more years to build the house. It's small, but it suits our needs. When Iara visits Buenos Aires with her husband, she stays in that little room in the back – Celia pointed.

– At the end of the yard, among the fruit trees and other plants and flares, there was a laundry area and a small, elegant bedroom with bathroom. It reminded him of a doll's house.

– I'd love to live in a house like this," said Alzira. – All neat, painted, organized. I really like a well-kept and organized home.

– Alzira was born this way – continued Arlete. – Since she was little, she would make the beds early in the morning, sweep through the rooms, and help mom in the kitchen. And she's really good at making both savory and sweet pastries.

– Celia was amazed.

– Do you like cooking?

Alzira nodded.

– I prefer sweets to savoury dishes. My mom taught me how to make some bread, sweet rolls that she had learned from my grandma. It seems that these recipes have been passed down through the generations.

Have you ever thought about making a living from it?

– No, Mrs. Celia. I'm thinking of studying literature.

– Do you want to be a teacher? – Celia asked.

– Arlete glanced to the side and upwards, indecisive.

– I enjoy reading the classics of Brazilian literature. I really appreciate Orfeu's Lessa and Erico Verissimo.

– Do you feel like teaching?

– I'm not sure.

– Close your eyes – Celia asked.

– What do you mean?

– Trust me, let's go. Close your eyes and hold my hands.

Alzira nodded and closed her eyes.

– Imagine that you're teaching, in a classroom full of students. You're teaching Brazilian literature.

– Alzira forced herself to think, closed her eyes tightly and began to imagine. Celia continued: :

What's the sensation?

– Hard to express. I don't feel anything.

– Keep your eyes closed.

Alright. And if, at this moment, you leave the classroom and enter a well-equipped kitchen with all the utensils? Imagine that you approach a counter and start preparing pastries, pies, and cakes.

– Alzira sighed and broke into a broad smile.

– No need to ask what I'm feeling. I'm loving being in this kitchen. My hands glide smoothly over the sweet dough. Oh! – Alzira was surprised. – Other girls have appeared; they're helping me. It's like I'm in a pastry kitchen. I can even smell the sweets!

Celia asked her to open her eyes.

– What do you prefer? Teaching or making sweets?

– Without a doubt, I'd rather spend the day making sweets – she admitted.

– You may love literature, but your soul wants something else. You can read all the books you want. Just because you like to read doesn't mean you have to be a teacher.

– We don't have the means to do anything. Especially now that Dad is dating Gisele.

– Why are you still living with him? From what I heard at Christmas, you're going to be nineteen soon – Celia pointed to Arlete – and you, Alzira, will turn eighteen. You're practically adults. Both of you are capable of finding a job. You can support yourselves and move out. – Part of the house is ours – Arlete said. – Dad is thinking of moving that tramp into our house. I won't allow it.

– Why not, Arlete? Do you really feel so powerless that you think you need the house your dad bought with his own money? Don't you feel you have the means to achieve what you desire on your own merit?

– No. My mom worked hard so he could make the house payments. She saved every penny she could. We even went through tough times because all the money that came in went toward the house payments. Then, in the past few years, he went crazy and decided he had to pay off the house. I don't think it's fair to hand it over to him and that tramp now.

– That house belongs to your father and mother. I won't deny that they are entitled to half of it, especially since the law gives them this protection. But are they going to stop living their lives to fight for half of that house? Are they going to give up their desires, dreams and accomplishments, put them aside, to make hell for a couple who, apparently, wants to try to be happy?

– This way, it makes me feel like the victim of the story. I'm the victim – protested Arlete.

– There are no victims in the world. We're responsible for everything that happens to us.

– I don't agree. I didn't ask to be his daughter – mumbled Arlete.

– Yes, you did. If you didn't ask, at least you were attracted to that house due to shared ideas. God never makes mistakes, my child.

– Arlete lowered her eyes and let the tears flow freely. Alzira approached and put her arm around her sister's waist.

– Don't be upset, Arlete. We're united and have the strength to face any situation. We lost our mom, whom we loved so much. If we could overcome that loss and move on with our lives, don't you think that fighting for that house is too small? Did you see what Mrs. Celia said? That we are capable. We can have our own house – Alzira said and turned to Celia. – I finished reading the novel *"Between Love and War."* I was fascinated. The book held my attention from beginning to end. It also made me see life in a more positive and less fatalistic way.

– Spiritist books have the power to stir us and, through light and pleasant reading, bring messages of comfort, hope, and peace. If you want, I have other spiritualist novels. I can lend them to you.

– Oh, I'd love that! – exclaimed Alzira.

Celia filled a coffee cup and handed it to Arlete. She then lent her a handkerchief.

– Thank you.

- Arlete, we need to be attentive to the treasure's life offers us. We need to pay more attention to the power of thought, which is a faculty of the spirit. See, thought is produced by suggestion, meaning the induction to do or act in a certain way. Beliefs arise from thought; they are conglomerates of thoughts imprinted on our emotional circuits. Beliefs determine the world around us.

- I thought was more powerful than anything - Alzira added. Thought has its power, but it's not as strong as belief. Belief is you accepting in your heart the imperative of a certain way of thinking.

- Arlete blew her nose, picked up her coffee cup, sipped the steaming liquid, and fidgeted on her stool.

- I've always wanted an independent life. The problem is we're very attached to that house. We grew up there, and if we leave, where will our memories of our mom go?

- Everything in life is cyclical and transient. We're not stuck in the same place forever. The emotional memory you have will never be erased, not even with the death of the physical body because it's an integral part of the spirit, and the spirit is eternal.

The young women agreed, and Celia continued:

- The phase you're going through now is challenging.

- A huge challenge - Arlete hissed. - Challenges move us forward. Through challenges, we move from the common ground to maturity, learning to deal effectively with ourselves. Challenges allow us to see the numerous possibilities of choices we have to meet our happiness. Each of you is your own master.

– I am afraid to leave home. I'm afraid to fail and ask my father for help again. I no longer want him to throw all the food he has given us since we were born in our faces. A father who loves his children would never talk like that.

– You attracted this father for the strengthening of your spirit. Look, Arlete, the way you were raised has made you a strong woman with your own opinions and a desire to grow, to be independent. If you had a father who spoiled you too much, you might be living a different reality and not realize the strength you have to shape your own destiny.

– I never thought about it that way.

– Everything you're saying makes so much sense – Alzira agreed. – We weren't raised to question differences between people. Since I was little, I've been wondering why we live in that house. And lately, I've been questioning life. Why did I lose my mom?

– You didn't lose your mom – Celia reassured her. – Josefa simply went to another dimension, to another world. Earth is a transitory world where our spirit reincarnates to learn to recognize its strength and expand its intelligence during a certain period of time.

– Do you really think we'll reunite with our mom?

– Certainly. Don't you remember our conversation at Christmas? We talked about spirits, your mom's death, your nightmares...

– It's true. That night was magical.

– It was magical and warmed my heart – added Arlete.

– I dreamed of her the other day – Alzira said. – Mom was in some kind of hospital with many beds, I think over a hundred stretchers, with many nurses and doctors offering treatment to the patients.

– Your mother's spirit must have been taken to an Aid Station that exists in the spirit world. She died from a cancer that destroyed her physical body and affected her perispirit. As soon as she is free of the energies of the disease, she can go to a Recovery Colony. Maybe soon you will be able to dream more about her and even go on a date.

– Really? – Arlete inquired.

– Yes. We never lose contact with those we love. Bonds of love are solid and eternal. At the right moment, you will have contact with Josefa.

– The sisters trembled with delight. They felt very comfortable in Celia's company. Alzira wanted to know more:

– What is the perispirit?

– Good question, Alzira – Celia smiled and answered enthusiastically –. Perispirit is the name given to the link between the spirit and the physical body. When the spirit incarnates, the perispirit serves as a link between the spirit and the body.

After passing away, the perispirit becomes the very body through which the spirit manifests itself and transitions into other dimensions.

– Do we live many lives? Is that true? – Arlete questioned.

- Yes, we live many lives, and we will live as many as necessary to expand our awareness, bringing maturity to our spirit.

The pleasant conversation continued throughout the afternoon. It was past six when Arlete suddenly got up.- I need to get ready. Ariovaldo will pick me up soon for a spiritual healing session.

- Celia smiled.

- You really like that young man. And he really likes you. You'll be very happy together.

Arlete felt an unparalleled warmth in her chest. She hugged Celia and thanked her:

- Thank you so much for saying these words. It's everything my heart wanted to hear.

She said her goodbyes, and Alzira also got up.

- Why are you leaving now? - Celia asked. - It would be a pleasure to stay for dinner.

- I would love to, but I need to help Arlete get ready.

- No way! Leave me, I'll get ready on my own - Arlete assured.

- What if Gisele is still at home? Promise you won't start a fight with her?

- Stay a little longer. What's the point of being cooped up in that house? The company there isn't the best - Arlete retorted.

- You're right. I can stay, Celia?

- On one condition.

– What is it?

– You'll teach me how to make a dessert.

– A dessert? – Yes. I have some in the cupboard. What's missing we'll ask Ariovaldo and he'll pick it up at the bakery

Alzira smiled happily:

– Alright. I'll make a carrot cake I really like.

Arlete admitted:

– Alzira's carrot cake is unbeatable. I've never eaten a better cake.

– Then let's have some carrot cake! – Celia said. – Let's celebrate because I feel that your lives are about to change for the better.

– Really? – Alzira asked, hopeful.

– Something very good is about to happen. Believe it.

The sisters exchanged happy glances.

– May God hear you, Celia. May God hear you.

– Arlete said goodbye to her sister and remarked:

– After this pleasant afternoon, nothing will take me off balance. Not even Gisele.

– That's right, Arlete. Always use this phrase with determination: "Within me, I am in charge."

– I'll never forget, Celia.

– And on her way home, only one phrase remained in Arlete's mind, which she repeated like a mantra:

– "Within me, I am in charge."

# Chapter 8

Valeria returned to Guaruja late at night. Her meeting with Elenice and Natalia had been wonderful. "It's so nice to be close to people who genuinely like me," she thought to herself.

He parked the car in the garage and turned off the engine. He went into the house and everything was dark. She turned on the lights, and soon one of the housemaids appeared.

– Do you need anything, Mrs. Valeria?

– No. I want to know where Dario is.

The housemaid blushed. She had heard Dario's and Marion's cries of pleasure for hours. The audacious couple hadn't even had the decency to keep their bedroom door closed. The girl, out of respect for Valeria, simply said:

– Miss Marion's driver picked them up two hours ago. They went to a party on Porchat Island. Your Dario said they don't know when they'll be back.

Valeria smiled with relief. She was tired of Dario, his drinking, antics, and that pointless relationship. She would wait for him to return and, the next day, end the relationship. It was the best thing to do.

- She walked to her bed, undressed and took a good shower. The heat was unbearable. He finished his shower and rubbed his body with a refreshing cologne. She dried off, put on a babydoll and turned on the room's air conditioner. She closed the window and drew the curtains. She leaned over to the bedside table and chose a record. He picked one from the Excelsior collection – The machine turned on the sound and he placed the vinyl on the turntable. He switched on the lamp on the bedside table and turned off the light in the room. He lay down on the bed and let himself be enveloped by the melodies of the record.

Valeria fell asleep and had a restful night's sleep. She woke up at ten in the morning. She opened her eyes, stretched, and noticed the record player's needle looping back and forth.

- I forgot that this device doesn't have an automatic shutoff.

- She got up, picked another record from the collection, and hummed the music as she opened the curtains and the window. From her bedroom balcony, she could see the sea. The day had dawned cloudy, and the rhythmic sound of the waves brought her profound peace of mind.

- Valeria reflected on recent events. She couldn't understand why she was stuck in a relationship without a future. She had failed the entrance exam and wanted to take a decorating course in Europe. She considered the institute in Florence, Italy. Americo had encouraged her to join the institute. Her uncle Adamo would be delighted to have her company.

– I will follow my father's advice, – Valeria said as she changed her clothes to have breakfast.

– She put on a new bikini and a beach cover-up. She left her room and encountered one of the maids.

– Would you like me to serve breakfast in the dining room or on the balcony, Mrs. Valeria?

– The day is cloudy but muggy. Please serve it on the balcony.

– Certainly, ma'am.

– Did Dario show up?

– He arrived just after eight this morning, Mrs. Valeria, in a pitiful state.

– Prepare the coffee and take it to the balcony. I'll check on Dario.

– Before that, Valeria called her father's office. Americo answered with a big smile on his face.

– Beautiful daughter! I miss you so much!

– I miss you too, Daddy.

– How's everything over there? Are you behaving yourself?

Yes, I am. Yesterday, I spent almost the whole day with Natalia and Mrs. Elenice. They do me a world of good.

– I greatly appreciate your friendship with Natalia. She's a good girl, and I've known Elenice for years. She may have lost her money, but she's still a woman of great character and a wise advisor.

- I called because I've been thinking about following your advice and enrolling in that decorating course in Florence.

- Americo opened and closed his eyes, showing extreme happiness.

- I'm thrilled that you're thinking about your future.

- I know that the course starts in August, that the school year in Europe is different from ours, but I am determined and I am going to prepare myself to enter the institute and perform well, I want you to be very proud of me.

- I already am very proud of you.

- Oh, before I forget, I also want you to know that I'll be breaking up with Dario.

-You don't know how happy I am with these decisions. It makes me glad to know you've been sensible and realized that this young man, even though his parents are my friends, is not the man for you.

- Thank you for supporting me, Daddy.

- Valeria, - Americo said with a quivering voice, - I love you very much.

- I love you too, Daddy.

Hey, this conversation sounds like a farewell.

- You're right, - she replied, her voice also trembling.

Would you like me to come down to the beach this weekend?

– It won't be necessary. I'll end the relationship with Dario and head to the mountains later today. Would you keep me company for dinner?

– I'd love to. I have a meeting with the Minister of Transportation, but I'll reschedule it for early tomorrow. You are more important.

– I love you, Dad.

– I love you too, daughter.

Americo hung up the phone but was overcome by great unease. He felt a tightness in his chest, as if something bad were about to happen.

– It's no big deal – he said aloud to himself – I'm having dinner with my daughter tonight.

– He pushed the thoughts aside and pressed a button on a device attached to the phone:

– Miss Mirtes, please. Cancel my meeting with the minister.

– Dr. Americo, he came to São Paulo just to talk to you.

– Tell him I had a bout of food poisoning, and we can meet early tomorrow wherever he wants.

– All right.

– Americo refocused his attention on his business. No matter how hard he tried to push it away, that bad feeling wouldn't leave his chest and now was churning in his stomach too. He got up, took an antacid out of the cupboard, mixed it with water and drank the fizzy liquid.

– It must have been breakfast. That slice of coconut cake didn't sit well with me.

Valeria hung up the phone and stood up. She walked to Dario's room, turned the doorknob, and opened the door. It was pitch dark inside. A mingled smell of alcohol and cigarettes invaded her nostrils.

– She entered and opened the window. The light flooded in, and Dario woke up, startled.

Hey, what's going on?

– Time to get up.

– I got back from the party after eight in the morning. I'm sleepy.

– You'll have the whole day to sleep. Now get up.

– Valeria approached the bed and pulled the sheet. Dario was naked. That image stirred something within her. Dario had a spectacular body. He was naturally muscular and had a bronzed skin tone. The mark of the swimsuit made him even more provocative, more sensual.

– We need to talk, – she said, her voice barely audible, trying to hide her excitement. It was hard to contain her emotions.

– Why am I so weak? – she asked herself while attempting to avert her eyes from her boyfriend's body. A voice whispered in her ear:

– Because I desire you, Valeria. I want you. You don't feel attraction for Dario, but you feel it for me. You're going to sleep with him, and I'll be able to experience pleasure through him. Come on, you want him. You desire him.

– Taviño's spirit spoke in a voice full of voluptuousness. It would be worth a try, but the spirit's strength over her will was far greater. Dario embraced her and the contact between their bodies made her forget about the promise to break, for now. Valeria lay on her boyfriend's body and they loved each other very much. Taviño brought his perispirit closer to Dario's aura and began to feel the same emotion as the boy. And he also controlled Dario's mind. Do it like this, now do it that way.

– After they finished making love, Valeria got up and realized she was famished. She fought with herself, and Dario asked:

– So, babe, shall we have our breakfast? I couldn't sleep, and I'm starving.

She didn't say anything. She put on her bikini, irritated herself, and left the room. She locked herself in the bathroom and cried. She asked for help from the heavens.

– Lolla, a spirit friend from past lives, approached and suggested, while stroking her long red hair:

– You need to strengthen your thoughts, my dear. You need to learn that you control yourself. Nobody has the power to manipulate your will. It happens because you let it happen. I can't keep Taviño away. You and Dario naturally attract him. The moment you feel strong enough to free yourself from both of them, they won't be able to do anything to you.

– Valeria stopped crying. She grabbed a piece of tissue and blew her nose. She washed her face and tried to smile at her reflection in the mirror. She felt disgusted with herself. She ripped off her bikini and stepped under the shower. She ran the loofah all over her body and soaped herself several times. She cried and prayed fervently:

- Please, God. Help me get rid of this feeling for Dario. I don't love him, and I don't want to be with him or anyone else.

- Valeria finished her shower, dried herself, applied some lotion all over her body, combed her hair, chose a short dress, slipped into flip-flops, and went to the balcony. She had an unpleasant surprise. Marion had just arrived.

Good morning, darling.

- Didn't you go to the party with Dario? Aren't you sleepy?

- No. I need little sleep. I'm young and full of energy.

- All right, - Valeria wanted peace and wasn't in the mood for an argument. - Join us for breakfast.

- Has Dario gotten up? I can't believe it.

- He must be in the bathroom. Nothing like a cold shower to wake him up.

- You're right.

- Marion served herself some watermelon juice and spread butter on a muffin.

- Do you really like Dario? - she asked straightforwardly.

- I do.

- With this enthusiasm? - Marion asked.

- Marion, I've known you for years, since we were kids. What's your angle? Are you interested in Dario?

- I... I...

– There's no need to stutter. Do you think I'm stupid? I'm not. I know you're throwing yourself at him. I'm sure you've already been together.

– Marion pretended to be surprised.

– Imagine, my dear! My friend's boyfriend is a woman. I would never do something like that to you, and...

– Valeria cut her off firmly:

– About me? Don't give me that nonsense, what about poor Thomas, why are you betraying him?

– Marion laughed, very typical.

– Thomas is a medium-term investment. He'll support me in launching my artistic career abroad, that's all. I can't get rid of him now. Dario picks on me, you know?

– You're worthless, – Valeria said with deep disdain.

– What's the problem?

Valeria sighed reluctantly. She shook her head.

– At the moment, your wish list strongly desires Dario. Am I right?

– Does that bother you?

– On the contrary. I'd love you to have him.

– Are you handing Dario to me on a silver platter?

– Before Valeria could answer, Dario asked:

– Who's handing me over on a silver platter? What's this conversation about?

– Nothing – Valeria diverted the subject. Marion did not want to miss the signal. It was just the right moment to cause the greatest confusion between the couple. It was now that she would clear the way to have Dario all to herself, even if it was only for a week or a month.

– Valeria doesn't want anything more with you.

– What do you mean? – he didn't understand.

– She's breaking up with you. She doesn't want to go out with you anymore. Did you understand?

– Valeria stood up from her chair.

– Marion, ease up.

– Why lie to Dario? Why make a fool out of him?

– Make a fool out of him? It's not like that.

– It is – Marion said, hysterically. – Valeria wants to break up with you, but she feels sorry for you.

– Don't put words I never said into my mouth, Marion.

– The two of them started a quarrel that almost escalated into a physical fight if it weren't for Dario intervening.

– Hey, what's going on? Why are you fighting?

– Deep down, he loved being the centre of that argument. He was tied to Marion and he also felt like breaking up with Valeria. But Taviño was close by, and their desires and wills were all intermingling. Taviño's spirit was furious.

– She can't leave you. Valeria is our little doll, our love. Without her, I don't know what we'll do.

– Dario felt a knot in his chest. He spewed out Taviño's words as if they were his own:

– Without you, Valeria, I don't know what to do.

– The two stopped their argument and looked at him in total surprise. Valeria didn't understand.

– What did you say?

– Taviño continued to whisper in his ear:

– She has to be yours, Dario. If you lose Valeria, I'll never be able to feel her again. I'll never be able to love her. You are the link that allows me to interact with her, you can't leave her, no way.

– You won't leave me, no way! – Dario shouted.

– Valeria widened her eyes.

– It must be the drug's effect. Dario doesn't know what he's saying.

– Marion intervened:

– Wouldn't you prefer to talk privately?

– I think it's an excellent idea – said Valeria. Your presence here doesn't help at all.

– Marion pouted and rubbed her body against Dario's.

– After you settle this matter, don't forget to give me a call.

– Marion said and left. Valeria remained silent and shook her head.

– Let's talk? – Dario insisted.

– I have a headache. I want to go up to the mountains.

– I'll go with you.

You can stay here if you want, Dario. We can talk some other time.

– No.

– Our heads are heated. It's better to cool off. We'll talk another day.

He picked her up in his arms and shook her with force.

– You won't leave me. You won't!

– For a moment, Valeria had the clear impression of having seen Taviño in front of her...

– It can't be, she told herself. I must be hallucinating.

– She opened and closed her eyes.

– Let go of me, Darío. You're hurting me – He let go and then said:

– I'll go up to the mountains with you. We can talk on the way.

– I don't think it's a good idea to go up to the mountains together.

– I came with you, and I'll leave with you. Get your things ready, and I'll pack my backpack. We'll leave in half an hour.

Valeria was tired of fighting, of arguing. It was better to go up to the mountains with Dario and have a conversation at another time. She was eager to get home and hug her father; that was her only desire.

– Half an hour later, they were in the Maverick, driving up the Via Anchieta. There were a large number of trucks that had refuelled at the port and the car was slowly making its way up. Dario was trying to overtake a truck, but then he had to stop for another one. He was getting annoyed.

– Damn trucks! – he muttered.

– Valeria grabbed a pop music tape and played the sound to lighten the heavy atmosphere

– Let's talk, – Dario insisted.

– We don't have anything to talk about for now. I'm tired of arguing with you.

– But I love you.

– Stop kidding, Dario. You love marijuana, cocaine, alcohol, and women. I know you're cheating on me with various girls.

– That's not true.

– You had sex with Marion yesterday, in my house.

– He squirmed in his car seat and didn't say anything.

– See? You're such an idiot.

– Come on, babe. It was just a joke. I have nothing with Marion. I'm crazy about you.

– Look at me and say: do you love me?

– Valeria asked frankly, from the bottom of her heart. She wanted him to be sincere. Dario was going to say no, but Taviño, sitting in the backseat of the car, intervened:

– There's no turning back now, man. She asked the typical woman's question and just pretended, looked her deep in the eyes and said "yes" or "I love you."

– Dario took a deep breath and said:

- I love you.

- That's a lie. You don't love me.

- He didn't know how to respond. He turned his face forward and concentrated on driving. Valeria opened her heart. She told him everything she felt. Dario, if he wasn't under Taviño's influence, would have understood everything and would have ended the relationship peacefully. But Taviño's insistence was painful. Taviño was nagging Dario's ear, heating it up by saying all sorts of terrible things and distorting everything Valeria was telling him.

Dario became increasingly irritated by it all. He didn't know if he was upset because Taviño talked too much or because Valeria wouldn't stop talking, or maybe because there were too many trucks, and he was tired of inhaling smoke. He turned around with eyes full of resentment and shouted:

- Stop talking! You will be mine, and that's it!

- The last thing Dario heard was Valeria's scream. He looked forward, but it was too late. He slammed the brakes, and the car skidded on the road. A truck coming from behind didn't have time to stop and crushed the Maverick, pushing it under the truck in front. The accident was so violent that when the highway police, doctors, and experts arrived at the scene, they couldn't distinguish the lifeless bodies or even separate them from the wreckage. It was a very tragic scene.

# Chapter 9

– It was a very sad scene... Arlete left the theatre crying. Osvaldo delicately took a handkerchief from his jacket and handed it to her.

– Were you so moved by "Falso Brilhante"?

– I've never seen such a beautiful show in my entire life. I'll never forget this night. The songs really touched me.

– Is that so?

– As the chorus of Belchior's song goes, "Despite all we have done, we are still the same, living like our parents," Arlete continued, looking down.

– This made me think of my intransigence towards my father.

– You don't get along with him?

– No. My father never cared about me or Alzira, nor even our mother. Sometimes, his eyes show great melancholy. It's as if he has no desire to be with us.

– I can't say anything because I don't know your father.

– He's very cruel. Mama died not long ago, and he's already thinking about getting married.

– Your father has the right to start over, or even to live his own life.

– Arlete felt her blood boiling.

– Are you defending my father? You men are all the same.

– Negative, – Osvaldo replied. – Your father owns himself. He's the one in charge of his life.

– But he has me and Alzira. He needs to think about us. He wants to get married and he wants that sweet Gisele to live under the same roof as us. That's disgusting.

– Why?

– Because, by law, half of that house belongs to me and my sister. I don't think it's fair for him to do whatever he pleases without consulting us.

– Can I ask you a question?

– Sure.

– Did you help your father buy the house?

– What do you mean? – Arlete asked, not understanding.

– Did you contribute any amount of money?

– Of course I didn't. When my father bought the house, we were still little.

– He has the right to do whatever he wants, after all, it was your father, Olair, who paid the instalments.

– Arlete stopped walking and stared Osvaldo in the eyes.

– You're a lawyer, and you know that my sister and I have the right to fifty percent of that house. It's the law, isn't it?

– Yes, together you both have the right to half of the house. If your father died today, I think it would be fair for you and your sister to have the property, use it to live, rent it for income, or even sell it and make a nest egg. However, it was your father who worked hard to buy the house. In my opinion, he can do whatever he pleases.

– It's not fair. My sister and I, along with my mother, went through hardships so he could afford the instalments. Is it fair that we're not rewarded for the sacrifices we made?

– Why? You lived in that house for years. You had a roof over your heads, didn't go cold, and had the luxury of taking warm showers...

– Arlete couldn't believe it.

– You sound just like my father. It's horrible!

– Osvaldo shook his head.

– Listen, Arlete. I understand that you feel somewhat "entitled" to the house. Brazilian law encourages and supports this line of thought. When our parents or relatives die, we want a piece of everything they've built. Unfortunately, I see cases where children demand "their share" before they legally own their inheritance. Whoever made the fortune should have the right to do as they please with it, as it happens in American law.

– I won't give up what's mine.

– You are no longer living your life, fulfilling your achievements thanks to a little piece of your home Don't you act this way because you're afraid to leave home and live your life independently?

– Arlete blushed.

– I'm dating you, Osvaldo. I believe we'll have a life together soon.

– I think so too. I want you to become my wife. However, I think we are all useful, intelligent and have many skills. I'd love for my wife to have a career, earn her own money, and feel her own self-worth.

– Who will take care of the house, then? And the children, who will look after them?

– Parents and maids, of course. A wife shouldn't do everything on her own, like our mothers were raised to do. I'm an advocate of sharing household responsibilities with my wife. No more of my wife just hanging out at the front gate, gossiping with the neighbours. The woman who will marry me should also think about herself, have a career, because work dignifies a human being.

– I don't have any qualifications. I finished high school and never even thought about going to college.

– Why not? – Osvaldo asked, curious.

– Insecurity, maybe.

– Or are you one of those who want to find a rich husband, get married, and stay at home all day, living a frivolous and uneventful life?

– Speaking like that, you offend me. I never wanted to touch anyone.

– They continued walking and stopped in front of a diner.

– I'm hungry, – Osvaldo said.

– Arlete checked her watch.

– It's late. I've never come home so late.

– We'll have a quick snack and leave afterward. I'll drop you off at home.

– Arlete's stomach rumbled. She agreed.

– Alright. A quick bite, and then we'll go.

– They entered the cafeteria and sat on stools, leaning their elbows on the counter. They placed their orders, and Osvaldo continued:

– Arlete, I genuinely like you. But I can't promise you marriage right now. I need to earn a bit more, clear some family debts. In about two or three years, I might be able to walk down the aisle.

– All of this?

– Three years go by fast, – he snapped his fingers. – I want to take a two-year preparatory course. First and foremost, I want to pass the judge or prosecutor's exam. After that, I'll be ready to make a marriage commitment. I will be able to make a down payment on a property, buy furniture, plan, in short, our married life.

– And I have to endure my father and my future stepmother for all that time?

– It's a matter of choice.

– I don't have a choice – she said tersely. Arlete spoke and picked up the straw in front of her. She put it inside the soda bottle and drank some of the liquid. Osvaldo amended:

– My dear, if you can't stand your father and your future stepmother, why not move out of the house?

– Where would I go? I don't have a job; I don't have an income...

– We can find jobs. There's always a job opening. Always.

– Where would I live?

– You and Alzira could move into a girls' boarding house. There are still very good boarding houses in the city. What do you think?

– I don't know...

– Trust life. When we want to do something for our own good, life always helps us.

– Arlete didn't respond. She didn't know what to say. Osvaldo was stating the obvious. If she wasn't happy at home, she needed to find strength within herself, believe in life, and move forward.

– On the way back, Osvaldo continued the conversation and motivated her immensely. Arlete thought about it and reflected. Osvaldo was right. There's no point in wanting to get married right now just to leave home, she thought. Osvaldo is right. I feel that I love him, but I wouldn't be ready to take such a big step. Not now. I'll talk to Alzira about it.

– Hey, a cruise through your thoughts.

– Arlete laughed.

– That's not nearly enough. You can increase the value.

They laughed, and soon Osvaldo parked the car on the curb. They said their goodbyes with an affectionate kiss, and Arlete thanked him once again for the enjoyable evening.

As soon as she closed the small gate and Osvaldo's car disappeared down the street, Arlete turned on her heels and let out a startled cry.

– What are you doing here?

– I should be asking you, – Olair barked, with his arms crossed and an unpleasant expression. Gisele was by his side, wearing a malevolent smile. She quickly said:

– Didn't I tell you, honey? – Gisele put on a childish voice and nibbled on Olair's ear. – This dad was a big mess inside the car. I ran to call you because it's so wrong. What will the neighbours say about you tomorrow?

– Arlete defended herself.

– She's slandering me, Dad. Osvaldo and I didn't do anything. He respects me very much. He just gave me a goodnight kiss.

– Gisele burst into laughter.

– A goodnight kiss? That kiss was like unclogging a sink drain. Disgusting.

– How can you be so mean, Gisele?

– Me? I just want your father's well-being. He's the best tailor in the region. I don't want his reputation to be tarnished because of a daughter with vulgar behaviour.

– Arlete felt her blood rise. She shook her head from side to side.

– You're wicked. You want to separate us from our father. And you speak incorrectly. It's "denigrated," not "degenerated," you fool.

– Gisele shrugged, and Olair slapped his daughter's face.

– That's enough! In addition to disrespecting me, you're dating in the car, right in front of our house, and you insult your future stepmother?

– Arlete reached for her face and felt it burn.

– I can't take this...

– Olair cut her off sharply.

– Shut up! Enough of your whining. I talked to Alzira and she's already packed. You'll do the same. You'll leave early tomorrow morning.

– Where to? – she swallowed hard.

– I don't know yet. But you won't stay in this house any longer.

– Arlete opened and closed her eyes. She had the urge to confront Olair and his girlfriend. What would be the point? Her father had never shown her an ounce of affection or consideration. Olair only cared about himself. Arlete was exhausted. She lowered her head, ascended the small steps, entered the house, and rushed to her room. Alzira had already packed her bags.

– She's really going to get us out of here! I can't believe it, – Arlete said.

– There's no use arguing, sis. Dad made the decision tonight. He said he's going to marry Gisele and wants to start a new life with her, without us around.

– He wants to erase us from his life. He'll regret it.

– Don't think that way, – Alzira replied. – Holding onto resentment won't help us. Right now, we need to be strong and trust life. – This was told to me a while ago by Osvaldo – trusting in life.

– You and I are healthy, and we can handle any kind of job. We can handle anything, even cleaning, if necessary. Any honest job dignifies a human being. Dad is going to take us to a boarding house. We'll find a job and move on with our lives. There's just one strange thing...

– What is it, Alzira?

– Dad said he met Mr. Ariovaldo and had a conversation with him. After that, he agreed and said, "even though I disagree, I'll have to take them there." Where is this "there"?

– I don't have the slightest idea. But Mr. Ariovaldo could have supported us and not given advice to Dad. It's like everyone is against us, my sister!

– Don't speak that way. I don't feel that Mr. Ariovaldo said anything to harm us. He and Mrs. Celia are our friends.

– Really? I feel so insecure...

– Arlete sat on the bed and put her hands on her face, covering it, and began to cry. She broke down in a heartfelt sob. Alzira sat beside her, and as her sister cried a river of tears, she gently ran her hand through Arlete's hair.

– Shh! Everything will be fine. We need to trust.

– The next morning, the girls woke up early. Alzira and Arlete freshened up, got dressed, and went to the kitchen.

Alzira took the coffee pot to prepare coffee and Olair appeared in the doorway.

- What do you think you're doing?

- I'm going to boil water and strain the coffee Warm up the milk.

- None of that. We're leaving now.

- I'm hungry.

- The journey will be long. I want to get back in time to open the tailoring shop.

- Alzira felt a knot in her stomach. She lost her appetite. Arlete entered the kitchen, hearing the same conversation.

- You'd better take us away. Or if you prefer, you can give us some money, and we'll manage. We know how to read. Just give us a map with directions. We don't need your unwillingness to take us wherever.

- Olair was about to slap her again, but Alzira stepped between them.

- Stop fighting. Let's just leave, once and for all.

- Arlete returned to her room and grabbed the two bags. Olair left and started the car. In no time, they were on the road, heading who knows where.

# Chapter 10

Dario's wake was crowded with curious onlookers, including many journalists. His father was a successful banker, and his mother was a socialite who lived in the United States. People from all over the country showed up, from businesspeople and high-society figures to politicians and artists.

The procession was televised and the death was featured in the country's major newspapers. Incredibly, the parents were not at all shocked by their son's death. Demetrio, the father, had a frown on his face and barely said hello to people. They said he was in shock. Maria Augusta, the mother, pretended to cry in grief. It was all an act. They never got along and raised their son with nannies and maids. That's why Dario had grown up without boundaries. Since they did not believe in anything, were completely disconnected from any creed or religion, they thought that death was the end. Maria Augusta was sure that at one time or another her son would put his foot down. Cold and calculating, she foresaw what happened and a year earlier had taken out life insurance on Dario, from which he would benefit.

- After the funeral, Demetrio went back to his duties, and Maria Augusta decided not to stay another day in the country. She was content with the insurance money she would receive. She asked the driver to take her to the airport. She boarded the plane and sat comfortably in her first-class seat.

- Dario had always been a burden, and she couldn't bear his antics any longer. Now, not only would she have no more problems, but she would also pocket a substantial sum of money, she thought, as she sipped a glass of champagne that the flight attendant had just served her.

- Not far from there, Valeria lay in a hospital bed. Américo and Natalia did not let go of each other for a single minute.

- They waited for the moment when she opened her eyes and came back to life. Valeria had been saved. In time, she would remember that tragic event in ever more vivid detail. When the argument became heated and Dario turned his face toward her, Valeria felt she was one step away from death. On instinct, she opened the car door and threw herself to the side of the road. Dario had no time for anything. Neither did the driver of the truck that had fallen. His death was instantaneous.

- Valeria had suffered some abrasions on her legs, knees, and elbows. Her face had a few scratches. Given the condition of the car and the remains of Dario, the young woman had miraculously survived.

- She slowly moved her face from side to side, opened and closed her mouth, and ran her tongue across her lips. She felt thirsty and tried to open her eyes. They seemed heavy, and she struggled to gather her thoughts. The images appeared jumbled and somewhat blurry.

– America dropped the newspaper on the small table and jumped to her feet. She approached her daughter's bed and leaned over. He put his hands in hers.

– How do you feel, my dear?

– I'm thirsty.

Natalia picked up a water jug from the bedside table and poured the crystal-clear liquid into a glass. She handed it to America, who gently placed the glass at Valeria's lips.- Drink, dear. Slowly.

– Valeria slowly parted her lips and took a sip of water. She ran her tongue across her lips and opened one eye. She saw her father and became emotional.

– Oh, Dad, I'm alive!

– America couldn't hold back her tears.

– More alive than ever, my love.

Natalia came closer and stood on the other side of the bed, placing her hands on her friend's.

– Valeria, my mother and I prayed for you all these days.

– How long have I been here?

– A week – her father replied.

– Slowly Valeria came to her senses and the scenes of the disaster came to her mind. She became desperate and began to struggle in bed.

– It was horrible! Dario didn't have time... Dario didn't have time...

– America pressed the nurse call button, and Natalia rushed to the door. A nurse entered the room and, seeing the girl's agitated state, administered a sedative. In a matter of seconds, Valeria fell back asleep.

– She's still in shock – the nurse said. – A few more days, and she'll be fine, fully recovered.

– Are you sure? – America asked, still unsure.

– Yes. Your daughter is in one of the best hospitals in the country, attended by excellent professionals. The X-rays showed no fractures. Valeria only suffered some abrasions on her body.

– But she will always remember the accident...

– Yes, Mr. Americo. When she is discharged, the doctor will probably recommend therapy sessions. Your daughter will be fine, believe me.

– The nurse spoke and left. Natalia approached America and hugged him.

– I know what you're feeling, Mr. America.

– The accident was horrible. I'm not sure if Valeria will ever be the same.

– She won't be the same, that's for sure. These tragedies change our lives.

– She didn't deserve to go through this.

– Are we the ones who decide what things we will or will not go through? We only have control over our free will. We live based on our choices.

– I don't understand why Valeria was dating that guy. I know his family must be devastated by his death, but Valeria and Dario didn't match.

– They definitely didn't match – Natalia replied. – But life is intelligent, Mr. America. Valeria needed to go through this tragedy to value life and reevaluate her beliefs. She is already a woman; she is capable of making her own life. She could no longer stay in this rain that does not get wet, in this unconstructive relationship.

– She nearly died.

– You said it: nearly. She's here, alive and kicking. She'll be able to return to a normal life, only more mature now. Valeria is strong and will overcome this tragedy. Her spirit will come out of this experience even stronger.

– America smiled.

– You talk about the spirit.

– Did you find that funny?

– Yes. It reminded me of an old girlfriend. She believed fervently in the spirit world. She was convinced that life continued after death.

– She was absolutely right.

– Are you sure? I find all of this very fanciful – America replied, sounding sceptical.

– I believe in spirituality, in the continuity of life. If I didn't, I wouldn't know how to accept the social and economic disparities in the world.

– Dying and coming back? Doesn't that sound like a soap opera? Like the one on TV, The Trip?

– Yes.

– What do you think about that?

– America stepped back. He bit his lip and replied thoughtfully:

– Isn't it a work of fiction?

– It's a soap opera, of course, but the show's scripts had the supervision of the journalist, writer, and professor Jose Herculano Pires, who is highly respected in the spiritist community.

– I've heard of Professor Herculano Pires. He seems like a serious man.

– Very serious, very intelligent and very studious. He dedicates himself with great love to spiritual studies, so he was invited by the author to provide guidance on the scenes dealing with the Kardecist doctrine. The novel clearly shows the basic themes of Spiritism, such as mediumship, the obsessions or influences we receive from the spirits, the communication between incarnated and disincarnated people...

– America raised an eyebrow.

– Incarnate and disincarnate?

Natalia smiled.

– I'm sorry, Mr. America. I forget that not everyone is familiar with spiritist terminology. We are incarnated, me, you, Valeria – she pointed to her friend on the bed, people who live in this world, in the body of flesh that houses the spirit. We are the incarnate. And the disincarnate are those who exist outside the physical body, who do not belong, temporarily, to the earthly world; in other words, the "dead."

– From what you're telling me, it seems like the dead are more alive than ever. Just like in the soap opera. Is that the case?

– Absolutely. The author, Ivani Ribeiro, is a spiritist. She's familiar with the subject and the topics being addressed. Furthermore, she based the soap opera on two spiritist classics: the books *"Our Home"* and *"And life goes on,"* dictated by the spirit André Luiz to the medium Chico Xavier.

– I'm a big fan of Chico Xavier. I saw him on TV a few years ago on a debate show. I was impressed with his confidence and how he conveyed so much tranquillity, serenity, and kindness to me through the TV screen. If he's part of a group that promotes this religion, it must be something.

– Allan Kardec has always been clear on this point. Spiritism is a doctrine with an experimental–scientific nature, with philosophical consequences. It shouldn't be seen as a religion, but it leads me to intense spirituality. I accept it as a natural religion, as Professor Herculano Pires teaches, with no connection to any particular religious denomination or ritual. It's the science of the soul, so to speak.

– America nodded.

– The science of the soul. Perfect.

– Moreover – Natalia agreed – religion means the belief in the existence of a higher power or principle. The word comes from *"religare,"* Latin for "to bind with" or "to bind again," meaning to reestablish a connection with this higher principle, which we call God.

- I'm impressed with your expertise on this subject. I've known you since you were a child, and I've never noticed this aspect of you before.

- After my father lost everything, he had built during his entire life, I questioned why we had to go through such a painful experience. From one moment to the next I lost the comfortable house I lived in, the school, the courses, the employees, the driver... Friends disappeared, and right after the shock, my mom and dad separated. It was a very tough time for both of us; we were practically living in poverty.

- Americo was about to speak, but Natalia gestured for him to stop.

- However, practically all the friends disappeared., but I must admit that you helped us a lot. You rented one of your properties to my mom for a nominal fee and never increased the rent. We will always be grateful for your assistance.

- I did what any decent person would do. I've always been friends with your mom, and when Amelia passed away, it was Elenice who helped me take care of little Valeria - he got emotional, cleared his throat, and continued - I should be thanking you. I never wanted to charge you rent.

- It's not fair, Mr. America. Everything in life is based on exchange. You gave us a home, and we pay to live in it, even if that amount is very small. We're happy to deposit the money into your bank account every month.

- Your outlook on life is fascinating, Natalia. I'm approaching fifty years, and I feel like I have less spiritual knowledge than you. I never wanted to connect with religion. I have always seen religion as something that tries to step on man and take away his strength, always with hidden, manipulative interests.

– We just need to have discernment to separate the wheat from the chaff. It's good to believe in something superior that governs life, as long as it touches our hearts and brings warmth. After we lost everything, my mom sought comfort and found in spiritual knowledge the strength to move forward. I confess that I wouldn't trade the life I have now for anything in the world, not even the life of luxury we used to have.

– A deep but melodious voice spoke from behind:

– After that entire conversation, I've become interested in the subject.

– Natalia turned around and was taken aback. She took a step back and felt her legs trembling. America opened a broad smile and extended his arms.

– My brother, how I missed you!

– The two embraced, and America introduced them:

– Natalia, this is my brother Adamo, who lives in Italy.

– She stretched out her hand and shook his. She felt a little shock, a very different sensation, pleasant and exciting.

– Pleasure.

– Natalia spoke and lowered her head. She tried to stop her legs from shaking. Adamo smiled, displaying perfect, white teeth. His lips were full, and his eyes were brown. He was well-built, stronger and appeared much younger than

America. The mustache and thick sideburns gave him a very manly appearance. He was an exceptionally interesting type. He fixed his gaze on Natalia's.

– I confess to being spellbound. I have never seen such a beautiful girl – She blushed and Americo cleared his throat. He knew his brother was gallant and seductive. She elbowed him and pointed to Valeria.

– Go see your niece.

– Adamo smiled, walked around the bed, and approached Valeria. He kissed her on the cheek and admired her delicate, albeit bruised, features. Natalia tried her best, but she couldn't take her eyes off that man. She remembered seeing his picture in a photo frame a few months earlier.

– He's even more handsome in person. I'm smitten, she thought while trying to figure out a way to hide her feelings.

# Chapter 11

– It had been more than forty minutes since Olair was driving his little Beetle. The girls, sitting in the back seat and holding their bags, were trying to imagine where they were being taken.

– Arlete couldn't bear such anxiety and asked:

– Where are you taking us?

– It doesn't matter. Be quiet and enjoy the scenery.

– Arlete swallowed her anger. Alzira closed her eyes and said a heartfelt prayer.

– Time passed; the car entered Via Anchieta.

– After driving a few kilometres, Olair left the highway and followed a sign. Alzira read it and asked:

– Rudge Ramos?

– Yes. We are in Sao Bernardo do Campo.

– Why did we have to cross the city? Weren't there more modest pensions in the centre? – Arlete asked.

– They're not going to a boarding house at all. A boarding house is for immoral women.

– A great place for Gisele to live, while the wedding of the century doesn't come to fruition – Olair released his right hand from the steering wheel and his arm flew back. The girls lowered their heads and it flew off.

- Don't say another word about my fiancée. I'll stop this car right here on the street and beat both of you. Now!

Arlete wanted to respond, but Alzira nudged her and made a pleading gesture, shaking her head from side to side. Arlete opened and closed her mouth and chose not to continue the argument.

A few minutes later, Olair turned onto a street and entered a small square, stopping in a quiet, peaceful street, with many trees and modest but well-kept houses with decorated gardens.

- The girls exchanged glances. Arlete said:

- Wow, this place is much nicer than where we live.

- Olair pretended not to hear. He opened the car door, got out, and folded the driver's seat.

- You can get out here. This is where you'll stay.

- They quickly got out of the car, each holding her bag of clothes. Olair took two steps on the sidewalk and stopped in front of a pretty two-story house, all covered in little bricks. The doors and windows were white. It resembled an English cottage, with a side entrance and a beautiful front garden full of various flowers emitting a pleasant fragrance. He paused for a moment, deep in thought, and rang the doorbell.

- Alzira asked:

- Is this a boarding house?

He didn't respond and rang the doorbell again. A drop of sweat ran down his forehead, and a large stain began to form under his arms. Olair was impatient and seemed very nervous.

- A friendly woman in her forties appeared at the side entrance and put her hand to her chest when she saw him.

- Olair?! Is that really you? - she asked, looking surprised.

- He didn't respond, and she walked to the gate. She looked over his shoulder and saw the girls. When she saw Alzira, she immediately remembered Josefa. They looked very similar. She tried to muster a smile. The girls remained quiet, not knowing what was happening.

- He was curt and rude, as usual.

- I never thought I'd see your face again. I'm not used to living with women of ill repute. But my conscience told me to bring the girls here. They need a home.

- Your conscience has a name: Ariovaldo.

- Olair didn't respond, and the girls exchanged worried glances.

Did you sell the house? Did you lose the tailoring business?

- I don't owe you any explanations.

- How not? You come to my doorstep, ring the doorbell, call me a harlot, and...

He cut her off abruptly.

- I don't want to argue. Let them stay with you. If you can't afford to house them, send them to a boarding house. But my conscience is at ease now. I did what I had to do.

– He spoke, turned around, and without looking at his daughters, got into the car, started it, and drove away. He went around the small square and the car disappeared around the bend.

– Arlete and Alzira didn't move. They felt extremely embarrassed by the whole scene. The woman hurried to open the gate and embraced them.

– My nieces, it's so good to see you.

– Are you Aunt Lurdes? – Alzira asked, moved.

– Yes, it's me.

– Oh, you don't know how relieved we are. We thought Dad was going to throw us in Billings Dam!

– Lurdes smiled and hugged them again.

– Olair is rough, but he wouldn't go that far.

– It's a shame that our mom married such a brutish and stupid man.

– Your mom married a stupid man because she didn't respect herself. I always liked Josefa, but her passivity bothered me. She never made an effort to change her attitude or confront her husband. That's what happened.

– Mom never had her own opinion – Alzira added. – She let Dad beat her and us. I would never let a man lay a finger on me. That's a lack of self-respect.

– Arlete nodded but was suspicious.

– Why did you say earlier that Dad's conscience is named Ariovaldo?

– Lurdes chuckled mischievously.

- I'll explain the story better later.

- First of all - Alzira intervened - can we stay at your house for a few days until we find a place to live?

- Of course! You will live with me.

- No, Aunt! - protested Arlete. - We don't want to invade your privacy. We don't even know if you're married or...

- Lurdes interrupted her with kindness in her voice.

- I'm single and live alone. I have a white cat named Smiles.

- Lurdes called, and the cat came running from the backyard. It passed through the iron gate and started circling the girls. Lurdes smiled

- Smiling is mischievous. He seems human. And he liked you. Good sign.

- Arlete bent down and picked him up.

- Hi, little friend, how are you?

- The cat wiggled his nose, opened and closed his eyes and let out a scream.

- He's happy with more people around - Lurdes added.

- I don't think it's fair for us to arrive here out of the blue. We were never allowed to have contact with you. Mom never told us anything about your separation.

- I'm sure Josefa must be behind it.

- Alzira and Arlete exchanged glances. Arlete spoke up:

- Sorry to inform you, but Mom passed away a few months ago.

- A tear rolled down Lurdes' cheek.

- I know. I attended the funeral.

- Really? - the sisters asked at the same time.

- Yes. I have a friend who lives in the neighbourhood and always gave me information about Josefa and you.

- Ah... you're friends with Mrs. Celia?

- Yes.

- That's why you mentioned Ariovaldo's name!

- We've been friends for a long time. I know everything about you through them. I watched both of you grow from a distance; after all, Olair didn't allow me to get close to his wife.

- Mom could have insisted. She should have stood up - suggested Arlete.

- Your mom was a very passive, submissive person, afraid to express her desires or even assert her will. What a shame.

- I'm not like her. If I marry Osvaldo, things will be very different! - exclaimed Arlete.

- I can see that both of you are very different from your mother. Unfortunately, Josefa suffered from rejection; she didn't know how to handle life's "no's." Rejection is not pleasant, but we need to learn to deal with it to strengthen our self-confidence. Maybe Zeta will learn that in the astral world.

- Mrs. Celia told us about the astral world. She said that mom did not die, but it was her flesh body that died. Mom lives in spirit and recovers from her illness in a hospital – said Alzira.

- That's right. Your mother is still alive in spirit, and who knows, maybe we'll be able to have contact with her soon?

- Is that possible? – Arlete doubted.

- Everything is possible, my dear. Now come, let's go inside and get to know the house where you'll be living.

- The girls picked up their suitcases and went inside. The cat accompanied them while Lourdes showed them around. It was a modest but very elegant house, with few rooms and very tidy. Lourdes was an organized woman and the house smelled clean, the furniture was old, but in good condition. On the first floor there was a living room, a kitchen, a bathroom and a small patio. In the back, in addition to the backyard, there was a small bedroom and a small laundry room.

- Upstairs there were two bedrooms. One of the bedrooms had a four-door closet, a chest of drawers, a dresser, a dresser and two beds. A nightstand separated the beds. On it was a small lamp. The curtain looked new, in a pinkish hue. The walls were painted pastel pink.

- Arlete remained suspicious.

- This room smells like new paint. The furniture is new. Why would you have a complete room for girls with two single beds?

Lurdes laughed cheerfully.

– Zefa used to say that you were always very observant and clever. You're right. I won't hide it. I knew you would come here.

– How?

– Ah," Alzira added, "Did Mrs. Celia tell you?"

– Lurdes nodded. The girls shook their heads.

– Have you been friends with Mrs. Celia and your Ariovaldo for a long time?" Alzira asked.

– We're very close friends. Josefa, Celia, and I were childhood friends.

– Mrs. Celia never told us that she was friends with Mom," Alzira commented.

– Or with you," Arlete added.

– Because Celia was afraid that if you said something at home, Olair would forbid you from seeing her.

– But why didn't Dad want her around or never allowed us to have contact with you?" Arlete inquired, curious.

Lurdes smiled.

– You're practically adults, and I don't intend to keep my secrets. No mysteries. One day, I'll tell you why Olair hates me so much and why he deprived me of your mother's friendship. At the moment, the important thing is to know that Ariovaldo convinced Olair to bring you here. This used to be a sewing room. I dismantled it and prepared it for you. The furniture is good; I bought it on instalment payments at a furniture store on Jurubatuba Street.

– The young women were delighted. They sat on the bed, felt the softness of the sheets, and the fragrance of the pillows. The closet was spacious for the few clothes they brought.

– It all seems too good to be true," Alzira said, pinching herself.

– Now you have a real home.

– Arlete got up from the bed and hugged her aunt. She kissed her on the cheek multiple times, deeply moved.

– I'll never have words to thank you. You're being more than a mother to us.

– Since you liked the room, I want to ask for something in return.

– What is it? – Alzira asked. – You can ask for anything.

– Don't call me "mrs." How about calling me "you"? Let's pretend that I'm the older sister of the two of you, can we do that?

– The girls laughed with satisfaction.

– You're very beautiful – Arlete observed.

– Thank you, dear.

– Arlete put her hand on her stomach.

– I'm sorry, Aunt, but we haven't eaten anything. Dad didn't let us have breakfast.

– Leave your bags on the beds, and we'll sort and organize everything later. Let's go downstairs; I'll make us a good coffee with milk.

– Lurdes and Arlete headed for the door, and Alzira remained sitting on the bed.

– Aren't you coming, sister?

– I'll be down in a moment, Arlete. Just a little while.

– Arlete put her arm around her aunt's waist, and they went downstairs. Alzira closed her eyes, smiled, and expressed her gratitude:

– Thank you, God. I was sure that everything would end well. Thank you from the bottom of my heart.

– A spirit in the form of a woman caressed her hair and kissed her forehead.

– Dearest Alzira, I couldn't stay by your side because the energy hanging over your house was dense and naturally repelled me. Olair's petty thoughts combined with Gisele's negative thoughts didn't allow me to get closer. Now, we'll be closer than ever. Nothing will be able to keep us apart. I love you very much.

– She spoke and disappeared into the air. Alzira felt a strong emotion and let a tear roll down her face. She felt an indescribable sense of well-being.

# Chapter 12

- It had been just over three months since Valeria left the hospital. She had quickly recovered from the injuries and bruises on her body. She had a few therapy sessions and gradually overcame the trauma of the accident. She was recovering, but she felt an unprecedented fatigue.

Valeria also had nightmares about the accident. In them, she argued with Dario, and then she vividly saw Taviño's face in front of her. Then, she would open the car door, roll onto the asphalt, and Taviño would try to catch her. Valeria screamed and woke up.

- Natalia was always there, helping her friend overcome all that torment.

- You need to react, Valeria.

- What intrigues me is not dreaming about the accident, but Taviño appearing in the scene. It doesn't make any sense.

- Natalia felt a shiver run down her spine.

- I have a feeling it does make sense.

- Imagine, Natalia - Valeria continued, shaking her head - Taviño died years ago.

– I've already told you that our physical body is the one that dies. Our spirit separates from the physical body and continues to live more alive than ever.

– I don't feel anything for Taviño anymore. Nothing. Why would I think of him?

– You may not be into him anymore, but who guarantees he's not still into you?

– Put that mouth over there – Valeria knocked on the bedside table three times. – I hope Taviño is far away from here. Do you feel anything?

– Natalia closed her eyes for a moment, took a deep breath, and exhaled. Then she opened her eyes and smiled.

– Funny, I don't sense Taviño's spirit here, or Dario's for that matter. But I feel a presence. I can't quite identify it.

– A good or bad presence? – Valeria asked, suspicious.

– Good. Very good. Very good indeed.

– You're good at dealing with these spiritual matters, Natalia. See if you can sense anything more, will you?

– Natalia closed her eyes and a very handsome young man appeared in her mind. His eyes were a deep green, his hair abundant and silky, and his smile was charming. He exuded pure love. She smiled and opened her eyes.

– There's a male spirit with you. A very handsome man, by the way.

– Valeria laughed.

– And? Is he as handsome as Pedro Aguinaga?

– More or less.

– Could it be that you're seeing my future boyfriend?

– I don't know – Natalia replied. – In the near future, you're going to Italy to study interior decoration, which you love. Who knows if you won't fall in love with a classmate there? An Italian guy, tall, strong, a handsome *"macho."*

– The two of them laughed heartily.

– They spent a good amount of time talking about the future and their dreams. At one point, Valeria mentioned:

– I'm trying, but something strange is happening to me. Do you think I might be spiritually disturbed?

– Natalia shook her head in denial.

– I don't sense any disturbance. I had felt a male presence earlier, but it was sweet and tender. Nothing that could disturb you.

– Valeria fell into deep thought for a moment.

– Maybe it was lunch and Marion's phone call. My stomach couldn't take it.

– Natalia shrugged.

– Marion keeps calling you?

– When Thomas came to visit me, she had a fit.

– Oh, Thomas came here? When?

– Last week. He was very polite and friendly.

– Natalia squinted her eyes.

– Look at that. Tomás has always been in love with you, Valeria. I still don't understand why you never gave him a chance. He's so nice, so responsible.

- I'll confess something: I got a little butterflies in my stomach when he entered the room.

- Hmm - Natalia smiled gleefully. - Thomas is quite a catch.

- I've been through so many problems lately. I'm not sure I'd like to start a new relationship. I still feel insecure. And to make matters worse, it seems that he's still dating Marion. - I can't believe it! Marion was interested in Dario.

- I thought that her relationship with Thomas had already expired.

- Negative. On the day of the accident, Marion confessed to me that she was interested in Dario, but she wasn't giving up on Thomas.

- Thomas and Marion don't match at all. They're like oil and vinegar, they can't mix.

- But they're still together, yes. Marion won't stop calling me because she got irritated that Thomas came here alone.

- She never changes. That girl is pushy and spoiled. A nightmare. How can she be so shallow?

- She keeps insisting. Marion has a terrible temper, she's stubborn, and she's nervous. A nightmare, just like you said. She called to inform me that she's coming to my house later.

- From what I've heard, she's been invited to make a cameo in an American movie.

- That's why I don't let Thomas go. His family has connections with people in the American film industry.

Marion doesn't love Thomas, but she sticks to him to become a star.

– A star – Natalia laughed dismissively. – Only if she's a shooting star. That girl has no sparkle, no charisma.

– But she's pretty, we can't deny that – Valeria added.

– Beauty doesn't last forever, my friend. One day, Marion will get old, and who knows what will happen to her.

– I wish you were by my side when she arrives. We can get rid of her quickly.

– Natalia said nothing. Marion's request seemed very strange to her. However, she preferred not to argue. Valeria walked very badly and the following month she would travel to Italy. She would miss Valeria very much, but the course would last three years and the time would pass quickly.

– How is the university? – Valeria asked.

– I'm loving it, studying the right course.

– I'll be a great architect.

– I know you will be.

– Who knows if we won't be business partners in the future? We could start our own firm, you handle the projects, and I'll decorate the houses, shops, and offices...

– I'd love that.

– The conversation continued cheerfully. One of the maids knocked on the door and announced that Marion was in the hallway.

– As soon as I mention her!

– Valeria sighed, annoyed.

– I'd better greet her now.

– I'll leave.

– No way – Valeria protested. – I want you by my side, I told you. This is my house, and you stay. Let Marion dare to ask you to leave. I'll go back to being the old Valeria and kick her out.

– Natalia laughed enthusiastically. However, her laughter didn't last long. Very little. Marion entered the room, accompanied by Adamo. Natalia felt her mouth dry up.

– After they met in the hospital, Natalia ran into Adamo when visiting Valeria. He was staying at the house and would only go out with his niece in tow. Natalia felt Adamo's eyes fixed on her, but she thought it was imagination on her part that interested him. Not to give a flag, she treated him seriously. He was no longer spontaneous and, in this way, Adamo understood that she did not feel any attraction towards him. But it was pure misunderstanding, she thought. Adamo was the man she had always dreamed of having by her side, for the rest of her life.

– Marion entered the room with enthusiasm, pulling Adamo by one arm and shaking the other while holding a magazine in her hand.

– Look closely, pay attention!

– She threw the magazine onto Valeria's lap.

– What is this?

– My passport to stardom.

– Valeria picked up the magazine and looked at the cover.

– You posed nude?

– Not exactly – Marion replied with great composure. – I did an artistic nude photo shoot.

– Artistic nude, I see – Natalia said with disdain.

– Status is a top-notch magazine.

– And being nude in a magazine guarantees a passport to stardom? Who said that? – Valeria asked.

– Many big movie stars started like this – Marion argued nonchalantly, shrugging her shoulders. – Marilyn Monroe, for instance. And there are artists who did much worse. I'm so happy. The whole country wants me. I'm beautiful, hot, and... rich! I just had a cameo in a Brazilian adult film.

– This conversation is quite enjoyable – Natalia mocked. – But why are we graced with the presence of the great adult film star?

– Funny. You can gloat with me, because what comes from below doesn't get to me – Marion spun around the room and sat down next to Valeria –. Adamo was helping me build my new name.

– New name? What do you mean? – Valeria asked, still confused.

– My parents are a bit nervous about the photos and the "cameo" I did in the Brazilian film.

– Well, Marion, don't you think you crossed the line? – Just because I show up naked, running on the beach. Can he? Look at this nonsense? My parents are very proper. Marion

Albuquerque Salles de Miranda is not the name of a star and it's aristocratic. It doesn't sell.

- Did Adamo come to a conclusion? - Valeria asked, looking at her uncle.

- Adamo smiled awkwardly.

- I gave some suggestions, but I'm not very creative. I'll leave you ladies alone. I need to take care of some things. Don't forget that we're leaving next month.

- Oh! - Marion pouted. - I'll miss you so much, Adamo.

- You have Thomas to make up for his absence, darling - Natalia retorted, annoyed.

- There are too many people in this room, Valeria. I wish we could be alone...

- Valeria looked at Natalia and bit her lip. Adamo approached and gently pulled her by the shoulders.

- We should leave the girls alone, Natalia.

- I'd rather stay with Valeria.

- I'm not going to kill her, honey - Marion mocked -. I'm going to talk about my future plans. Now see if you can leave me alone with her. Go and make room for Adamo, go on.

- Natalia was about to respond, and Adamo led her out of the room.

- Why do you get so nervous around Marion? - he asked, intrigued.

– For no reason – Natalia replied, still upset. – Let's go downstairs. We need some tea.

– We need to get rid of that annoying woman.

– Adamo shook his head.

– Come on, I'll ask them to prepare some tea for us. Are you coming?

– Natalia blushed and nodded.

– As they walked down the stairs, in Valeria's room the conversation raged.

– I'm going to change my name to Marion Krystal.

– Really?

– Yes. My agent suggested it. People will associate it with actress Sylvia Kristel, who starred in Emmanuelle.

– That movie was banned in the country, Marion.

– So what? Everyone is interested in what's forbidden. The movie may have been banned in theatres, but everyone knows the actress. I'm going to pursue a film career now. Since I posed nude, I keep receiving offers. I'm starting to taste success.

– Success under these circumstances is short-lived – Valeria pointed out.

– I'm going to enjoy my youth.

– One day you'll grow old.

– I'll grow old, but I'll always be beautiful. I'll take care of myself, exercise, follow a diet, and use expensive creams to delay aging. Money will keep me forever beautiful and young.

- I think relying solely on beauty is quite shallow. Don't you believe it's too little, too superficial?

- The world is superficial - Marion replied. - I'm superficial. That's life. I was born beautiful and rich. I'll die beautiful and rich.

- You don't think about getting to know yourself better and. - Marion interrupted her with a quick wave of her hand.

- All nonsense, garbage. What counts in the world is beauty, silky skin, the audacity of participating in an erotic movie. I was born to be a star.

- I hope you're lucky!

- Marion chuckled and twirled around again.

- Did you know I'm going to get engaged to Thomas?

- I had a suspicion.

- I didn't like him coming here alone.

- Why? Did you think I would devour him?

- Marion suppressed her anger.

- No, of course not, but...

- What, Marion? - Valeria asked, changed. You seem to be chasing me. You always wanted to have my boyfriends or my lovers.

- Me?!

- Yes. I started dating Taviño in school, and you chased after him. Then I dated Dario, and you went after him too. - Big deal. It seems like all your boyfriends die. Are you going to become a genuine black widow?

- How mean.

- Nothing stupid, Valeria. We're of the same ilk. I manage you. Now the situation is reversed. You want my fiancé. Or rather, my future fiancé.

- Thomas? No. He's rich, he's part of our social circle. He's a catch.

- That has nothing to do with it. Thomas is a friend.

- A friend who always had a crush on you.

- Oh, come on...

- Marion interrupted her sharply.

- Do you think I never noticed?

- So, what, Marion? You can have him.

- The weather wasn't very good. Marion said irritably:

- Thomas' father knows some Hollywood producers.

- Now I understand the reason for this engagement. - Yes. Thomas will be the yellow brick road that leads me to stardom.

- You're using Thomas.

- I am. That's why you won't get near him, at least not now.

- How degrading! Using a person to achieve your goals.

- The world is smart, Valeria. You know - she said, while trying to remove the red polish from a nail -, I'm going to use Thomas as I want. He's handsome, but weak and very manipulable.

- He's not that dumb. If he realizes you don't love him...

– Marion laughed.

– Love? Oh, I had forgotten. You're one of those people who believe in love! How naive.

– Thomas will eventually figure out your hidden agenda.

– When he does, it will be too late. Do you think I won't be courted by a big shot from the movie industry in America? I'll trade Thomas in a heartbeat. With this body – Marion ran her hand over her curvaceous figure – I'll always be desired.

– I'm tired. Would you mind leaving?

– I didn't plan to stay here much longer anyway. I only came to give you the warning. Don't mess with Thomas.

– Marion spoke with fury in her eyes. She grabbed the magazine from the bed and walked hastily to the door. She slammed it shut.

– Suddenly, Valeria felt sick. She lay down on the bed. I was not feeling well. Very tired and sick.

# Chapter 13

– Marion descended the stairs swiftly. She passed by the employees with their heads held high and made her way to the kitchen.

– Adamo, I'm leaving, – she said.

– Adamo asked, – Aren't you staying for tea?

– Marion replied, – I don't like tea. And I don't like certain company, – looking sternly at Natalia.

– Natalia retorted, – If you're uncomfortable, you can leave.

– Marion placed her arm on Adamo's shoulder and said, – Before I go, Adamo, I wanted to give you this copy. I'll sign it with my new name.

– Adamo remained silent as Natalia, upset, got up and announced, – I'll go to the kitchen to check if the tea is ready.

– Marion took out a pen from her bag and wrote on the magazine's cover. She then handed it to Adamo and kissed him on the cheek.

– If I didn't need Thomas to get along in America, I swear I'd sleep with you. What a shame!

– She whispered in his ear, got up and walked away, clicking her heels. Adamo smiled and shook his head to one side.

– Adamo smiled and shook his head, exclaiming, – Women!

– Natalia approached with a tray containing a teapot and two cups.

– Talking to himself? – Natalia approached carrying the tray with a teapot and two cups.

– Adamo responded, – I'm just amazed by human vanity. Vanity punishes and hinders the progress of our spirits towards a greater good. Poor Marion.

– Natalia commented, – She's quite shallow.

– Adamo said, – However, I do not condemn her. Everyone knows what he does best. And, what's more, we reap what we sow. Instead of judging, I hope Marion has a chance to review her beliefs and change her stance before it's too late.

– Natalia expressed her dislike, – I don't like her. Just by her passing through here, I sensed her negative energy.

– Natalia felt herself blushing.

– How so?! I'm not understanding.

– Adamo waited for her to sit down and served the tea.

– After taking a few sips of the hot and flavourful liquid, he spoke seriously, – I've been studying the world of energies and how they influence us.

– I read something about it. But I don't engage so easily with people's energy. And I was born with a lot of sensitivity and I easily pick up everything people think.

– I'm a sponge!

– And a sponge because you want to be. It's up to each of us to select what does and doesn't enter our auric field. There are no victims in the world.

– Natalia tried to hide it.

– I'm not saying I'm a victim, but I suffer from the bad mind of others.

– You let yourself get involved, yes. I saw how disturbed you were by Marion's presence.

– Adamo noted, – You do get affected. I saw how disturbed you were by Marion's presence.

– Natalia confessed, – She's terrible. She's a shallow and selfish person who only cares about physical beauty. What's the point of being like that? The body ages, and what truly matters is the spirit. I have nothing against physical beauty.

– Adamo asked, – Do you think Marion is a beautiful woman?

– Of course she is! – Adamo said, sincerely.

– I can't believe it! – she exclaimed, annoyed.

– Marion is beautiful. We can't deny that. If she uses her beauty to achieve things and if she believes that only through beauty, she will have everything she wants, that is a problem with her, with her ideas, with the way her spirit has been living throughout some incarnations. Is it you or me who points fingers and says what is right and what is wrong?

– Natalia complained, – Her behaviour has nothing to do with spirituality. That irritates me.

– There is nothing spiritual about the way you act. That irritates me.

– Why are you angry? Does she irritate you or are you irritated by her?

– Natalia replied, – It's the same thing.

– No – Adamo continued, serious –. We were raised as victims. We blame God and the world for our misfortunes. Others blame their failures on past incarnations.

– Natalia acknowledged, – That's true.

– Adamo explained further, – But it's not quite that simple. While today we are a product of all our past existences, we can't attribute everything bad in our lives to the past. If the past had such a strong influence on our current life and was the only decisive factor, there would be no point in reincarnating. We are perfect at our current level of evolution. We are on this planet for two reasons.

– And what are they? – Natalia asked, as she took a sip of her tea.

– Adamo answered, – To learn to be impersonal and, with that, to reach our happiness more easily. We reincarnate for happiness...

– Natalia defended herself, – I am impersonal.

– You are not. You get carried away by others. If the person is angry, you get angry. If someone says something you don't like, you shut down and get hurt. Now, we cannot depend on people's influences. We are the commanders of our body, our mind, our spirit. We must impose our will above all else. If someone thinks differently than you, you must learn to understand that everyone has the right to be and say what they want.

– Adamo interrupted her, – Listen, Natalia. You can't let yourself be influenced by others. You need to learn to be firm, to be master of your thoughts and not allow the energy of others to invade you so easily. We need to create our energetic barriers to fight negativity in the world. It is time to create a positive magnetic field around you, to become aware of your power to rule your own life.

– Natalia explained, – I've learned that I have to show empathy for others' pain. I get involved. If my friend Valeria is sad, I become sad too. That's just who I am.

– Adamo pointed out, – A serious problem for your spiritual maturity, because you will never be well enough to help your friend and, above all, to help yourself.

– Natalia reasoned, – I can't help it. I care about Valeria.

– Adamo concluded, – Because you like your friend and you need to be impersonal. A lot of people confuse impersonality with coldness of feeling. It's nothing like that. Impersonality and don't mix with other people's energy. If the other person is not well, I need to be well to help them. What good is it if I feel bad too? What good will it do if I feel bad too? How will it help?

– Adam sighed and said, – The courage to see and accept oneself is the secret to evolution. Close your eyes.

– Natalia placed her teacup on the table, settled into her chair, and closed her eyes.

– Adamo instructed, – Start saying to yourself with strength: "I decree my power."

– Natalia repeated, – I decree my power.

– Adamo continued, – I am the one in charge of myself.

– And she repeated. Adamo then spoke a few impactful positive phrases and gently touched her hand.

– He reassured her, – For now, that's all. Your energy pattern has already shifted.

– Natalia felt relieved, – Wow, I feel like a weight has been lifted off my shoulders.

– Adamo explained, – You were connected to other people due to their troubled thoughts.

– I'm sorry, I shouldn't have been angry with Marion.

– Adamo comforted her, – You get angry because you take everything personally. When we accept the insults of the world, we become disturbed. When you are disturbed, the disturbance increases. When you are balanced, disturbance doesn't come in.

– Natalia reflected, – You have a very different perspective on life.

– Adamo shared, – I learned the hard way. I've always had a keen sensitivity and would pick up all sorts of energies, good or bad, from the living and the deceased.

– Natalia related, – It sounds just like me!

– Adamo admitted, – And I just got hurt. I thought I had to suffer for past debts. So, I studied spirituality more deeply and learned that I am responsible for everything good or bad that happens to me.

– Letting go of the world's blame is not a dignified way out.

– And blaming the world for your misfortunes isn't worthy either? Adamo asked seriously.

– Natalia shivered.

– The world causes us a lot of suffering.

– Let's change the way we look at this situation. You suffer because you let yourself be affected by the world's suffering, which means you're affected because you want to be.

– You speak as if I were irresponsible. It's my sensitivity...

– Sensitivity is a gift. Understanding and using it to your advantage will only help it grow in the world. Sensitivity is a reward, not a misfortune.

– I learned differently.

– Then unlearn, Adamo said firmly. Use your strength for your growth and happiness, not to cause yourself pain.

– I think I need to reevaluate my entire belief system.

– Accept it. If you continue to think and act this way, like a victim of the world, you will suffer needlessly. I see that you are a beautiful and talented and intelligent young woman. First of all, you need to do away with the belief that suffering and suffering makes you grow. Suffering hurts a lot all the time. Suffering hurts a lot. Wouldn't you rather grow in life through intelligence rather than pain?

– Those words deeply affected Natalia. Adamo's perspective was entirely contrary to what she had learned and considered valid as a belief. She believed that pain and suffering were essential and useful tools for her spiritual evolution. Adamo was now suggesting that it was all a matter of perspective. Her mind was challenged, and after this conversation with Adamo, Natalia would see life with different eyes.

# Chapter 14

– Olair was feeling like the happiest man in the world. He had gotten rid of those two nuisances. He had never really liked his daughters, and now he was free to live happily with his beloved Gisele.

– Everything was done to please Gisele. He painted and redecorated the house, bought new furniture, appliances, everything just the way she wanted it. He even splurged on a color television, something expensive and not yet present in many households at the time.

– Don't you think you're spending too much, man? – asked Ademar, one of his clients.

– Olair replied with a smile from ear to ear:

– I've saved money my whole life, and now I can afford to spend it on my new wife.

– But hey, didn't you say you didn't have money to pay for a private doctor for Josefa?

– I lied. Did you think I would spend money on that lousy illness? Zefa was doomed to die anyway. Why would I waste my hard-earned money on a dying wife?

– Ademar shook his head.

– Olair, that's not nice. Josefa was a good wife. She always took care of the house, of the girls. She was very reserved and discreet.

– And he lived at my expense. I put food on the table. If she took a hot bath and had a TV to watch her shows it was because I paid the electric bill. I paid for her clothes, I paid for everything! She did nothing but her duty. And, if you ask me, she did very little. I don't miss her.

– Not even your daughters?

– No. Arlete and Alzira have always been a thorn in my side. They interfered with my life. If I hadn't brought them into this world, I could have saved more money. But I had to spend on school supplies, clothes, uniforms, more food on the table... – Olair paused, took a drag of his cigarette, and continued: – They cost me a lot. I'm very happy they're far away from here.

– Ademar shrugged. He had known Olair for many years and knew that the man was hot-headed, touchy, and stubborn. He didn't like being contradicted, and his word was law. He tried to change the subject.

– Are you happy with Gisele?

– Very – Olair was all smiles. – This is a woman with a capital "W," my friend. She fulfils all my desires and is always ready for love. She gives herself to me every night.

– Does she take care of the house?

– Imagine! Are you crazy? And do I want a woman smelling of bleach? No way. I want Gisele always clean, well-dressed, and perfumed, with her huge red nails to scratch my back. I hired a maid for the heavy work.

– I see you've become a different man now. Who you were and who you are now! – exclaimed Ademar.

– Time passes, we age, but we get wiser. I was used and stayed stagnant in life because of three women who gave me nothing. It's as if I'd been at a standstill all these years.

– Where are your daughters now?

– I left them with a relative over in Sao Bernardo. – Olair could not bear to talk about his sister. He was terrified of remembering the shame he had experienced with Lourdes, years before.

– So now it's just the new wife?

– That's right, you know I'm even thinking of giving her a trip? A wealthy client of Jardim Franca told me that the *finegranes* travel to Bariloche. I'm thinking of splitting a trip for the two of us.

– Look, Olair, I'm impressed with your devotion. I hope this love lasts a good long time.

– It's for a lifetime, – he replied, seriously. – Gisele loves me, and we're going to live many years together.

– So be it!

– The customer finished trying on the suit, got dressed, and left. It was almost seven o'clock in the evening, time to close the tailor shop. Olair turned off the lights, locked the iron door, and put on the padlock. He turned the corner and went to the bakery. Gisele didn't like – and didn't know – how to cook. She said it was boring to have to prepare food and end up smelling like seasonings. Olair agreed, and it became a habit: every night, he would stop by the bakery, grab some bread rolls, a bit of ham and mozzarella, and a bottle of guarana. He would arrive home tired but happy.

- He walked around the small iron gate and climbed the small step. As he reached for the doorknob, the door swung open, and Rodinei came out, looking serious.

- Rodinei, what a surprise!

- Olair, I came to talk to Gisele about the house. She's pressuring me, and...

- Olair interrupted him with a kindly tone in his voice:

- Nonsense. She's like that because she wants you to transfer the deed to us.

- I'll arrange that for next month, okay?

- Of course. Rodinei, you're like a brother to me. If I didn't trust you, I'd never have transferred the house into your name, just so my daughters wouldn't have any claim to the inheritance or anything.

- Rodinei chuckled, and his gold canine tooth gleamed.

- Clever of you, my friend. You took advantage of Josefa's illness. I remember the day you made her sign the deed.

- Josefa thought it was a life insurance document for the girls. She was simple, naive, and didn't dare oppose me. But, thanks to you, my dear, I managed to keep this property all to myself.

- And for your new wife, right? - Rodinei added.

- Of course, for Gisele.

– Rodinei said goodbye and left. Olair entered the house, put the bakery packages on the kitchen table. Gisele was taking a bath.

– Taking a bath at this hour, darling?

– Rodinei was wasting my time, my love. I'm sorry for only bathing now. I know you don't like it, and...

– Gisele didn't finish speaking; she got a big surprise. Olair took off his clothes and pulled the shower curtain and stepped into the tiny square. I want to love you now!

– Gisele smiled and closed her eyes.

– How long do I have to give in to this jerk? I hate this dirty man with his horrible breath. I'm only making this effort because Rodinei asked me, she thought to herself.

Olair continued to indulge in his wife, and she pretended to enjoy it. She kept thinking: Rodinei is a real man. He just left here and left me dizzy with pleasure. Now I have to pretend to enjoy this nobody. I can't wait to take the house for myself and throw this miserable man out. I'll do the same thing he did with the girls.

– Gisele was tired. She had spent almost the whole afternoon in Rodinei's arms. She had no desire to continue with this rubbing. She grabbed the shampoo bottle and deliberately poured it into Olair's eyes.

– Ouch! My eyes are burning.

– Oh, my love, I'm sorry – she said in a fake, childish tone. – I got confused. I'm sorry. Rinse your eyes under the water.

– Gisele detached herself from the brute and grabbed a towel. She handed it to her husband.

– There you go, Olair. The pain will pass. Let's continue.

– I've lost the desire. My eyes hurt. Go set the table. I bought bread and cold cuts.

– Gisele smiled. She had achieved her goal. She dried herself, put on underwear and a nightgown. She went to the kitchen and set the table. She made sandwiches, filled a glass with guarana, and sat in the chair.

– I'll wait for another month and then make my move. I'm going to take everything from this old scoundrel – she muttered under her breath while chewing her sandwich with her mouth open.

– Gisele had been ecstatic for days. Now she would finally conclude her devilish plan. And what was this diabolical plan?

– Let's go back in time to when Josefa got sick. Gisele came from the city of Aquidauana, in Mato Grosso do Sul – in those days, the city was still part of the state of Mato Grosso – to try her luck in the big city. She tried Cuiaba, Belo Horizonte, Rio de Janeiro, and eventually arrived in São Paulo. After various odd jobs, she met Rodinei.

– Gisele fell deeply in love with the bar owner. Rodinei was from the Northeast, with a rugged face marked by acne scars, and he was as macho as they come. In a conversation with him, she learned that Olair, the owner of the tailoring shop, had a seriously ill wife, dying of cancer.

– She's very sick. They say it's cancer – said Rodinei.

– I had an aunt who had that disease, and she also died – Gisele commented.

– The man is nervous. If his wife dies, half the house will belong to his daughters. He doesn't want to share the house with anyone.

– Why not?

– Because he said he worked hard to achieve everything he has, and none of his daughters helped him at all. The man just put together some money and paid off the house at the bank. I think Olair is right.

– Gisele poked her head out to think. And the bright idea came up:

– Why don't you offer to take the house?

– What do you mean, Gisele? I'm a man, and I don't have the money to buy a house.

– This little house must be worth very little.

– Even so, I don't have the money. I live in the back of the bar.

– A mischievous gleam passed through Gisele's eyes.

– What if he transfers the house to you as if he had sold it?

– I don't understand.

– It's simple. You offer yourself as a buyer. You go to the notary, Olair writes the deed in your name and, after the old lady dies, you and I get the house. All front.

– He won't be foolish enough to transfer the house like that, for nothing.

– You said it yourself that Olair doesn't want to share the house with his daughters. I'm sure he would agree to make a deal, and I'll go further: he'll thank you for offering to lend your name.

– I don't know. After that, he might go to the police station, file a report, and prove that he never received a dime for the house. I want to stay away from the police.

– Silly – said Gisele. – Olair won't be able to prove anything. And if he wants to go to court, as slow as the justice system is, he'll never get the house back.

– You are my queen, and you should be well treated. I swear I'd do anything to give you comfort.

– Then put your head to work.

– It's not a bad idea. A little house from heaven, without having to pay anything... I'm starting to like it.

– Gisele smiled maliciously and threw herself onto Rodinei. She did everything he liked in matters of love and convinced the young man to accept the plan. It was all straightforward. She would get close to Olair and show him attention. After Josefa died, they would get married. After some time, Gisele would request a divorce and go live with Rodinei in the house that would be theirs. And, of course, Olair could go to hell. Everything went according to plan. Josefa signed the sale of the house and died a few months later. Olair fell for Gisele's deceit and they got married.

– Now it was time to reveal the truth to Olair and ask for a divorce. Gisele was tired of living with that dirty man with rough manners. She couldn't wait to be with Rodinei, the man she truly loved.

# Chapter 15

- Life was flowing peacefully, and the days seemed to be getting better for Arlete and Alzira. Lurdes's company did them a world of good. Gradually, they adapted to their new routine.

- The week they arrived at Lourdes' house, Arlete called Osvaldo and told him what had happened. The boyfriend went to see them and got Arlete a job as a typist at a car assembly plant in São Bernardo. As the months went by, Lourdes noticed Alzira's gift for cooking and encouraged her niece to prepare sweets and salty snacks to sell. Before long, the neighbourhood and Arlete's co-workers were making requests. Alzira had fairy hands, they said.

- One Saturday, Osvaldo came to pick up Arlete at home. They were going to the cinema to watch the thrilling *"Jaws."* Lurdes invited Alzira to visit a couple of friends and play cards.

- No, Aunt. I'm tired. We made a lot of sweets and pies this week. I'd like to have a snack and go to my room to read. And I have to keep an eye on the cat.

- The cat? - Lurdes asked, surprised. - Smiles is independent. He loves to go out at night and walk around the neighbourhood's rooftops. Why this concern about the cat now?

- Alzira didn't answer. Lurdes had been worried about the girl's behaviour. Alzira didn't feel like going out, she had no friends, and she didn't want to date. Every weekend, she would grab her worn copy of "*See the lilies in the field*" and lock herself in her room.

- You already know this story inside and out. Wouldn't you prefer to read another novel?

- Mrs. Celia once lent me a spiritualist novel.

- What did you think?

- I liked it a lot. But Verissimo's book has marked me deeply. I have great affection for it - she said while caressing the book's cover.

- Lurdes had plenty of time and sat on the couch next to her niece.

- What makes you like the book so much?

- I fell in love with Olivia. She loves Eugenio in such an unselfish and sublime way, so beautiful!

- I haven't read the book, but I know the story - Alzira's eyes filled with tears.

- Do you think I'll ever love like Olivia? Young people don't want anything serious. They've always called me a stick-in-the-mud.

- Come on - Lurdes reassured her. - Arlete is a year older than you. She's dating a nice young man and they're thinking about marriage. Why couldn't you have the same luck?

– Because Arlete is carefree, she has a very different attitude from mine. She's extroverted. I'm shyer and more reserved. It's hard to find someone.

– It depends on you. If you stay locked up at home every weekend, it will be hard to find a boyfriend.

– I don't feel like going out, Aunt. I feel like I belong to another world, to another century. I don't like all this modernity.

– Making friends is good.

– I have your friendship – Alzira said affectionately – I have my sister's friendship, and the friendship of Mrs. Celia and Mr. Ariovaldo.

– It would be nice to get to know young men and women your age.

– Osvaldo insisted that you go to the cinema with them. I saw the sadness in Arlete's eyes when you declined the invitation.

– Imagine! Would I be the third wheel?

– They both laughed.

– Arlete enjoys your company.

– I know that, Aunt Lurdes. The thing is, I don't like the Saturday night hustle and bustle. And, if it were to watch a romantic movie, I might consider it. But watching a horror film? It's not my thing.

– You prefer to stay at home.

– I do. You can go out and meet your friends, play cards. I'll be just fine in the company of my book.

– They heard a car horn.

– It's my friends. If you want to go out, there's a spare key inside the potted ferns, near the little gate.

– Lurdes kissed her on the cheek and left.

– Alzira had a snack, drank some juice, and then grabbed the book and sat in the armchair. Her eyes gradually began to blur, and sleep started to creep in. She closed her eyes, drifted off, and had a dream.

– Alzira found herself sitting in a chair on the veranda of an old colonial-style mansion from the late 19th century, looking out at the green fields in front of her. She looked at herself and was amazed.

– I'm wearing old-fashioned clothes. From the past century!

– She was touched to see the cameo delicately attached to the wine-coloured velvet dress. She looked ahead and saw a man with a stern expression approaching. Alzira felt a chill in her stomach.

– What are you doing here? – she asked, irritated.

– I want to see my daughter.

– Carolina is not your daughter – Alzira snapped.

– And this house is mine!

– It's not yours either.

– If I had known that your sister's husband was the buyer of this house, I would have never sold it. You used me.

– I want my house and my daughter back.

– You're more interested in the house than the daughter, aren't you, Malaquias?

– So what? If that girl – he pointed inside the house – helps me reclaim my inheritance, what's the problem? What's it got to do with you?

– It's got everything to do with me! – she shouted. – You don't lay a finger on the girl!

– Well, well. Now you've become a brave woman? – the man asked. – You've never had the courage to do anything in your life. You got married, and your husband left you because you're barren, and you'll never be able to bear a child. What man would even like you?

– I won't tolerate you coming to my house and speaking to me in this manner – she protested.

– All right. I don't want a fight. I want to see my daughter.

– She's not your daughter, Malaquias. My sister married someone else. The daughter is his.

– The man's eyes were filled with anger.

– Before she married that idiot, your sister, that slut, slept with me. She married that dandy for money. And the idiot outsmarted me, buying this house for a pittance.

– You sold it because you wanted to!

– If I had known he was the buyer, I would have never made the deal.

– You're saying that now because you lost your wife and the property.

– Malaquias slapped her across the face. Slap!

– You animal! – she screamed and jumped out of her chair. – Don't ever lay your dirty fingers on me again.

– Right now, I don't just want to lay my hands on you – he said in a profane and highly disturbing tone.

– Alzira blushed and anticipated what would happen. She shivered. She tried to steady her voice.

– Don't you dare!

– Get out of my way. I want to see my daughter.

– Alzira didn't think. She lunged at the man and began slapping him all over his body.

– Damned man. I hate you!

– He turned to her and slapped her again. Then he tore off her dress and lay on top of her.

– Alzira immediately found herself in another place. She was now sitting on a bench. There was a beautiful garden around her. She saw a woman approaching and smiled:

– Lolla, how are you, my dear?

– It's so good that you appeared! Malaquias came to beat me, and...

– Shh! Calm down. That's part of the past.

Lolla sat down next to Alzira and gently placed her hands on the young woman's hands.

– Your hands are cold.

– It was fear. Malaquias abused me

– That's in the past now. It was many, many years ago. We were sisters. You, me, Anamaria, and Judite. Why didn't you come back?

– Because I decided to stay. You and your sisters returned.

– Do you remember the plan?

– Mother.

– Yes. Judite would be my sister, and Anamaria would be our mother.

– Exactly. Josefa and Arlete are by your side.

– Josefa passed away.

– She transcended. She completed a stage in her evolutionary journey. Soon, you'll be able to reunite.

– Alzira smiled, then furrowed her brow.

– I still feel anger just thinking about it all. He was brutal, and I was a helpless woman. – Alzira spoke as tears streamed down her face.

– Don't torment yourself anymore. It's time to free yourself from that past existence. Your spirit is the same, but you're living a different reality today.

– He was the reason I'm afraid to love.

– No. You attracted that situation to become stronger. You were a woman who would despair over anything, with no firmness in your decisions.

– I grew up surrounded by affection. After my parents died, I lost my way. My sisters and my niece were responsible for me staying alive.

– You need to forgive Malaquias and free yourself from this stain on your soul.

– It's difficult. No matter how hard I try, I can't think of forgiveness.

– When you realize that you are responsible for everything that happens to you and that Malaquias was nothing more than an instrument of life to strengthen your spirit and make you strong and self-reliant, maybe you'll consider forgiveness. In fact, forgiveness is meant to soothe our souls and heal the holes in our aura. True forgiveness makes us stronger and clearer-headed.

– I'll try.

– You have a good heart, Alzira. You have everything to be happy.

– Me, happy? I don't believe it.

– Stop punishing yourself. Free yourself from the past and give happiness a chance to appear in your life.

– Alzira embraced Lolla.

– Why aren't you with us? I miss you so much.

– I've already said it. I didn't plan to reincarnate with you, Josefa, and Arlete. My spirit has other aspirations. What are fifty, seventy years apart? It's nothing in the face of eternity. Your lives will pass in the blink of an eye, and soon we'll all be reunited, assessing the steps taken in this blessed incarnation.

– Blessed incarnation? – Alzira asked, astonished. – Malaquias reincarnated as my father and kicked me and my sister out of the house. Is there a harsher proof than that?

– Malaquias acted based on the past incarnation. Olair still feels tied to the past. However, you and Arlete had a chance for a better life. You live with Lurdes, and, between us, you live much better than in that small house.

– Thinking about it...

– Alzira, life gave you the opportunity to be reborn alongside someone you had conflicts with and undo the knots of bitterness and animosity. Josefa, you and Arlete overcame a difficult but significant phase in this incarnation, and from now on, you have everything to live happily. Josefa is recovering well and will soon live with me. This incarnation was very useful for her. Now she realizes how much she put herself down. She promised me that she'll be strong and never bend to the world's ideas again.

– I was a bit traumatized by everything. I lost my mother, my home, and I feel like I'm going to die single.

– Are you being dramatic?

– Not at all!

– Lalla laughed.

– It seems quite dramatic to me. Malaquias reincarnated as your father, and you're not even together anymore. Free will separated him from you and your sister.

– Thinking it over, calmly and with balance, my life improved a lot after he entrusted us to Aunt Lurdes' care.

– See? Everything got better. Forgive your father. Free yourself from him sincerely. Say a liberation prayer for Olair and detach him from your life. Or do you prefer to hold onto resentment and come back together in another life, going through the same experiences again?

– Alzira knocked three times on the bench's wood.

- God forbids!

- Then think carefully about everything I've told you. And, regarding your father, say firmly with feeling: "I am guided to my true place. I release all things and people that no longer belong to God's plan in my life, setting them free to be happy in their own lives and purposes. In the name of God."

- Alzira repeated it and felt a great sense of well-being.

- Practice this phrase as many times as you like. It works as a powerful tool to distance yourself from people and situations you no longer need or want to be around.

- I'll use that regarding my father.

- Do that, and you'll see that your life will improve even more. After all, when we make room to sincerely release people and things that are no longer a part of our lives, we open up space for interesting people and things to come into our path. Give it a try.

- I'll wake up and forget everything.

- Maybe you'll forget our conversation, but I'll help you remember the powerful phrase.

- Alzira embraced her warmly.

- You're an angel in my life, Lolla. Thank you so much.

- Lalla returned the affection and smiled.

- I need to go now.

- Oh, already? I enjoy your company so much.

- You'll return to your body, wake up, and leave.

– I don't want to leave. I don't like anything. It's all too modern. I wish I could live like in my previous life.

– Everything changes with time, my dear. Life has become more dynamic, helping people on the planet rebalance more quickly.

– I like the quiet, the antique furniture...

– You can live in this world while maintaining the essence of the past. For example, you can live in the countryside and decorate your house with period furniture.

– That's a pleasant idea.

– And if I were you, I'd risk taking a little stroll. Just a little stroll.

– Why are you telling me this? – Alzira asked, suspicious.

– Go out and see! It's my time. I need to go.

– Lalla hugged Alzira, kissed her affectionately on the cheek, and left. In a few moments, Alzira shifted in her armchair and opened her eyes. The cat was sitting on her lap. She smiled:

– Smiles! Have you been with me all this time?

– The cat meowed, as if understanding and answering the question. Then it jumped and curled up at Alzira's feet. It meowed once more and dashed away, leaping out of the living room window.

– I went for a walk! – she exclaimed.

– Alzira remembered the dream and smiled. She was aware that she had dreamed of a beautiful woman, but she didn't know her well. She remembered her father, and the words flowed easily, like a memorized text, in a loud and clear voice:

– I am being guided to my true place. I release all things and people that no longer belong to God's plan in my life, setting them free to be happy in their own lives and purposes. In the name of God.

– Then, she said:

– I release you, father. – Alzira closed her eyes and thought of Olair. She tried to imagine him smiling and continued: – You are no longer part of the divine plan in my life, and so I set you free to be happy in your life. In the name of God. Now and always!

– Alzira opened her eyes and felt a light sense of well-being. She felt thirsty and got up. She picked up the book and placed it on the small table in the living room. She went to the kitchen and drank a glass of water. – Maybe I need to go out for a little while. This dream has stirred me up.

– She walked to the backyard and looked up. The sky was full of stars, and a pleasant breeze touched her face. Alzira decided:

– I'm going for a walk.

– She dressed up, tied her hair in a bun, applied some perfume, and grabbed her purse.

– Arlete and Osvaldo went to see a movie at the Astor cinema. I know how to get there – she said to herself.

– She locked the door, crossed the street, and caught a bus that took her to the top of Consolação Street.

- An hour later, she got off at the corner of the street and Avenida Paulista. She walked to Conjunto Nacional. She was amazed by the crowds. She went to a bookstore and started flipping through a cookbook.

- Alzira checked the time, and there were twenty minutes left for the movie to end.

- I hope I find them - she said quietly while her eyes examined the photos of the recipes.

- Do you like the book? - a young man asked, very politely.

- Alzira raised her head and looked into his eyes.

- Very beautiful. But my recipes are much better.

- He laughed.

- Why don't you write a cookbook?

- The young woman sighed. She closed the book and put it back on the shelf.

- I wish I could.

- Why not? Don't you believe in your potential?

- Of course, I do. I'm a great cook.

- Then writing a cookbook is a natural step for someone who knows how to cook.

- Certainly, here's the translation of the text from Portuguese to English:

- No. There's a big gap between making sweets and selling them to the neighbours and publishing a successful recipe book like this one - he pointed to the book on display.

– If your desire to write comes from your soul, nothing will stop you. Whatever the soul wants, we can achieve.

– I've wanted many things in life and didn't get them.

– Maybe it wasn't meant for your soul. It might have been a desire of the mind.

– I can't separate what's from the soul and what's from the mind. It's all the same thing.

– A friendly salesperson approached and informed them that the store would be closing in ten minutes. The young man said something in the salesperson's ear, and Alzira quietly left.

– She left the store and went to the cinema's lobby. The movie would end soon.

– I hope to find Arlete and Osvaldo – she said to herself while checking the clock again.

– The young man approached, and Alzira was startled.

– Hi.

– Hi – she replied in a shy manner.

– You left me alone in the store.

– They were closing. You went to talk to the salesperson, so I decided to come to the cinema's lobby.

– The young man took a package from a bag and handed it to Alzira.

– What is this? – she asked, apprehensive.

– A gift. Open it.

- Alzira delicately tore open the package. It was the cookbook she had been browsing through in the store just minutes before.

- Oh my God! You bought the book?

- Mm-hmm.

- It's expensive. Why did you do such a crazy thing?

- The young man laughed heartily. - It's a crazy thing that's worth it.

- Alzira looked closely at the young man. He was a handsome guy, of average height, wearing prescription glasses that hid his big black eyes. He had dark hair, neatly styled. He wore an orange turtleneck and jeans. The fragrance he exuded was subtle, and she blushed.

- We should introduce ourselves because I'd like to write a dedication in the book. Can we?

- Sure - she said, somewhat awkwardly. - My name is Alzira, and you?

- Eugenio.

- Alzira shivered. She felt a slight dizziness, and Eugenio held her in his arms.

- What's wrong?

- Nothing.

- "Nothing"? I say my name, and you nearly have a fit?

- She tried to hide her emotions and replied:

- Nice to meet you. My name is Alzira.

- Eugenio pretended to shudder.

– What's wrong?

– You already said your name. I'm just teasing you. I want to know why you got so worked up when I introduced myself.

– It was nothing.

– An ex-boyfriend with the same name?

– She waved her hand in the air.

– Imagine! It's nonsense. Complete nonsense.

– I love nonsense – Eugenio responded.

– You'll laugh at me.

– I'd never do that – he said seriously.

– Well, I, um, I'm passionate about a book by Erico Verissimo. There's a character in one of his books that really affects me.

– Ah! You must be talking about *"See the lilies in the field."*

– Do you know it? – she asked, bewildered.

– I do! – sighed Eugenio. – My mom had contact with that book when she was still a girl and asked my dad that if they had a son, he should be named Eugenio because of the character. Can you believe it?

– Alzira wanted to scream and say yes, she believed in dreams, in witches, in anything. She was too emotional. The young man in front of her was named Eugenio because of the book she loved so much. What to say? That she had found the man of her life in less than fifteen minutes? He would probably think she was crazy and run away scared.

– She bit her lip and replied:

– I believe. And I would love to meet your mom!

– My goodness! What did I just say? I'd better keep my mouth shut, she thought to herself.

– Eugenio was about to respond, but the cinema doors were opened. Alzira raised her head.

– Are you waiting for someone?

– My sister and her boyfriend came to see a movie here. Well, at least that's what they told me.

– A few minutes later, she saw Arlete and Osvaldo, holding hands and smiling. When Arlete spotted her sister standing there, she was startled.

– What are you doing here? Did something happen to Aunt Lurdes?

– No. I decided to go out and meet you. I swear. But I absolutely don't want to be a third wheel.

– You won't be a third wheel – said Osvaldo as he greeted her. Then he noticed the young man behind Alzira.

– Eugenio! What are you doing here, man of God?

– They hugged each other, and Arlete pulled Alzira aside. – You never leave the house. Suddenly, I find you here at the cinema entrance on a Saturday night, next to a handsome guy. Am I hallucinating? Did the shark movie mess with my head? – Arlete pinched herself.

– No – Alzira replied, laughing. – It's just that I had that dream again.

– On the farm?

– Yes, the same scene. But this time, it was worse. I felt something very bad. I woke up startled. Aunt Lurdes went out with a couple of friends to play cards. I didn't want to stay home alone. I had the urge to go out and took a chance to come here.

– And the guy?

– We met at the bookstore.

– When?

– Less than half an hour ago! Can you believe he's named Eugenio?

– Yes, so what? – Arlete asked.

– He has the name of Olivia's great love. Do you understand?

– Arlete nodded up and down. Osvaldo approached the girls.

– Darling, this is Eugenio Salles, a school friend. He was doing a specialization course in the United States.

– Eugenio nodded. Arlete lifted her face, and they exchanged little kisses.

– Nice to meet you. I'm Arlete, Osvaldo's girlfriend, and Alzira's sister.

– Eugenio gave a big smile.

– The pleasure is all mine. In the letters I exchanged with Osvaldo, he always mentioned you. But he never told me that his girlfriend had such a beautiful sister.

– Eugenio spoke and looked at Alzira. She blushed, and Osvaldo added:

– I never mentioned anything because I'm very reserved. Besides, you were dating Celiña.

– The relationship ended. Celiña met an American politician and they got married. She's pregnant with their first child.

– Are you dating? – Arlete asked.

– I just arrived from the United States. I'm thinking about setting up my law firm and establishing myself here. I love my country.

– Osvaldo noticed Eugenio's interest in Alzira. He changed the topic and suggested:

– I'm starving. How about grabbing a sandwich nearby?

– I'm hungry too – Arlete replied.

– I was just walking around aimlessly – Eugenio said. – I've barely arrived, and I haven't had the chance to catch up with the few friends I left here.

– Alzira remained silent. She was very emotional. She felt something very strange. Her face was warm, her heart seemed to want to jump out of her mouth, and a little chill persisted in her stomach.

– Is all of this love? – she wondered as they walked to the sandwich shop.

– Alzira looked at the sky and gazed at the stars. She felt an indescribable happiness.

# Chapter 16

- It was only a few days before Valeria would embark for Italy. The plane tickets had already been purchased. She had packed her bags and would be traveling with her uncle Adamo.

- I'm going to miss you so much, Natalia said as she hugged her friend.

- I don't know why you don't come with us.

- Me?! Are you crazy, Valeria? I've worked so hard to get into university, and you expect me to drop everything?

- Without the drama, Natalia. You can defer your enrolment.

Come and study at the same school as me. If you don't like it you go back and start the course here again. You'll lose a year. What's a year in the face of everything you have to live for?

- You're so optimistic. You're a wild one. Have you forgotten that we have a simple life? I can't afford plane tickets or pay for this course.

- I've already told you that's not a problem. You're like a sister to me, Valeria added. My father has said he'd be happy to pay for your plane tickets and the course.

– Well, then, get used to it.

– I'm afraid of things that come too easily into my hands.

– Why?

– My father always said that everything that comes easy goes away easy. Look what happened to him. He lost everything he had.

– Your father lost everything he had because he was irresponsible, Adamo retorted.

– Natalia widened her eyes. She felt like the ground had opened beneath her. She wasn't sure whether to keep looking at Adamo or avert her eyes. Valeria noticed and intervened:

– Uncle, may we have a moment? I need to change.

– That's all right. But remember – he said looking fixedly at Natalia – that your company will do me a lot of good – Adamo spoke and left, closing the door softly.

– Natalia did not move a muscle. She stood still in the middle of the room like a statue. Valeria made a graceful up and down motion with her hand, drawing her friend's attention:

– Hey! Did something happen?

– Natalia snapped back to reality and sat on the bed, dishevelled.

– Is it just me, or is your uncle interested in me?

– Interested? Valeria asked with a mischievous smile. He's very interested. I noticed it a few days ago. He was constantly circling around, asking to invite you for tea. I think you've hooked him!

- I can't believe it, Natalia put her hand on her chest. I was interested in Adamo, but I started to dismiss the idea of a serious relationship.

- Oh, come on, Natalia! That's a silly comparison, Valeria said. What's the problem with that age difference? I don't see any problem. My uncle is handsome, single, intelligent, and doesn't look his age.

- There's a big difference, Natalia said. He lived abroad for many years; he has experience...

- Experience enough to come to the conclusion that it's worth opening his heart to you. I never knew my uncle Adamo was interested in another woman before. He never introduced us to a girlfriend.

- And you're immediately interested in me? An ordinary girl with no great attraction?

- Stop putting yourself down. You need to value your qualities. Not everyone is interested only in physical beauty. If the person has no content, the relationship will not move forward. Beauty will one day go away, but what we are and what we feel - Valeria put her hand to her chest -, no one will be able to take it away from us.

- I confess that I am calmer. Adamo touches me very much.

- Stop being afraid. Let's travel together, let's live together. We are practically sisters. Your company will do me a lot of good.

– I'm going to talk to Mom.

– That's right. Think it over and...

– Valeria stopped talking. She felt a numbness, an incomparable nausea. She covered her mouth with her hand and ran to the bathroom. Natalia followed her.

– What happened? – she asked, anguished.

– I don't know. I've been feeling sick for a few days. Why didn't you ever tell me anything?

– Nonsense, Natalia. It must be the anxiety of the trip. We'd better consult a doctor.

– No. It happens.

– One of the maids knocked at the door.

– Mrs. Valeria, your tea. Where can I place the tray?

– There, on the dresser – Valeria instructed.

– She wiped her mouth, flushed the toilet and poured some water down her throat.

– Are you feeling better? – Natalia asked.

– Yes.

– But, as she approached the tray and smelled the aroma of the cookies, Valeria felt sick again and ran back to the bathroom.

– It's not normal – assured Natalia –. Something you ate attacked your liver. Whether we like it or not, we are going to the doctor.

– Valeria protested, but Natalia would not calm down until an appointment was made. She agreed and in the late afternoon they went to the doctor's office. The doctor asked the usual questions and ordered some tests. Despite waiting for the tests, the symptoms were clear. Valeria felt nauseous first thing in the morning, her breasts were swollen and her period was late.

– Natalia was sure of the result, but waited for the doctor to tell Valeria, days later:

– You are pregnant.

* * *

– On that same afternoon, Arlete returned from work feeling exhausted. She had been typing reports all day, and her fingers hurt. She entered the house, threw her bag onto the side table, and stretched out on the sofa.

– Alzira followed shortly after.

– She is tired. What was it?

– Nothing. A working day like any other.

– You don't look so good. Did you have a fight with Osvaldo?

– Not at all. The relationship is going very well. Although I'm tired – said Arlete smiling – I have an announcement to make.

– What is it?

– Osvaldo wants to get engaged – Alzira covered her mouth with her hand.

– Really?

– Yep, he wants us to get engaged on Christmas. And we're planning to get married in two years.

- Alzira ran and jumped into Arlete's arms.

- Give me a hug, my little sister. How happy I am for you.

- Arlete got up and they embraced excitedly.

- I am going to marry the man I love and we will be very happy.

- I'm sure of that.

- What about you and Eugenio?

- We're doing well. We've started dating. I'll meet his mother next week. He's hosting a lunch to introduce me to his family, Alzira said with some apprehension.

- Why are you so anxious?

- We're not wealthy. We received a good education from our mom, and we have manners. But we don't have money.

- Eugenio knows about your situation, and he likes you just the way you are. It seems his family doesn't care about differences in social class. You're a wonderful person. Who wouldn't fall in love with you?

- Alzira hugged her tightly. - After everything we've been through, I can't believe how well this year is going.

- Exactly! We started the year feeling down, discouraged, and without any motivation. Dad kicked us out of the house, and we thought our lives would be terrible. In the end, everything improved.

- Alzira nodded in agreement, and they heard Lurdes' voice coming from the hallway:

– Everything has improved and will continue to get better with each passing day. We deserve the best.

– The two sisters approached Lurdes. They hugged their aunt and placed a delicate kiss on her face.

– We don't know how to thank you, Aunt Lurdes – said Alzira, excited.

– I will never forget your generosity. We love you very much.

– Lurdes smiled, her eyes welling up. She adored her nieces. The encounter with them had been the best thing that had happened to her in years.

– Father was very harsh with us – said Alzira. – We were afraid of you.

– Why? – asked Lurdes, curious.

– Because your name couldn't be mentioned at home. And father called you a harlot when he left us here. I'm sorry to speak like this, aunt – said Arlete.

– No need to apologize – replied Lurdes.

– I don't want to pry, but why doesn't your father like you? – Arlete asked, curious.

– Lurdes gestured for them to sit. The girls nodded and settled on the couch. Lurdes remained seated between them.

– They are adults and are experiencing love – They nodded and Lourdes continued:

– Maybe they will understand what happened to me. Olair and I come from a very large and very poor family. We come from Jutaf, in Amazonas, and we were the only ones who had the courage to go down through the country to São

Paulo. Some brothers stayed there, others went to Goiás. I no longer have contact with any of them. I was the only daughter among nine siblings. They all got married and continued to live their lives.

– Arlete and Alzira nodded, and Lurdes continued:

– Olair was my protector. We were very close and good friends.

– Hard to believe – said Arlete. – Father has always been rude and stupid.

– I believe Olair became like that because of me.

– What do you mean? – asked Alzira.

– * As I said, we were very close. Olair met Josefa, they fell in love, and decided to get married. I went to live with them.

– We never knew about this – Arlete interjected.

– Because your father is ashamed of me. I started dating a young man also from a humble family and we had plans to get married, we got engaged and he set the date. But he fell in love with someone else and broke up with me.

– How sad! – sighed Alzira.

– That wasn't a reason for father to hate you so much.

– It wasn't – Lurdes agreed. – After a month of the breakup, I found out I was pregnant.

– The girls swallowed hard. Lurdes continued:

– Olair couldn't accept it. He called me all sorts of ugly names. Josefa tried to defend me, but in vain. My brother, feeling betrayed in his honour, kicked me out of the house.

- And what happened next, aunt? - asked Alzira, almost in tears.

- I went to live in a boarding house for pregnant women in Santana. In the third month of pregnancy I had a severe haemorrhage and lost the baby. Then I wanted to start my life again. I became friends with Celia and Ariovaldo, who were newlyweds living near the boarding house at the time. They were very good friends with a couple who lived here in Rudge Ramos and they took me in. I got a job at an automobile manufacturer and went on with my life. From time to time I corresponded with Zefa. I would send letters to Celia's house, and Zefa would do the same, writing and sending me letters. So, I followed their growth, Olair's bad behaviour, which got worse and worse over the years, Josefa's illness... - Lourdes got up, walked to the hallway and opened the door of a small chest of drawers. From there she took out a large box. She took it to the sofa and, when she opened it, there was a pile of letters yellowed by time. He showed them the packet of letters delicately wrapped in a satin ribbon and showed them a photo.

- Mom had this same photo, but it was cropped when I was 10 years old.

- We took this picture just after your parents got married.

- At that time, we were very happy.

- And then aunt, what happened? - Alzira asked, anxious.

- Mrs Carmiña and Orlando, the couple who took me in, passed away a few years ago and, as they had no children, they left me this house as an inheritance, I kept working and I retired for seniority last year. Retirement is not about those things, but it's enough to pay the bills and have a modest life, without luxuries.

– Have you heard from your ex-fiancé again? – Arlete asked.

– No – answered Lourdes, looking at an undefined point in the room –. And I didn't want to know more either. If the baby had survived, maybe I would have looked for him. However, after everything that happened to me, why pursue someone who doesn't love us? I learned to value and love myself.

– You are right, Aunt. We should value those who love us. That's why we don't want to know more about our father – said Arlete, dryly –. I'm not going to invite him to meet my fiancé or to my wedding. I'm going into the church alone.

– It's not your father's fault it's like this. Olair did the best he could.

– Aunt, he kicked you out of the house and didn't provide shelter or even protection. How can you defend him? – Arlete was irritated.

– Because I've known your father since we were children.

– So what? That doesn't justify his bad upbringing.

– Our parents didn't give us love and affection either. We had a very tough life, and I was a model perfect sister. When I got pregnant, my brother felt angry because I had given in to a man who traded me like one trade in a market. Olair felt anger toward my boyfriend, but he took it out on me. If he could have done better, he surely would have had a different attitude.

– I can't accept this! – protested Arlete, while Alzira focused on the letters written by her mother to her aunt.

– It's not a matter of accepting or not, my dear – Lurdes spoke kindly. – Olair did the best he could. No one can give what they don't have. Besides, I forgave myself and forgave your father. Forgiveness brings liberation, and we can move on with life.

– I have been making that statement of forgiveness every day – nodded Alzira – and I have been feeling better and better.

– Forgiving oneself and others does us a tremendous amount of good – declared Lurdes. – Look at all the good things that have happened to me over these years: I gained a home, and now, I gained two girls as a gift. I love you both as daughters.

– Arlete and Alzira were moved. Their eyes welled up, and both hugged Lurdes. They stayed like that, united and in silence, for a good while.

– From above, colourful lights were sprinkled like snowflakes over them and over the house. From the colony where she was, Lola smiled and said to herself:

– The three of them are in great harmony. It's time for our little Carolina to return to the world.

# Chapter 17

– Valeria paced back and forth in the room, distressed.

– It's over. Everything is over.

– Don't say that, my friend – Natalia protested.

– How can I not? How am I going to study? What am I going to do with my life?

– Move forward. You're going to have a child. That won't stop you from studying and building your career.

– If you hadn't accepted Uncle Adamo's proposal and hadn't come with me, I swear I would have given up on the trip.

– Never! You, me, and the baby will be very happy in Italy. You know – Natalia was radiant – Mom dreamed about me and you. She said she saw us a few years ahead. She swore that your child will only bring you joy.

– That doesn't cheer me up.

– Well, it should, Valeria.

– You don't understand – Valeria shouted. – This child is Dario's!

– What's the problem?

– I could never have imagined getting pregnant! And on top of that, it's Dario's.

– I know you only slept with him – Natalia replied.

– But you yourself told me that nothing had happened between the two of you for a long time.

– And nothing did. I swear!

– This child is not the result of the Holy Spirit – Natalia said, raising her hands and shoulders at the same time.

– I was weak. I tried to control myself, but I was weak!

– Do you remember when you slept with Dario?

– It was on the day of the accident – Valeria replied, perplexed.

– That morning, I wanted to talk to Dario and end everything. I went to wake him up and couldn't resist. But I swear – she was in tears – it all happened very quickly.

– Quick enough for you to get pregnant.

– I can't have this child!

– Calm down.

– If the pregnancy weren't so advanced, I would consider ending it.

– Natalia glared at her.

– Do you have any idea what you're saying?

– It's the pure truth. I don't like children. I can't stand them. I dread them.

– That's not a reason to consider ending it. Spiritually, I wouldn't advise you to do that.

– And I want to know if removing this foetus is spiritually right or not? – Valeria shouted. You know I've always hated children, Natalia.

– So what? People change with pregnancy.

– How do you know? You've never been pregnant!

– Intuition.

– I won't be a good mother.

– Don't say that.

– I didn't wish for this child.

– You better not talk like that. The foetus is developing, but the spirit is already suffering – she pointed to Valeria's belly –. Everything you say or feel is passed on to the baby.

– To hell with what I feel or think! To hell with this child. My God! A child of Dario! – Valeria was inconsolable.

– Imagine the happiness of his father. Dario left a little seed, an heir!

– I simply do not strike you now because you are my friend. However, this is my will. Stop talking nonsense!

– You stop – Natalia said, firm. – Valeria, get real. You're pregnant, and you're going to give birth to a beautiful child. I'll help you raise this baby.

– Valeria threw herself into her friend's arms.

– I'm desperate. I'm scared, very scared.

– Calm down.

– Adamo knocked on the door and entered the room. Valeria pulled away from Natalia and composed herself. She wiped away her tears with the back of her hands.

– Hi, uncle.

– How are you?

– Fine. Talk to America.

– You have another one – said Valeria, raising her voice. – My father will skin me alive when he returns from the trip.

– No. Americo loves you very much. He's upset, yes. It's not easy for a father to see his daughter pregnant without even being able to demand that she get married or that the baby's father assume certain responsibilities. After all, the baby's father died.

– I betrayed my father's trust. I was his little princess.

– And you still are – Adamo replied. – Nothing changes. America is a man with a generous heart. He's obviously surprised, but we know that everything passes. When he holds this child in his arms, he'll fall in love and even thank you for giving him a grandson.

– I don't know, uncle.

– It's true – Natalia intervened. – Your Americo is a good man. He'll give you all the support you need. You only have him.

– That's right.

– And you also have me and Natalia – said Adamo, smiling.

– I want to leave, but I'm afraid.

– Soon, the months will pass, and you'll be a mother – Natalia added, happily.

– Just thinking about having a child gives me chills – Valeria said, crossing one arm over the other.

– Adamo looked at her seriously.

– If you weren't ready, you wouldn't be pregnant. It's time to face your fears and learn to be a mother.

– Valeria felt sweat bead on her forehead.

– Why are you being so harsh with me?

– Because you're acting recklessly.

– I made a mistake. I don't think it's fair to carry this stain for the rest of my life.

– How dare you speak in that tone? – Adamo asked, dismayed. – How can you speak like that about a child who could bring you so much joy?

– I'm confused – said Valeria and threw herself into her uncle's arms –. My father is not coming back from this business trip and I need to board him. I don't know if I should leave.

– What do you prefer to do?

– Stay. Have my baby here and then go to Europe.

– And who will take care of the child? – Natalia asked. – Please, help me," pleaded Valeria. Tears flowed incessantly, and Adamo stroked her hair.

– Hush! Don't worry. Natalia and I will take care of you and this baby.

– You're not alone – added Natalia. – I'll always be by your side. I promise to be his or her godmother.

– Promise? – Valeria asked, in an almost inaudible voice.

– Yes. We'll help you.

– Adamo let go of her and smiled:

– We need to prepare ourselves. Our plane takes off later tonight.

– We'll postpone the departure. I prefer to wait for my father to return from Argentina – protested Valeria.

– Not at all – answered Adamo –. Your father will meet us in Italy next week. He has a business meeting in Rome. Then he's taking a train to Florence.

– Valeria bit her lips apprehensively. She felt a great fear of giving birth. She dreaded dying shortly after childbirth, as had happened to her mother.

– But it's not just that, she thought. This fear seems to be ancient. Becoming a mother could bring me misfortune.

– Valeria's mind was far away. In fact, deep in her soul, there was a fear that came from the past. The experience of becoming a mother was ultimately unsuccessful.

– Her life and her spirit rejected the idea of having to relive unpleasant experiences linked to motherhood.

– You may be going through similar experiences, but the ending may be different. It all depends on you – said a friendly voice, next to her. Valeria neither saw nor heard; however, an enlightened and smiling spirit tried to give her calm and balanced energies. After all, she was carrying another spirit in her womb and her emotions went directly to the foetus.

– She's weak, that's what she is – exclaimed a voice from further back.

– The guy spoke and took a step forward. He was shock.

– Ouch! – he screamed in pain.

– Stay away from her – the illuminated spirit said, a serious tone in his voice.

– It's not worth it – replied Taviño, irritated.

– How come? Thanks to your contribution, your influence, Valeria got pregnant. I must admit the manner was not elegant at all, but we achieved our goal.

– That deeply irritates me. I should be the child's father. Valeria is mine.

– Nonsense – said Eliel, the spirit of light. – Valeria would have gotten pregnant by Dario anyway. You hastened the pregnancy and Dario's passing.

– Am I responsible for his death now?

– That's not what I said – Eliel spoke, in a measured voice.

– You, from the light, don't you say everything happens by free will?

– Yes. So what?

– I knew Dario would die in that accident. I just wanted to participate in the event. I was glad he was getting away from Valeria. On the other hand, I was sad because Dario was the only link that bound me to her, now without him around I have no way to get close, but I will find a way.

– For now, you won't succeed – Eliel said, patiently. – Valeria is pregnant and has extra protection. The spirit she carries in her womb is a close friend of mine, and I won't let anything or anyone interfere with the pregnancy.

– Ah! That's all I needed – protested Taviño. – I'll wait for the remaining months. Soon, I'll attach myself to someone and make that person interested in Valeria. And I'll love her again, you'll see.

– No, you won't.

– How?! Just because you're part of the enlightened side of the universe, you think you can forbid me?

– Not only forbid but also threaten. Valeria will change a lot after the pregnancy and will no longer have energetic affinity with you. You better look for someone else to satisfy yourself or else...

– Or else what?

– Well, come with us.

– For what? – Taviño grumbled. – To live in the middle of wheat fields? Spend the day playing the harp and meditating? I'm out.

– Who told you our place is like that? You were taken to a rescue station and then escaped. You've been wandering here on the planet for a few years.

– I saw it on TV. It was in a soap opera.

– You're mistaken – Eliel smiled. – Our city is bustling, quite lively. We work, study, and have many responsibilities. The spirit, when it leaves Earth, has more activities than when it was incarnated.

– I don't believe it.

– See for yourself, Taviño. Come and spend a day with me. If you don't like it, I'll let you go back to the planet. However, know that you won't have a chance to get close to Valeria.

– Taviño felt a chill in his stomach.

– She's mine.

– Forget that possession. You're stuck in adolescence. You're still eighteen.

– I did the math. If I were alive, I'd be twenty-three.

– With the mind of an irresponsible boy. Many of your friends on the planet got married, others are studying, and some of them will soon pass away. Life changes for everyone.

– And I died – he said in a disheartened tone.

– Disincarnated – corrected Eliel.

– Disincarnated, dead, it doesn't matter. I didn't turn nineteen, didn't have other girlfriends, didn't have the chance to meet other people, to study, to become someone in life. It's not fair.

– Nature doesn't make mistakes – Eliel added, kindly. – Your time was short. You were very irresponsible in your last incarnation. You could have lived many years, but you threw yourself into the vices of gambling and drinking. You passed away too early.

– Useless talk. I don't remember any of that. My name is Octavio Mendes Leyte Junior, alias Taviño. I had a rich childhood, but I never had the love of my parents. I had no siblings, I grew up alone and, when I turned fourteen, my father gave me a motorcycle. Then he let me take his car to learn. My father never set limits for me. If he was more energetic with me, I would be alive.

– Hmm, don't blame your father for your death. You were responsible for your own passing.

– Taviño, after many years, felt a deep melancholy. I just have the impression that Valeria was his greatest love.

– No. You yourself said you never had your parents' love. When Valeria gave you a little affection and attention, you felt true love and poured onto her the pent-up love you never knew how to give.

– Why didn't I receive love from my parents?

– Learn to value and love yourself unconditionally. Consciously or not, you have only harvested your parents in this incarnation. We always attract perfect parents for us. It all depends on our vibration, the pattern of our feelings and beliefs over many lifetimes. Taviño thought for a moment and a quick image of his penultimate life flashed through his mind. He saw himself lying on a sidewalk, drunk and with no control over his body.

– Leave the past behind and come with me – Eliel invited. – As I said, where we live, we don't hold anyone. Everyone is free to stay or leave.

– I don't know – Taviño hesitated.

– Try. Just for one day.

– All right. I'll go. But promise that Dario won't get close to her?

- Dario is in the same rescue station that took you in. The trauma from the accident was very strong. He'll still be hospitalized for several months. Rest assured that during these months when Valeria will carry this child, no spirit with negative influences will get close to her.

- Taviño nodded, and the two spirits disappeared from the scene.

- At that moment, Valeria felt a gentle breeze touch her face. She smiled and grabbed her bag. The fear of being pregnant had diminished, but an uncomfortable sense of insecurity still lingered around her.

- She brushed away the thoughts with her hands and went down with Natalia and Adamo. The driver was waiting for them.

- Where are Mrs. Elenice and Milton? - she asked, settling into the back seat of the Opala.

- They're already at the airport - Natalia assured.

- The friend got into the car, and Valeria squeezed her hand.

- Everything will be fine, Valeria. Trust.

- Valeria nodded, and the car left the Morumbi mansion. Shortly afterward, they were at Congonhas, ready for the trip.

- Minutes before boarding, someone touched Valeria's shoulder. She turned around and widened her eyes, surprised.

- Thomas?! - she asked, surprised. - What are you doing here?

- I came to say goodbye.

- Valeria swallowed hard. The presence of the young man stirred a lot within her.

- Where's Marion?

- She's filming a movie in Rio de Janeiro. I don't know when we'll see each other.

- I'll be boarding shortly.

- I know. I want you to know how much I like you.

- Valeria felt weak in the legs.

- It's not right, Thomas. You're going to marry Marion. If you tell me not to get married, I won't.

- Don't say that.

- I love you, Valeria. Please give me a chance.

- Valeria ran her hand over her belly and remembered the baby. She wasn't emotionally prepared to start a romance. Something inside her wanted to scream yes. But reason prevailed. She remembered the child she carried within her and Marion's possessive temperament.

- As if being pursued by that crazy woman wasn't enough, she thought.

- Thomas was deeply moved.

- For you, I'll do anything.

- Why are you telling me this now?

- Because I realized that it's you, I love.

- Marion is crazy about you.

– Nonsense! – Thomas protested, with a hand gesture. – Marion is interested in me because my father has contacts with film producers abroad.

– Valeria felt like throwing herself into his arms and making Thomas spin with her body entwined with his, as in romantic American movies with a happy ending.

– Thomas continued, – Let me go with you to Italy.

– Valeria smiled.

– You're special, Thomas. I swear that if it were another time, I would accept your request.

– Accept it.

– However, it's not feasible now.

– Why?

– Because I...

– Adamo appeared and said, patiently:

– Our flight is about to depart.

– I'm coming, uncle, just a minute.

– Adamo greeted the young man with a nod and walked away.

– What were you going to say? – Thomas asked.

– Nothing. I need to go.

– Valeria tilted her head and kissed Thomas on the cheek near his lips. She felt a thrill of pleasure and blushed. Then she turned and increased her steps toward her uncle and Natalia.

– Thomas shook his head from side to side and walked away, dejected and sad. Very sad.

– The farewell was emotional. Valeria was sensitive because of the pregnancy and cried a lot. An hour later, the plane took off. Elenice and Milton accompanied the three and then rushed to the upper floor where they could see the planes taking off.

– May God protect our girl! – said Milton.

– He will protect her, yes – replied Elenice, moved. – Natalia will be very happy. She'll have a beautiful career and marry the man she truly loves.

– Milton put his arm around his wife's waist. They smiled happily.

# Chapter 18

– Gisele was radiant and happy. The day had come when she would finally be rid of Olair's disaster.

– It took a while, but it came. Today I get rid of this stupid pig.

– She wore her best outfit, a golden polyester jumpsuit, with huge flared pants and platform shoes that made her very tall. Gisele put on her makeup. She lined her eyes with black pencil and wore red lipstick. She sprayed an excessive amount of cheap perfume on her body. She looked at her reflection in the bathroom mirror.

– Way to go, girl!

– She blew herself a kiss and left smiling. He went to Rodinei's bar. When he saw her, he smiled and walked away from the customers. He gestured for her to go around the counter and head to the back of the bar.

– What about today? – he asked anxiously. And today we're going to throw the old man out of the house?

– Gisele smiled and pouted:

– Yes. Today that house will be ours. All of it, wow!

– I feel sorry for Olair.

– The idiot trusted me blindly.

- He gave me the house with a kiss.

- A fool. He deserves to be damned - Gisele opened Rodinei's shirt and tangled her finger in his chest hair -. And we're going to love each other forever, aren't we?

- Of course I do, honey. If it weren't for you, I wouldn't have that house.

- Gisele looked at her watch.

- It's about time. The idiot must have already closed the tailor's shop and is on his way home. Will you show up in half an hour?

- Hum, hum - she said affirmatively -. I'll close the bar early and run there.

- Okay then. See how beautiful I look? - she pouted, as she turned her body.

- You went a little overboard with the perfume.

- You can wash it off later, in the shower - she said insinuatingly.

- Rodinei kissed her on the lips for a long time.

- Now go away. Do everything as we planned.

- It's all right.

- Gisele kissed him again on the lips and left. She arrived home in a few minutes. She walked in, turned on the light and ran to the bedroom. She looked around the corner and smiled.

- Olair still had me to thank. I packed his bags.

- He won't leave the house with only the clothes on his back.

- Then he lay down on the bed, reached over to the bedside table and turned on the radio. He hummed a song that was very popular at the time, in the voice of Barros de Alencar:

- I know that a man should not cry,

- For a woman who abandons him.

- I no longer care about your love,

- Because all my tears have dried up with a new love.

- Olair entered the room and asked, with a strange smile covering his face.

- Lovely to see you singing like that, dear.

- Did you like it? - Gisele asked as she turned off the radio.

- I liked it. And I'm burning with desire for you.

- Olair spoke, quickly took off his clothes and threw himself on Gisele in his underwear and socks. She turned her body and got up from the bed. She jumped up and Olair fell on the mattress.

- Naughty girl! Want to play with daddy, huh?

- No.

- Gisele changed her tone. She began to speak quickly. He was tired of pretending. And even more tired of sleeping with that pig.

- Nothing, get dressed and get ready to leave.

- Olair didn't understand. He sat on the bed and ran his hand over his face.

- I don't remember planning a trip. Where are we going?

- Better change the question. Where are you going? - he asked, putting the emphasis on you.

- I don't understand.

- Look toward the corner of the room," Gisele pointed.

- Are you packed? Let's just travel and that's it? And here I am thinking about our trip to Bariloche. You're faster than me. Damn!

- No, Olair. Stop being an idiot, man. Can't you see they are your bags? I want you to leave this house immediately.

- What do you mean, get out of the house?

- Besides being stupid and deaf? - Gisele was irritated. The party is over. The sham marriage is over too. I don't love you anymore.

- Just like that, without any explanation? - Olair was trying to piece together his thoughts. It was difficult to organize them. There was too much information to process in such a short time.

- I want you out of my house.

- Our house. Anyway, it's my house. I'm the one who bought it. You should be the one to leave.

- Gisele laughed.

- Me, leave?! No. You're the one who's leaving. Now.

- Olair became irritated with the woman's persistence. His face started to turn red with anger.

– The house is in Rodinei's name, you stupid woman. I do it like this – he snapped his fingers – and he transfers the house to me. Of course, after I separate from you, you slut.

– He spoke, jumped up from the bed, and lunged at Gisele with his hands around her neck. She widened her eyes, feeling the man's fury. She tried to defend herself, scratching Olair's back, while mentally pleading for Rodinei to arrive.

– Rodinei appeared with two strong, intimidating-looking men. He commanded:

– Stop it, both of you.

– Olair remained clinging to Gisele's neck. Rodinei signaled with his head, and the two brutes approached and forcibly pulled him away. They threw the man onto the bed. Olair grumbled and faced Rodinei.

– I don't know what brought you here, but it was by the grace of God. If you hadn't come, I swear I would have killed that bitch.

– It won't be necessary – replied Rodinei, his voice calm but as cold as ice.

– Now, please, Rodinei, take this slut out of my house. Out of my house – he emphasized.

– She's already leaving – Rodinei replied. – But first, I need you to grab your bags and go.

– Huh? – Olair didn't understand.

– Grab your bags and go, Olair. You have one minute to leave this house before my men take the necessary measures.

– Gisele is the one who should leave – Olair argued. – This house is mine.

– The blonde intervened, nervously:

– Idiot. Did you believe Rodinei? Do you think he was your buddy and did you a favor? Do you really think he's going to give you back the house? Wake up, man! You've been deceived.

– Deceived – corrected Rodinei. – Truly deceived.

– Olair glanced from Rodinei to Gisele and back to Rodinei. The realization hit him.

– You used my trust to take my house?

– Yes.

– You want to keep the house I worked so hard to pay off early with the bank?

– Exactly.

– I'll go to court. This house is mine.

– It won't help, Olair. You were very stupid. You had your wife sign a sales contract.

– It was an informal agreement. I can break it at any time.

– No, my friend.

– Don't call me your friend! – Olair shouted.

– Rodinei smiled and continued:

– I went to the notary and transferred the deed to my name. This house is mine, and no one can take it. Now I can think about getting married and having a home, starting a family. This townhouse may not be a palace, but it's neat, a good size. After a good renovation, it will be perfect – he said, pinching his thumb and forefinger to his ear.

– This can't be true.

– Of course it is, idiot – Gisele yelled. – Rodinei played you for a fool. Now grab your bags and get out. Leave here the same way you did with your daughters.

– Olair felt the blood rise. His eyes were injected with rage. He had never felt so much anger in his life, not even when he hit Josefa or pulled the belt on the girls. He even felt a twinge of pleasure. Sadistic pleasure. He wanted to kill the criminal couple. But those brutes were very strong, and inevitably, he would come out worse.

– Olair thought and thought. He seemed lost. A thousand scenes flashed through his confused and anger-filled mind. He stood up and was about to say something, but he didn't have time. He felt a sharp pain and clutched his chest.

– You'll pay for this... – he mumbled.

– And he felt lifeless to the floor. Olair had a sudden heart attack. He died instantly.

– Gisele looked at the body and touched it with the tip of her foot.

– Is he dead?

– Looks like it – Rodinei confirmed.

– He bent down and placed two fingers on Olair's neck.

– The old man couldn't handle such strong emotions.

– What should I do?

– Call the police, of course. Your husband was too happy. He wanted to love her, got carried away with sexual play, and had an attack. It happens every day. Normal stuff.

– I'm afraid of the police.

– You're married, I mean, you were married to the deceased. Olair isn't hurt.

– His back is scratched.

– Another reason for them to believe Olair died while you two were dating – Rodinei added.

– Gisele agreed. She went to the hallway and picked up the phone. She dialled the police.

– After signing the papers and Olair's body was taken to the Forensic Institute, Gisele ran to Celia and Ariovaldo's house to inform them of his death. She asked, pretending melancholy, for them to call and inform the daughters.

– Celia and Ariovaldo received the news with some sadness. They weren't friends with Olair, but they felt compassion for him. They knew he had put his foot in his mouth and was completely immersed in the sea of illusions of the world.

– After she left, Celia closed the door and felt a shiver down her spine.

– What's wrong, my love? – Ariovaldo asked, concerned.

– My goodness, there's something bad stuck to Gisele. I couldn't identify it.

– It must be because of Olair's death. She must be disturbed.

– Disturbed? Gisele? Don't even think about it. I didn't feel a drop of sadness from her. She's not upset about Olair's death.

– Really?

– You can bet. However, it's not our place to judge others here. Let's sit on the couch and say a prayer for Olair's spirit. I feel that he's not doing well – Celia concluded.

– Gisele closed the little gate of Celia's house and burst into laughter.

– The plan worked out better than expected. I was afraid Olair might come after me, bother me, and make my life hell. But the idiot had a weak heart, and – poof – he died. Poor thing. Now I have to get ready for the wake and put on a sad widow face for those unbearable girls. I do everything for the man I love and the house we inherited – she muttered under her breath.

– Gisele turned the corner and didn't notice a shadow of hatred practically glued to her. Olair had passed away, and his spirit had immediately detached from the physical body. His spirit, full of resentment and hatred, would be trailing Gisele for a long time.

– Poor thing – he said, in a furious and gloomy tone. – Get ready because, from now on, I'm going to turn your life into a sea of unhappiness. You can bet!

*  *  *

– Alzira was convinced by Eugenio to rent a small salon near her home on a busy avenue to set up her own commercial establishment, manufacturing and selling sweets and savoury pies.

- I feel a knot in my stomach just thinking about having my own business, - she said, excited.

- You're competent, you know what you're doing, - Eugenio replied. –I don't understand administration.

- Learn. Take courses about it. Your Aunt Lurdes will help you a lot, and I'm sure the shop will be a success, - Eugenio continued, smiling as he hugged her from behind and cheerfully chose the name for the venture.

- Marion noticed Thomas's interest in Valeria. She was furious.

- Now that Thomas' dad is going to get me an interview with American producers? I can't lose this man now, not now! - She shouted loudly, as she formulated a way to win him back and have him for as long as she wanted.

- As soon as Valeria left for Italy, Marion ran to tell Thomas about her friend's pregnancy.

- Valeria is pregnant with Dario's child. I always knew she loved him - she said, in a tone full of pretense.

- Thomas listened to everything in silence and, just when he was about to think about being alone and rethink his love life, Marion arrived with a surprise that would make him lose his way: she was pregnant and they should get married, immediately. I

– At the end of that year, Valeria gave birth to a beautiful baby boy, named Federico. Two years later, Arlete and Osvaldo married and, in the summer of 1980, their daughter, Olivia, was born.

– Time passed and life, cleverly weaving the web of its coincidences, made that, many years later, Olivia and Federico met. Or better yet, they met again.

# PART II

## The rejection between parents and children

# Chapter 19

– Alzira finished signing some checks and handed them to Lurdes.

– There you go, aunt. These are the last checks for the purchase of the spot in the shopping centre. Another "*See the lilies in the field!*" store – she exclaimed, with pleasure.

– I'm worried. Don't you think you're biting off more than you can chew? – Lurdes asked, anxious.

– I know you're nervous because of the slip-ups we had at the beginning. But we learned the hard way.

– After the courses we took at SEBRAE we became successful entrepreneurs. We failed mainly in two fundamental issues: prior planning and structuring and business management. These are aspects to which we cannot fail to pay close attention. All the efforts we made to learn, and there were many, have supported the viability of our business to date.

– Why the fear, then? – Alzira asked, smiling. – You're right. I never thought we'd have more than one store. I was content with just the store in São Bernardo do Campo.

– This new store in the shopping centre will bring us more prosperity. We'll continue on an upward path of progress.

– You're correct – agreed Lurdes. – I retired, and I never thought I'd have such a busy life. It's good to feel useful and do what you love, even in old age.

– Alzira stood up from her chair and hugged her aunt.

– Imagine, old lady! You look great for someone in their sixties. You still have a chance to find a companion.

– Me? That's not for me. I'm too independent.

– You stopped playing cards and started attending dance dinners on Fridays. You have a bunch of men after you.

– I have a lot of work.

– Work, I know... I see how some customers come to our establishment just to see you.

– Lurdes blushed.

– Don't talk nonsense.

– True, aunt. Your José from the grocery store, for example. He can't stop sending you little notes.

– I don't want to hear about José, Manuel, or anyone else. Matters of the heart are closed in my book.

– Just because you had a romantic disappointment years ago? Is it fair to close your heart and have no one?

– Lurdes shivered and missed her boyfriend.

– My God! It's been over forty years, and I can't forget him.

– Why not go after him? At least to find out if he's still alive.

– I don't even I don't even think about that – objected Lourdes –. He's the one who should be looking for me. If he hasn't looked for me, why should he be here?

– Alzira gave her aunt another hug. She understood why Lurdes was acting that way. Kind of taken by a sense of expanded consciousness, she continued amiably:

– You know aunt, when a romantic relationship ends, it is common for us to feel depressed, feeling discouraged. We are tempted to look for someone else, even more so when it wasn't you who wanted to break up. Being abandoned by another, feeling abandoned, being left here can cause us great harm – Alzira pointed to her chest –; however, this can be overcome with time. The problem occurs when you feel rejected and unable to look for a new relationship and, in the face of such rejection, the fear of being left alone for the rest of your life arises

– In a way, that's what happened to me – said Lurdes, tearful.

– Alzira nodded up and down and continued:

– Rejection is directly and deeply linked to low self-esteem.

– It's not easy to overcome abandonment.

– Because you feel totally insecure, you feel rejected and this feeling affected a lot the way you chose to relate all these years. You tried to distance yourself from men, putting a fence around your heart, as if that imaginary fence was capable of making you stop feeling.

– Lurdes was deeply touched. A tear escaped from the corner of her eye.

– People can better handle rejection when they are very secure – she spoke, trying to feel strong. Alzira nodded in agreement and continued:

– When they are very secure and have various support pillars, such as a good family structure, a fulfilling job, and, above all, self-confidence. You have all these pillars, very well structured, I might add.

– I do, but...

– Auntie, I learned this over the years. The lower the self-esteem and the higher the insecurity, the harder it is to cope with the feeling of rejection. And this can repeat itself throughout life.

– I'm too old to engage in relationships.

– Who said there's an age limit for relationships?

– I've acquired many habits. I no longer have the dream of love. Deep down, I'd like to find a companion, someone to talk to, date... but marriage is out of my plans. I have my house, my money, and I'm the boss of my work and my life. Am I going to get married? Trouble? For what?

– Alzira laughed. Lurdes continued:

– Society also doesn't accept that a woman my age can love. My body may have aged, but my soul is still young.

– We can't care about society, aunt. I know what it's like to receive accusatory glances from people. Remember when I returned from the honeymoon trip? The world expected me to be pregnant.

– If I remember!

– Eugenio and I chose not to have children, and we're crucified by many people. It's as if, by choosing not to be a mother, I was committing a great sin.

– Just because a woman is born doesn't mean she's obliged to have children.

– Thank God you understand me. I even considered the possibility of having a child. However, after Olivia was born and started visiting my house, I no longer felt that need.

– You're more of a mother to Olivia than Arlete.

– I didn't mean any harm. It's pure affinity. Arlete doesn't understand her daughter, and vice versa. They've lived in this conflict forever. Arlete wants everything her way, and Olivia is stubborn, just like her mother. I try, in my own way, to make Olivia accept her mother more naturally.

– Why are they so distant from each other?

– Everything is explained by understanding that we are born and die many times, Aunt. Reincarnation explains my sister and niece's case perfectly. I know that there is a feeling of love that one has for the other, but, on the other hand, I perceive a certain distancing between the two, a strong feeling of rejection.

– Arlete never rejected her own daughter – protested Lurdes.

– Olivia has always rejected her mother, ever since she opened her eyes. Remember how she used to cry every time Arlete picked her up?

– That's true – agreed Lurdes. – Olivia only calmed down in the arms of Osvaldo, mine, or yours. And I never noticed any behaviour from Arlete that would cause this repulsion from the daughter towards the mother.

- I do my best for both of them to get along. I believe this estrangement comes from past lives.

- Thinking like that, it's natural that this feeling of animosity between them is related to the past.

- The conversation took that direction and was soon interrupted by a knock on the living room door. Alzira's and Lourdes' eyes widened when they saw Olivia enter, nervously, crying. The little girl ran to Alzira and hugged her.

- Aunt, I don't want to go back to my house anymore. Never again.

- Why?

- My mom... I can't take it anymore with my mom! - she exclaimed, between sobs.

- What happened? - asked Lurdes. - Did you fight with your mom again?

- Olivia nodded while sniffling and kept her head on her aunt's shoulder.

- We fought. She wants me to take a computer course. She said that when she was young, she took a typing course, and thanks to it, she got a job. I don't need and don't want to work yet.

- Lurdes intervened, kindly:

- Didn't your dad promise you that you would go on an exchange to England next semester?

- Well, aunt. After my mother messed with me with that contest, my father is also trying to persuade me not to go to England. He said English can be learned in the corner of your house.

– Oh! – said Alzira, while stroking her silky hair. – It's good that you don't need to work yet – she emphasized the last word – however, your mom is concerned about your future and well-being.

– She wants me to do what she wants. I'm tired of being a pawn in her hands.

– Don't exaggerate – mended Lurdes. – Arlete genuinely cares about you. She wants you to develop your skills.

– By doing computer stuff?

– The two didn't answer.

– I want to do an exchange and then a theatre course in England. I want to be an actress! – The girl spoke and cried again in Alzira's arms. As Olivia burst into tears, Alzira looked at Lourdes and they both shook their heads. The story was always the same and it seemed that it would never end...

✱ ✱ ✱

– Since she began to babble her first words, Olivia insisted on the same idea: when she grew up, she would be an actress. Her father thought the idea was great and boasted about it. Arlete, on the other hand, did not conform to her daughter's desire.

– My daughter was not born for the stage. Olivia will be a proper young lady, Arlete insisted.

- What is that? Osvaldo asked. - We are almost in the 21st century, and you talk as if we were living two hundred years ago.

- You indulge every whim of this girl; Arlete gritted her teeth.

- I will do it and continue to do it whenever I can, as long as her whims make her happy, responded Osvaldo.

- To make matters worse, Olivia was born with mild convergent strabismus, one of the most common forms of strabismus. Her left eye was slightly deviated inward, as if the deviated eye was looking at her own nose. In short, Olivia had a squinted eye.

- As vision is fully developed at around seven or eight years of age, early diagnosis helps enormously in obtaining a highly satisfactory outcome, practically achieving a cure. Osvaldo soon tried to consult a strabismus doctor, a specialized ophthalmologist. Olivia wore an eye patch and, at fifteen, still wore glasses. Her strabismus was much improved, although she still had a slight deviation of the eye.

- The vision was not compromised, but the appearance was. The girl suffered from tasteless teasing at school–names like "cross-eyed," "squinty," "crooked eye," and other unfortunate nicknames were common in her childhood and adolescence. Olivia was confident that one day she would be "normal" like the other little girls.

- Eventually, she wanted to be one of *Xuxa's paquitas*. No one could dissuade her from the idea. When she learned that the stage assistants had come of age and that a new group of fifteen-year-old girls would replace the old ones, Olivia harassed the family. She had her father take her to Rio de Janeiro to participate in the audition. There were hundreds of candidates for the position.

– Arlete changed the registration dates, and when Olivia arrived in the city, the registrations had closed.

– You did this on purpose! She shouted at her mother when she arrived home.

– Don't speak to your mother like that, Osvaldo requested. – She changed the dates. She got confused.

– Liar! Mom did this because she doesn't like me.

– Imagine, Olivia. Arlete loves you more than anything in this life. You are our little princess.

– I'm your princess. She doesn't like me, she repeated.

– I'm sure your mom did this for your own good.

– She doesn't want me to be a star, Dad. She wants me to do computer science, study accounting. She said that a solid career is the one that puts money on the table.

– She's right.

– Netiño's father, who studies with me in school, was laid off. He has a degree in accounting. He was fired due to cost-cutting. What good is a solid career? By the way, Dad, what is a solid career?

– He was always of the opinion that a person should do what he liked, what gave him pleasure. From a young age he was passionate about studying and understanding the law. He graduated as a lawyer, passed the bar exam and the judicial officer's exam. A few years later, after nights and nights of bad sleep, studying textbooks and devouring law books, he managed to pass a competition for Labor Lawyer. Osvaldo loved what he did and earned well. He felt fulfilled.

- If his daughter wanted to know about the stage and the spotlight, why not let her follow her heart?

- He stroked Olivia's brown, long hair and smiled.

- You can be whatever you want.

- I always knew that. Mom says, though, that because I'm still a little cross-eyed and wear glasses, I'll never be an actress. She says why she says famous actresses don't wear glasses. I can wear contact lenses now, can't I?

- You can. Of course, you can.

- There are actresses who are a bit cross-eyed. They are successful. Strabismus can be charming, don't you agree?

- I agree.

- Dad, let me go on an exchange and get to know England.

- Why? Do you want to be away from me? Osvaldo asked, smiling.

- No way. After Mom played this trick on me...

- Osvaldo cut her off:

- Watch your tone. Your mom didn't play a trick on you.

- Olivia nodded:

- Well, after Mom unintentionally - she emphasized - changed the dates for registration for the Xuxa Park audition, I might as well do a year of exchange. Then, if I like it there, I can reconsider my professional future.

– We have good courses here. Why go abroad?

– Because it gives more prestige, Dad! Olivia exclaimed, in a playful way.

– Osvaldo laughed and kissed her on the cheek.

– Let's think about it.

– Promise me one thing, Dad?

– What is it, my dear?

– Can you try to convince Mom to let me do a year of exchange?

– If that's what you want.

– That's all I want.

– All right. Together, let's convince your mom.

– Arriving from Rio, having better assimilated the feeling of feeling defeated and not having arrived in time to sign up for the *paquitas* test, Olivia imposed on her mother her desire to go on the exchange.

– Too young to leave home, was the dry response.

– What if I took a theatre course?

– Don't even think about it! Arlete objected. An artist in the family? Never. A thousand times never.

– You made me miss the "*paquita*" audition. Now, are you going to forbid me to go on an exchange or take a theatre course?

– I will.

– What kind of life is this? How can it be so bad?

– I'm doing this for your own good.

- My good? Olivia was amazed. She widened her eyes and said, "You always find a way to screw me over!"

- Arlete hated that Olivia used that word. She raised her hand and got close to her face. The girl challenged her:

- You complained that you were beaten by your father, but you're crazy to lay a hand on me too. What's wrong? Do you also want to kick me out of the house?

- Olivia became furious:

- It's not the same thing! And more: I want to meet other people, experience different cultures. I can't stand being stuck in Sao Bernardo anymore.

- I love living here. Now you're going to complain about the city where you were born?

- You twist everything! Olivia responded sadly. - It's not that I don't like it here, but there's a whole world out there to be explored. I want to see the world, Mom.

- It's better to get to know the world with a computer course. I saw a report on *Fantastico* that said computing will dominate the world in a few years. See how I think about your best interests?

- I don't need you to think for me. I have a brain!

- Arlete was losing patience.

- Enough! No TV for a week.

- I won't be punished.

- Arlete approached and glared at her.

- Don't challenge me, girl. I'm your mother.

– Olivia swallowed hard, spun on her heels, and ran out. She slammed the front door with force, crossed the street, and minutes later arrived at her destination. She needed to talk to her aunt.

– Only Aunt Alzira understands me – she said to herself as she walked through the garden and entered her aunt's house.

– Arlete brought her hands to her face.

– I don't know what to do anymore, Osvaldo.

– He embraced his wife from behind and whispered in her ear.

– Let her go on the exchange.

– Olivia is very young.

– She's fifteen. She's in the second year of high school. She's a good student.

– Alone in the world?

– And we raised our daughter for what? For the world, of course! I'm insecure, dear.

– What about the theater course? She likes it.

– I'm afraid.

– Of what?

– That trickster Gisele was a model and actress.

– Osvaldo burst into laughter.

– Gisele?

– That's what they said in the neighbourhood.

– Nonsense. Gisele was never an actress or a model. It was a pure invention.

– I don't know, Osvaldo.

– She's young and has dreams. If her soul leans towards theatre, she'll be a great actress. Otherwise, she'll meet other people, from other cultures, and maybe develop an interest in another profession. She might express herself artistically in a different way. Everything is possible.

– I'm afraid Olivia will get lost in life.

– Our daughter has our blood. She would never bite off more than she can chew. She was born to dream, just like I was born for the laws, and you were born for me!

– Arlete smiled and kissed him on the lips.

– I've known you for almost twenty years, and you're still gallant! You're the love of my life.

– And you are mine – he replied, his voice filled with kindness. – Don't try to impose too many strict rules on our daughter just because you and Alzira suffered at the hands of your father. It's difficult.

– Why?

– I don't want our daughter to suffer.

– We can't prevent that from happening, my love. Olivia is growing up; soon she'll become a woman and will have to face the world. She'll experience heartbreak, hear the word "no," deal with jokes about her slight strabismus, and she'll have to manage. We've always been partners, and we decided to raise our daughter for the world, not for ourselves. You and I love her so much, and we want to be her friends.

Every argument you have with her drives her further away from us.

- You're right. I'll call Alzira.

- Why?

- Because Olivia always goes to Aunt's house when she fights with me.

## Chapter 20

– Frederico stretched luxuriously in bed. He was radiant and happy about the trip to England.

– I'm dying to be back in Europe – he said to himself as he got up. He put on his slippers and walked to the bathroom. He turned on the shower and took a long bath.

– After dressing up and applying cologne, he went downstairs for breakfast. He found America sitting at the table, having his breakfast and reading the newspaper.

– Frederico circled the table and bent down.

– Good morning, Grandpa – he greeted, kissing him on the forehead.

– America lowered the newspaper and smiled.

– Good morning. What's the news?

– The economy seems to be getting on track.

– Yes, grandfather. The Royal Plan seems to be working. It should. It included contributions from several economists, received by the Minister of Finance, Fernando Henrique Cardoso. You know it was because of the plan that I decided to study economics?

– And you're going to take care of my company.

– I don't know. Maybe I want to have mine.

- You're my only heir. I want you to manage mine, sorry, our companies.

- You did your part. You created and managed the companies. They are yours.

- But one day they will be yours too. Who am I going to leave my legacy to?

- To your daughter.

- Valeria doesn't like dealing with my business. Your mother has always been good at decoration - he grumbled. - She became a highly recognized professional in the market. You have a fondness for supermarkets. It's natural for you to manage the business.

- Frederico opened a wide smile. He felt very good by his grandfather's side. He replied sincerely:

- You can count on me, Grandpa. I'll be your right-hand man.

- And left-hand too - said Americo, laughing. - When you retire...

- Americo cut him off sweetly.

- No way. I'll only retire when I die. I'll work until my last breath. If I stop working, I die.

- You'd better enjoy life. You've done a lot. You created this empire. You could put business aside for a while and focus more on your emotional life.

- Me?! - Americo asked, surprised.

- Of course! I'm past the age of dating.

– Spare me, will you? You can fool my mother and my uncles, but not me.

– I don't know what you're talking about – America feigned.

– I saw you the other day caressing an old photo, a very old one. And, curious as I am, after you went to bed, I went to check the photo. It wasn't my grandmother Amelia in the picture.

– Americo shifted in his chair. His breathing was laboured by now. He cleared his throat and changed the subject completely.

– How was your night?

– Federico shook his head and smiled. He knew his grandfather well and knew when Americo didn't want to pursue a topic that caused him discomfort. He took a sip of café con leche and, while spreading cheese on toast, replied:

– Good. I slept well.

– No nightmares?

– I had none last night. Yesterday I went with Aunt Natalia to the spiritist centre.

– How is your spiritual treatment going?

– It ended yesterday.

– Thank God! – America said, raising his hands.

– Frederico continued:

– The mediums told me that I am practically free from obsession. Obviously, the long-term success of the treatment depends only on me.

– I don't understand much about it, but your uncle Adamo told me that it was a spirit bothering you. So, the success of the treatment depends not only on you.

– I have to change my way of being – the young man said as he sipped his cup of milk coffee. – In fact, I have talked a lot with Uncle Adamo, and I know there is something in my behaviour that attracts this spirit.

– Why do you think he was tormenting you? You're such a kind, good boy. –Spirits approach us by affinity of thoughts, grandfather. If I am well, I attract good spirits around me. If I don't feel good about myself, I end up attracting lost spirits or enemies from the past.

– What to do? – America asked, seriously. – It seems you're left with no way to improve.

– Absolutely not! – Frederico said, shaking his head negatively. – The lesson to get rid of obsession is to take better care of our minds – he pointed to his head – and cultivate good thoughts.

– See how smart you are? You are my pride.Frederico laughed.

– You're my grandfather, and you're suspicious to talk about.

– No way. You're a sweet, gentle, intelligent, and very handsome young man. By the way, you take after me.

– I see old photos, and I really look like you when you were young.

– There's a bit of your grandmother too. You have Amelia's eyes.

- I wish I had some resemblance to my mother - Frederico said, saddened.

- Don't be sad. You are as clever as Valeria.

- Clever, I know... - Frederico cleared his throat. - She doesn't like me.

- America placed the newspaper on the side table. He understood his grandson's feelings. Frederico felt a great rejection from his mother. He couldn't understand if her feelings were due to him being Dario's son or if she had to change the course of her life when she found out she was pregnant.

- Before answering, America nibbled on his lip and closed his eyes. He quickly went back to a not-so-distant past...

* * *

- His daughter's pregnancy had taken him by surprise. And, upon discovering that Darío was the child's father, Américo felt completely helpless. He wanted the boy to take care of his son and marry Valeria. Américo was a man raised in other times. He himself had gotten Amelia pregnant and had to smother his love for another woman to commit to marriage, even though he did not love his wife.

- In my time, people married out of obligation, he thought.

- I know what's going on in your mind, Adamo said.

- You don't know.

- Of course, I do. The same thing happened to you.

– To me? America asked.

– Yes, Adamo replied. You impregnated Amelia when you were in love with another woman.

– It was a mistake. We were at a party, drank too much. We were carried away by the emotion of the moment.

– And it led to what it led.

– I lost my love, but gained another one, Americo grumbled. Valeria is everything I have. I raised her alone. You should be proud of the accomplishment.

– Quite the opposite. Today, I feel like a failure. Just because my daughter got pregnant before getting married?

– Now, Americo, you've realized that everything you idealized for your daughter doesn't correspond to reality. Isn't that it?

– I dreamed of another life for my daughter. Now she's pregnant, and I can't even demand that the father take responsibility and marry her.

– He really can't do that. Unfortunately, Dario died in that accident. Valeria will be a single mother, just like you were a single father.

– Being a single father is one thing. Being a single parent... well, society is unforgiving and makes snide remarks behind people's backs.

– And what do we owe to society? Adamo asked.

– Times have changed, and it doesn't matter what people think, but what you can do for your daughter. Supporting her at this time is the best thing.

– I know that. I would never stop supporting my daughter. I would never put her out on the street because of this pregnancy.

– I don't understand your concern.

– I broke off my engagement and married Amelia. I didn't expect her to die after childbirth. It's different.

– Different is how it happened, but the result is the same for both of you. After the experience you've had all these years, it's better to accept your daughter's pregnancy and help her as much as possible.

– I think it's better for Valeria not to embark for Italy.

– Well, I believe the best thing to do is to let her go.

– I am her father. I can't allow my daughter to embark for an unknown country without me being present to help her. You know very well that I can't leave the business.

– I understand. Natalia and I will be by your daughter's side. We'll shower her with affection and care. This child will be born into an environment full of love, warmth, and understanding. Later, Valeria can resume her interior design course and graduate. You'll see; everything will work out, my brother.

– America wanted to believe in this story with a probable happy ending. However, the story took another turn because during the pregnancy, Valeria experienced depressive episodes and hit her own belly. Miraculously, she did not lose the child.

– When Frederico was born, she refused to hold him in her arms. Then, when it was time to breastfeed the baby, she was so shocked that her milk would not come out as if it had frozen and she would rather feel the horrible pain than try to breastfeed her son.

- Years passed and her estrangement with her son became evident. Valeria finished the heart-to-heart course, returned to Brazil and Americo gave her the studio as promised. He partnered with Natalia and, in time, the establishment became a well-known and respected architectural firm in the city.

- Valeria felt fulfilled as a professional but a failure as a mother. She acknowledged that looking at her son meant having to relive her mistake for the rest of her life. That morning in Guaruja when she lay with Dario repeated in her mind day after day. She tried therapy, but the scene persisted.

- She thought and decided that the best thing to do was to stay away from her son. And so she did. Valeria avoided staying at home, immersed herself in work, and took on project after project. She didn't even take a break for leisure. She was afraid of getting involved with another man and getting pregnant.

- It's a good thing Valeria had been attracted to Tomás years ago. After Federico's birth, she tried to establish contact with the boy. She discovered that Tomás had married Marion and, according to the celebrity magazines, they were very happy.

- "I missed the chance to be happy," she repeated to herself many times.

- Determined not to get involved with anyone else and avoid contact with her son, Valeria constantly travelled outside the country, claiming that travel, international fairs and contacts with foreign suppliers were important to keep up to date and become more and more capable in the profession. Federico grew up surrounded by the love of Natalia, Adamo and his grandfather. As soon as they got married, Natalia discovered that she could not have children, had no desire to adopt a child either, and took care of her nephew as if he were her son.

– "I am your aunt. Valeria is your mother," she always said, even against her will.

– Natalia didn't want Frederico to completely distance himself from his mother. However, that's what happened. He and Valeria barely spoke.

– Frederico was a good young man, but when he felt the rejection from his mother, he was obsessed by the spirit of Taviño. Unable to approach Valeria, Taviño started wandering the world and feeding on the energy of people who felt a high degree of rejection, as he deeply felt rejected, believing that Valeria had chosen Dario over him.

– After the birth of the child, Valeria changed her attitude significantly, and consequently, the content of her thoughts. Taviño could no longer get close to her, but he discovered in Frederico a new source of energy to stay in the earthly world. When the boy had relapses due to the feeling of rejection, Taviño approached and drained his energies.

– Many times, Natalia had to take her nephew to the doctor's office, thinking that the boy's weakness and discomfort were due to some illness. Adamo warned her that Frederico's problem was spiritual. They regularly took the boy to the spiritual centre, and Frederico improved. However, when the feeling of rejection increased for some reason, Taviño "attached" himself to the boy.

– Until the day Frederico underwent a complex treatment for disobsession, and the energy ties between him and Taviño were broken.

– He will have a new relapse, and I will be back," Taviño vociferate during the disobsession session.

– Eliel, a friendly spirit and family protector, shook his head:

– No, he won't. Frederico is changing the content of his thoughts. He is becoming a more emotionally balanced young man and will learn to deal with the feeling of rejection in a way that won't hurt him anymore, and consequently, won't give you the opportunity to get close to him again.

– One day he will change, lower his standards, and...

– Eliel cut him off:

– Here in this family, you have no more chances. It's over.

– Taviño's eyes were filled with fury.

– I don't want to die. I want to stay here.

– You passed away more than twenty years ago. Why do you insist on staying and not accepting the destinies of life? Why not do as Dario?

– He was weak! He died and naturally accepted the new condition.

– And he lives very well. Dario learned to be less reckless, learned to balance his emotions. He works at a rescue station near the planet, specialized in welcoming young people who pass away in car and motorcycle accidents.

– He is a fool. He didn't want to know about Valeria. He didn't even want to meet his son.

– Because he wasn't supposed to meet him, of course.

– I'm afraid to move on. Go where?

– There are numerous places for you to live.

– Can I choose? – Taviño asked, curious.

– No. Places in the astral world are not chosen by will, as on Earth, but by energetic affinity. The content of your aura will determine the places you can visit.

– I'm tired," Taviño was being sincere. – I'm still infatuated with Valeria.

– You are attached to this feeling because of the past. You have had an emotional relationship with Valeria, just like Dario and Frederico. At the moment, what matters for her spiritual growth is trying to live harmoniously with Frederico.

– Is it true that I can reincarnate? Return to the planet?

– Yes. We all are born and die many times.

– I want to come back. I like it here.

– Then come with me. I will take you to a very interesting place, full of young people like you. And there are other girls for you to be interested in. What do you say?

– Taviño opened a wide smile.

– Hmm, so I can meet a girl and date?

– Yes, you can.

– I accept!

– Eliel smiled satisfactorily, and that same night, Taviño followed him to a rescue station near the Earth. After that night, Frederico improved significantly, and away from Taviño's influence, he began to wish to get rid of that feeling that brought him down so much and, consequently, pushed him towards contact with less balanced spirits.

– Guided by Eliel, Frederico decided to study in England. He would leave in two weeks.

– Certainly! Here's the translation with dashes used for dialogue:

– I confess to being quite relieved.

– I was talking to a friend and learned that not just anyone can pass the proficiency exam, – America added.

– It requires a lot of language fluency, you know.

– America felt an unparalleled pride.

– My grandson will study at the Faculty of Economics at the University of Cambridge in England!

– Frederico is a very dedicated young man. I'm sure he will graduate with merit, – Natalia said as she served herself a slice of cake.

– No university in the world surpasses the more than eighty Nobel Prizes associated with Cambridge. Isn't that something to make a grandfather proud? – America asked, happy and smiling. Icons of science like Isaac Newton, Charles Darwin, and Stephen Hawking have passed through there as students or professors.

– It's true, – replied Natalia.

– How was the admission process? America was genuinely interested.

– You know, students who wish to enter the university for an undergraduate degree submit their application dossier to an individual college of their choice. In general, most colleges admit students interested in studying any discipline offered by the university. The in-person interviews are similar to an oral exam and cover specific questions about the subjects studied by the candidate in the last two years of high school.

– Interesting, – America said, running his fingers over his well-trimmed white beard.

– This boy is going far, – Natalia added.

– And you can bet I will, – Frederico replied, with a hint of enthusiasm.

– Natalia noticed her nephew's radiant expression. She placed her cup on the saucer and looked at Americo. He shrugged and smiled.

– "I need to talk to Valeria," he thought. "My nephew can't leave like this, without a conversation with his mother."

# Chapter 21

– Valeria responded to statements in a terse and cold manner, without taking her eyes off the model.

– I know.

– He can't leave like this – Natalia said.

– Like this?

– Sad.

– Who told you he's sad?

– I feel it.

– He's going to live in England. We're going to pay for his studies. Frederico has a unique opportunity for personal growth, and I'm sure he'll love the experience of living on his own.

– Agreed. You and I lived abroad, and we know how life in Italy did us a world of good. But I feel that Frederico is still sad.

– What do I have to do with that, Natalia? If Frederico is a sad young man, what can I do? I offered to pay for therapy. He refuses.

– The problem with your son is not therapy but a lack of love.

– Valeria made a grimace and continued to focus on the drawing.

– Again, with this story of lack of love? Are you going to tell me for the umpteenth time that Frederico grew up like this because of me?

– And it wasn't? – Natalia asked, upset. – You never liked your son.

– It's not a matter of liking or not. You are too dramatic – said Valeria.

– She finished touching up the model.

– There we go. The client will love it. If I win with this decoration project, we'll be rich.

– We already are – replied Natalia, curtly. – What good is so much money if you feel so sad?

– I don't feel sad.

– Of course, I forgot the details; you are sad.

– Valeria became exasperated.

– Did you make it your mission to annoy me today? What is it? Did you fight with Adamo?

– No, I didn't fight with my husband. Everything is fine. I just don't like looking at my nephew and seeing his sad little eyes.

– Don't look at him.

– How can you be so cold, Valeria?

– I'm not cold. Frederico is almost a man. In a little while, he'll turn twenty. He'll get to know a fantastic country, another culture, meet interesting people, graduate, find a good wife, and be happy.

- Why do you repel him so much?

- You talk as if I feel repulsion for my son.

- And don't you? - It's not that. I've told you millions of times. Looking at

- Frederico reminds me of that morning, years ago. I was weak and slept with Dario. I'll never forgive myself for that moment of weakness. Never.

- Don't you think it's time to leave the past behind? So what if you slept with Dario? It happened, and what's done is done...

- Valeria interrupted her:

- What's done cannot be changed. I don't have the power to go back to the past and change the course of history.

- Adamo entered the room at that moment. He had just heard Valeria's response and intervened:

- You can't change, but you can transform. Life gave you a beautiful, healthy, loving son, full of virtues. Frederico is a sweet, intelligent boy, and he feels your rejection deeply.

- When Adamo spoke, Valeria listened. She knew her uncle was a fair and impartial man. Adamo helped people without getting emotionally involved in their problems. A tear rolled down her face.

- It's stronger than me, uncle. I can't treat him differently. Every time I see my son, I... I see Dario. And now that he's grown up and a man, he looks just like his father. It's too much for me.

– Frederico is not to blame for anything. It doesn't matter that he was the result of a slip. What matters is that you have a lovely child. Life gave you the chance to raise a son.

– Many of us dream of this gift – added Natalia.

– You speak like that because you can't have children. I don't want to be rude or mean to you – Valeria was emotional and hugged her friend. – I know how much you love Frederico. I love my son, but I can't have a better relationship with him. I'm not a perfect mother. Patience.

– You could at least become his friend. At this point in the game, all Frederico needs is people who give him affection, attention, support...

– If I couldn't overcome this rejection, it won't be now, almost twenty years later, that I'll be able to.

– Natalia loved Valeria. She considered her friend a true sister. She knew that both had been sisters in a past life, and between their spirits, there was a strong bond of understanding and, above all, affection. She also knew that Valeria and Frederico's relationship was a knot of misunderstandings created over many lifetimes that needed to be untangled in this life.

– Frederico had made Valeria suffer a lot in past lives. However, centuries were able to appease this suffering, and he learned to love and respect her. He didn't feel anger toward his mother, but deep sadness because his spirit had already unravelled the knots of misunderstandings.

– Valeria could have had a different kind of behaviour if it weren't for the stumbles in her affective relationships. If she had had a man by her side, perhaps the upbringing of her son would have been different. Natalia caught this thought and said bluntly:

– If you had married, your relationship with Frederico would be completely different.

– That's not true.

– You don't fool me, friend. I know how bad you felt when you found out about Thomas and Marion's marriage.

– That marriage was a done deal. I was pregnant. Do you think Thomas would have married me in that condition?

– Thomas would have married you pregnant or in any other way. He did the right thing when he accepted Marion's proposal. She was pregnant. If she wanted, she could have looked for him after a few years.

– For what? So, he could divorce Marion, and she would make my life hell? – Valeria asked bewildered. – I can endure many things in life, but I can't stand a jealous and vengeful woman. Marion is a thorn I don't want in my shoe.

– Thomas separated from her some time ago.

– So what? Don't you follow the life of the "big star" in magazines and on television shows? Marion loves to appear on sensational TV programs to trample on someone and, in this way, get a bit of attention. Today, she is more known for being a troublemaker than for her talent. I mean – Valeria corrected herself – talent she never had. She has always been a good b, that's for sure. She took advantage of her sensational body and used it to make a career. However, time passes, and the body doesn't stay young forever.

- Marion is over forty years old and will pose for a male nude magazine. Her body still haunts the minds of many men - asserted Valeria.

- She may even be successful at the moment, but it's all temporary. Soon she'll reach middle age, and the body naturally won't be the same as in her youth. Marion is not ready to grow old.

- Whether she is ready or not, what matters is that the path for you to resume your story with Thomas is open.

- He doesn't even remember me anymore, Natalia. We haven't seen each other in twenty years.

- Natalia smiled.

- Don't remember? Let's see.

- She left the room and then reappeared with a beautiful and sophisticated bouquet of red roses.

- What beautiful flowers! - exclaimed Valeria.

- They're for you.

- For me? What do you mean?

- Read the card, come on.

- Valeria smiled and took a step forward. She took the bunch in her hands and inhaled the delicate perfume of the flowers. Then she picked up the card and read it. She blushed.

- They were sent by Thomas!

- Didn't I say he still remembers you?

- But why did he send flowers only now? - she asked, curious.

- Natalia shrugged.

– If I were you, I would call him. Thomas is a successful businessman. He managed to dissociate his image from the rich father he had. He made his own fortune and gained more sympathy when he separated from Marion.

– He separated from Marion over a year ago. Why did he send the flowers only now?

– You're well-informed about him, huh? – Natalia teased.

– Valeria waved her hand.

– There are always bits of news here and there in the newspapers. Call him.

– Should I?

– Of course. Call to thank him for the bouquet of roses. Who knows, you might go to dinner and catch up on these twenty years?

– You won't give up – protested Valeria. – You want to see me with someone.

– Of course. Your son is grown up, and soon he will have his own family. Are you going to stay alone for the rest of your life?

– It's not that...

– Sit here next to me – Adamo invited.

– He gestured, and Valeria followed him. They sat on a sofa, and Adamo, firmly, said to his niece:

– Listen carefully: we all feel rejection, to some degree.

– I don't feel it – Valeria declared.

– You may deny it, but you have felt rejection, indeed. You reacted with anger because you didn't have a mother. You grew up afraid of having a child because you feared dying like Amelia, right after childbirth.

– Valeria said nothing. She bit her lower lip and looked at the floor. Adamo continued:

– Rejection, in a way, makes us deny our desires. Unresolved, it brings terrible consequences to our spiritual progress. You created the image of a tough, independent woman who doesn't need anything or anyone. You forced a veneer that is not yours. You ended up not being authentic.

– I'm not fake!

– That's not what I'm saying – Adamo continued. – You stopped being yourself, being the cheerful and flirtatious Valeria, for fear of attracting relationships similar to those you experienced with Taviño and Dario. This happened when you were very young, many years ago. Life's experiences turned you into another woman. You can overcome this fear and seek your happiness.

– I can't – Valeria was stunned by the conversation.

– Yes, you can. Nothing is difficult or impossible. Understanding and mastering rejection removes the fear from things, life, situations, and, realizing that it cannot destroy us, we feel strong enough to understand and deal with it better.

– The world is bad.

– That's an old belief we acquired over incarnations to avoid making significant changes for our spiritual growth. It's convenient to stay in one place and not face it. It's easy to feel like a victim of the world. But it's all an illusion.

– I've never been lucky in love relationships.

– Did you choose to close your heart because you can't stand hearing a "no" anymore, or because you don't want to be deceived again?

– I'm afraid...

– Valeria was deeply touched and moved by the conversation. Adamo smiled and continued.

– First of all, you need to change the way you see yourself. You need to pay more attention to yourself, look at your needs, and try to fulfil them. After that, you'll be able to better assess your attitudes towards your son.

– I think it's too late for that. Frederico is already a grown man.

– You have a whole life ahead of you – said Adamo, excited. – Let's forget the past and focus on today, on what can be changed now.

– I'll try.

– Adamo spoke and looked at his wife. Natalia nodded and stood up. She walked to her desk, opened a drawer, and took out a small box. She settled back on the sofa and handed it to Valeria.

– What's this?

– Open it.

– Valeria opened it, revealing a gold necklace. The pendant was a Japanese ideogram: the kanji.

– It's so delicate and beautiful!

— Adamo and I bought it for you when we visited Tokyo.

— The ideogram means love – added her uncle.

— Adamo continued:

— I want you to wear this necklace, and whenever the feeling of rejection becomes strong, just hold the ideogram with your thumb and forefinger and say to yourself: "I won't let myself suffer."

— Valeria hugged them.

— I have no words to thank you for such a kind gesture.

— Don't thank us. Wear it and feel the love for yourself, long overdue – concluded Adamo.

— Natalia stood up and delicately placed the golden necklace around her friend's neck.

— I'll let you reflect on what we talked about – Adamo said and kissed her cheek.

— Natalia made the same gesture and, before leaving and closing the door, said with a smile:

— Please, don't forget to call Thomas.

— Valeria nodded and held the pendant for a long time. She felt loved by the universe and was sure that from then on, her life would be very different.

# Chapter 22

– Arlete called her sister's house and was reassured by the automated response:

– Don't worry; she's with me and Lurdes. Eugenio will arrive soon, and we're going to have dinner. Afterward, he'll take Olivia home.

– This is too much, Alzira. I can't allow Olivia to run to your house every time we have an argument.

– You are very stubborn.

– Arlete sniffed:

– Me, stubborn?! Are you defending your niece?

– I am. You've been hard on Olivia ever since she was born.

– Not true.

– Yes. You might not even realize it, but you're tough on Olivia.

– She's a tough cookie.

– Weren't you like that when you were young? Remember how you stood up to Dad?

– Arlete laughed on the other end of the line.

- You're right. Sometimes I catch myself thinking about our adolescence and how we faced Dad. He used to give us a good slap, and we didn't care.

- Don't try to do the same thing to your daughter that Dad did to us.

- Don't compare me to that scoundrel. I gave my daughter a few spankings, but I never beat her.

- You need to stop deciding Olivia's future.

- She's only fifteen. She wants to be a *"Paquita."* Can you believe it?

- And accidentally - emphasized - you got the audition date wrong.

- Arlete blushed.

- I did it for her own good.

- You're not inside your daughter to decide to this extent. If Olivia were involved with bad company, if she were dating a troublemaker, I would fully support you in intervening and taking some action. The thing is, your daughter is so sweet, so gentle. She has never caused any trouble at school and has never been involved with a boy.

- That's true. In that regard, I can't complain about our daughter. Osvaldo and I are proud of the education we gave her.

- If she wants to be an artist, let her be. A lot of water will flow under the bridge. Olivia is young, and desires change over time. Let her dream.

- I'm afraid, Alzira.

- Afraid of what?

– That she becomes another Gisele.

– What does Gisele have to do with Olivia? – her sister asked, bewildered.

– Gisele claimed to be an artist. She said she was an actress and a model.

– Alzira laughed over the phone.

– Gisele made that up. She wasn't an actress or a model, not in a million years.

– Really?

– Of course. Ask Osvaldo. He handled the process that evicted her from the little townhouse. In the legal documents, besides her eviction, her occupation should be stated.

– Changing the subject – Arlete didn't like to remember her father or Gisele – what do you think about Olivia doing an exchange program?

– A wonderful idea.

– Are you sure?

– Of course, Arlete. This trip will positively transform Olivia's life. Moreover, I'm sure that your relationship will improve when she returns.

– She doesn't like me.

– Nonsense. Your daughter loves you.

– She likes her father. It's all like this – Arlete joined her thumbs while keeping the phone against her neck – with Osvaldo.

– He doesn't bother her. Osvaldo talks to Olivia, listens to what she feels, and is more a friend than a father. You should be less of a mother and more of a friend to your daughter.

– I'll take it easier on her, believe me.

– I'm glad, my sister – Alzira said and heard Eugenio's voice. – My big man just arrived. Send a kiss to Eugenio. I miss him.

– I'll send it. Now I have to hang up, and Eugenio will take your little one home as soon as we finish dinner.

– Agreed.

– Arlete hung up the phone and felt a slight sense of well-being.

– Alzira is right. I need to be more of a friend to my daughter.

– She spoke and got up. She walked through the corridor and bumped into the sideboard, full of photo frames. One of them fell and shattered on the floor. Arlete bent down to pick up the shards of glass that had scattered.

– I should have moved this sideboard a long time ago – she said aloud as she picked up the glass fragments with her hands.

– Then, she picked up the fallen photo. It was a picture of her and Alzira crouching and hugging, still girls. Behind them, standing, were Olair and Josefa.

– She smiled at the photo.

– Mom, how I miss you. I hope you're well.

– Then, she fixed her gaze on Olair. She made a face and shrugged. She vividly remembered the day her father had died, and after the shock of the news, Celia had read to her a passage from the novel "Between Love and War," referring to her father's fate:

– "The laws of divine justice, immutable, repay each according to their deeds. And time, a constant friend, takes care of restoring the truth in the intimacy of being."

– She repeated the phrase and concluded:

– I hope you're well, Dad – Arlete said and felt a shiver down her spine.

– After all, what could have happened to Olair and Gisele?

– Let's go back to the point where Olair passed away. The man didn't die of a heart attack but of pure hatred.

– As soon as he passed away, Olair's spirit detached from the physical body. He looked at his lifeless body on the ground and at his perispirit. He saw Gisele and Rodinei's disdain. Hatred surged again, and Olair felt a stabbing pain in his chest. Then, he found himself behind Gisele. After he shouted, and she didn't hear, Olair became disturbed. He tried to slap her, but his hand passed through Gisele's face as if it were smoke. Olair looked at his hand and momentarily forgot about the treacherous lover, returning to the room where he died.

– What happened? he asked himself while palpating his own perispiritual body. A tormented spirit, covered in astral larvae around its body, approached him. Olair took a step back, feeling a strong sense of repulsion. The smell emanating from the spirit, due to the larvae sticking to its body, was unpleasant, reminiscent of a garbage truck.

– What do you want from me? Olair asked, eyes wide.

– I won't hurt you, said the spirit. I'm part of a group of astral vampires that feed on the little life energy left in your physical body.

– Olair looked at the ground and saw himself.

– How did I return to the room? I was on the street, and–

– The spirit chuckled sinisterly. When we die, we can move in this world in a different way, at a different pace. I want to feed on this, the spirit pointed to the silver cord still connecting Olair's perispirit to the physical body.

– A very bright light appeared, and a spirit of light emerged in front of them. The spirit covered in larvae jumped backward, while Olair remained static, wide-eyed.

– The spirit's voice was firm and unfriendly: You won't feed on anything, for now. If you do, Olair will feel great pain.

– And so what? – the embittered spirit retorted. – The pain won't last long. I need to feed.

– Not here. If you want, go to some cemetery. There are many recently departed there at this very moment.

– I know, but to enter the cemetery, I need authorization. That's why I grab one dead here and another there.

– You can leave – the voice was powerful.

– The darkened spirit shrugged, uttered some insults, and departed. Olair approached and inquired:

– Who are you?

– I'm Lolla, a friend of Josefa.

– I don't know any Lolla.

– You don't remember me. I didn't reincarnate with you this time.

– Olair's expression showed complete unfamiliarity.

– We don't have much time to talk. I came because Josefa asked me to.

– Josefa? Asked you to come here?

– Although she is still in the hospital, she asked me to help you in the process of passing away.

– I don't understand anything.

– Lolla smiled and stared at him firmly:

– You died.

– Yes, but I'm talking to you. I don't understand.

– Your physical body died. Your spirit is still alive. Simple as that. The death of the body is not the end of life. Life never exhausts. It is eternal!

– If I died, what do I do now?

– You can come with me, and we'll go to a help centre. You'll be attended to by dedicated and competent doctors. Afterward, we can discuss the colony where you can live according to your energy vibration.

– I can't leave. I have to settle scores with Gisele and Rodinei. They tricked me, and I won't let them get away with it.

– That's part of the past. You died, and everyone reaps what they sow. Later, after clarifications, you will understand why Rodinei and Gisele did this to you.

– I never harmed them.

– In this life. And in another?

– What other?

– We are born and die many times, Lolla spoke didactically. You have lived with Gisele and Rodinei before. Had another life, another body, in another era, but beliefs and attitudes haven't changed.

– I don't remember having lived before.

– You will remember soon. In the last life, you deceived a peasant couple. Took away their lands and, consequently, the family's livelihood. You did it out of greed, and Rodinei and Gisele, after passing away, couldn't forgive you.

– Something inside Olair said it was true, but he brushed the idea aside and raised his voice:

– Will they live happily like this, getting away with it?

– The probability of them being unhappy is very high. Let's leave both in God's hands. Let's follow our path.

– I won't. You can't force me to leave. I want them to pay for the deceit. I won't rest until I get revenge.

– Don't even think about it, Olair. Vengeance is a feeling that corrodes the spirit, just like rust corrodes iron. It's not worth it.

– You say that because you weren't deceived.

– I don't have permission to stay here any longer.

– Then you can go. I'll stay until I settle the score with these scoundrels.

– Lolla shrugged and sighed:

– What a pity! I hope to see you soon.

– She spoke and disappeared into the air. Soon, the brightness was gone, and Olair found himself alone in the room, next to his body. The spirit full of larvae reappeared and, in an instant, pounced on the silver cord, violently breaking it and greedily sucking the little vital fluid that lay there, much like a vulture over carrion. Olair's perispirit felt a sharp pain and collapsed.

# Chapter 23

– After dinner, Olivia agreed to go back home. On the way, she engaged in a conversation with Eugenio.

– But, uncle, my mom is very controlling.

– Eugenio listened to the conversation and said nothing, just nodding his head up and down. At a certain point, he asked his niece:

– Why is there this feeling of rejection towards your mom? I don't understand.

– I feel that you feel a strong rejection towards Arlete.

– Oh, uncle, imagine – Olivia tried to dissemble.

– I don't like to meddle in anyone's life; however, you have always had a hostile attitude towards your mom.

– Are you defending my mom? – she asked, bewildered.

– I'm not defending anyone, but I am outside your relationship. Whoever is outside the conflict can see the situation with total impartiality. You had difficulties being born. Arlete took hours in a difficult labour that almost cost her life.

– I never knew that.

– Now you know.

– What does that have to do with our relationship? I love my mom.

– I know you love her, but there are certain components in your behaviour that keep you away from her.

– And I might as well! Mom always prunes me. She won't let me do anything I want.

– I'm not talking about that. Arlete has this behaviour because she wants to protect you. It's the behaviour of an overprotective mother.

– I don't feel that way.

– Eugenio shook his head from side to side.

– You do feel that way. I'm sure this animosity between you two comes from past lives.

– Nonsense. I don't believe in that.

– Don't believe or are you afraid to see the truth?

– Olivia shifted in the car seat. She pretended to fasten her seat belt and turned her face toward the car window. Her aunts Lourdes and Alzira studied and believed in the continuity of life after death.

– Olivia was in adolescence and in the phase where she only believed in what was proven to her. She had grown up listening to conversations and, speaking of "proofs", she had fresh in her memory a day when she visited Celia and Ariovaldo. The couple received Arlete and Osvaldo with great affection and were, as usual, very kind to Olivia.

– So far, nothing out of the ordinary. However, at a certain moment, Celia called Olivia to help her in the kitchen and commented:

– Are you still having that dream?

– Which one?

– The dream where you find yourself in a hospital and are afraid to return to our world.

– Celia referred to the dream that Olivia had since she was thirteen years old and still recurred. The scene repeated itself, as at the beginning of this story. However, there was a part that always marked Olivia significantly:

– Are you going to tell me that my mom will be there too?

– It's necessary to reconcile, there is no use forgiveness here in the astral world, if the same does not happen in the next stage of reincarnation, with the veil of oblivion over past memories. She will go through some experiences so that her spirit can overcome this rejection.

– The young girl lowered her head. She knew that overcoming rejection would be a significant step in her evolutionary journey. She felt that she needed to face situations that would make her confront this monster that had hurt her so much in some existences. She took a deep breath and stared intently at Lolla:

– I'm ready. I know I am strong, and I have friends here in the astral who will inspire good thoughts in me. I will overcome it.

– She always woke up after this part. Celia turned to her and asked:

– Will she overcome it now?

– Olivia shuddered and asked, sweating:

– How do you know that? I never told anyone about this dream, not even my aunt Alzira.

– Celia smiled and said nothing. From that day on, Olivia began to read spiritualist books and became interested in the subject.

– Olivia moved her head to the side and said to Eugenio:

– I lied, uncle. I believe that life continues after death.

– If you believe, you can open your mind and your heart to better understand the difficult relationship you have with Arlete. What does it cost you to change the way you are?
– Me?! It's her who has to change!

– If you positively change your way of being, I guarantee that the people around you will also change. Your mother is one of those people. Why don't you try?

– I don't know – Olivia felt insecure.

– What have you got to lose? If you come to understand yourself better, you will understand your mother's attitude better. Arlete and your aunt Alzira had a difficult life and have a very different outlook on life than you. While you think about doing theatre or going to England, your mother, when she was your age, was taking care of your grandmother Josefa's illness and living with a brutal and stupid father.

– Before she could open her mouth to retort, Eugenio added:

– I know that everyone has the life they deserve. I also know that there are no victims in the world. Your mother and aunt took advantage of the parents they had growing up. All

I can say is that it costs nothing to open your heart and listen to your mother with different eyes and ears. You are young, smart and know what you want. You have a mother and father who love you very much and always want the best for you.

- Olivia nodded, touched.

- You're right, uncle. I need to be less stubborn. I loved talking to you, as always!

- He parked at the curb and hugged her.

- Do everything you can to get along in life, my dear. Give yourself a chance to improve your relationship with your mother. Arlete is a good person. If he wasn't, he'd be the first to invite you to live with me and your Aunt Alzira. But you have wonderful parents. Talk to them, tell them about your desire to go to England without imposing your wishes in a haughty way. Go with that. If all goes well, I promise I'll give you round-trip tickets

- Olivia rejoiced with joy.

- You're kidding, uncle?

- Mm-hmm.

- She hugged him and kissed him several times on the face.

- I love you and Aunt Alzira so much!

- We love you too. Now go in and show them that you are a good daughter.

- They said goodbye. Eugenio started the car and left. Olivia took a deep breath and smiled. She entered the house and found Osvaldo and Arlete in the kitchen, talking. She took a deep breath and walked through the hallway.

– I'll pretend everything is fine. I need to be friends with my mom, understand her better to win the trip to England, she thought.

– Olivia walked into the kitchen. She kissed her father on the cheek and walked over to her mother. Arlete stared at her:

– No way! Why did you disturb your aunt's life? Was it worth staying at home? Can't we solve our problems within these four walls? – He pointed to the sides.

– Osvaldo got up from the chair and was about to position himself between the two. He knew his daughter was going to retaliate hard. To his surprise, Olivia smiled and nodded her head up and down. She hugged Arlete with great affection.

– You're absolutely right, Mom. From now on, I won't bother Aunt Alzira or Aunt Lurdes with my complaints. As the old saying goes, we should air our dirty laundry at home. I'm going to change my ways, and we won't fight anymore.

– Olivia spoke, kissed Arlete on the cheek, and walked to the sink. She looked to the side and saw the steaming pot on the stove.

– Hmm! You made yam soup with chopped kale. How I love that! Too bad I just had dinner. Can you save some for me to have tomorrow?

– Arlete didn't know what to answer. Osvaldo put his hands on his hips.

– Did you drink or smoke something strange?

– No, Daddy. You know well that I don't like alcohol or cigarettes. I just had pleasant moments with my aunts and my Uncle Eugenio. I'm happy, that's all.

– She turned around and hugged Osvaldo. Kissed him on the cheek and said:

– I'm going upstairs, to take a shower and, when I come down, I want a glass of milk with burnt sugar, like you used to make me when I was little, remember mom?

– I remember – Arlete was monosyllabic.

– The girl turned on her heels and left the kitchen. She walked up the stairs to the bedroom. Arlete was really surprised. She didn't know what to say. Osvaldo was stung and said with his mouth open:

– This is not our daughter! Olivia was abducted by extraterrestrials!

– They both laughed.

– That they did She put a little sense into her head. Olivia always comes back well from my sister's house. Maybe you've heard some good things about Alzira.

– I don't know – Osvaldo stroked his chin. – Olivia showed a different behaviour. I was prepared for a fight between the two, and yet the atmosphere was one of harmony and peace.

– She's treating us like this because she wants to go to England.

– Is that all, my dear? Haven't you noticed a different brightness in our little one's eyes?

– I did.

– How long has it been since Olivia gave you such an affectionate hug and kiss?

– Arlete put her hand to her face.

– I confess to being taken by surprise.

– Olivia is growing and changing.

– I'm afraid she might get lost in the world.

– Unfounded fear. Olivia has common sense. I feel that the exchange program will do her a world of good.

– We'll be alone.

– Alzira has invited you numerous times to work with her.

– Maybe now I'll accept the invitation.

– Let's trust because life always does the best for us.

– Osvaldo spoke and hugged his wife. Arlete felt a lump in her throat. She hugged her husband tightly.

– Don't leave me, my love – the words came out of her mouth automatically.

– I love you – he replied. – I promise to be faithful to you until death.

– Until death?

– Yes. After death, everyone goes his own way! – Arlete patted her husband on the shoulder.

– Joker! So, you mean we'll be married...

– As the saying goes: till death do us part.

– She laughed and hugged Osvaldo again. She felt a great love for her husband and daughter. She didn't understand why Olivia had rejected her so much since she was a little girl. But now it seemed that everything would change for the better. Arlete had every reason in the world to believe that.

– That night, after having a glass of warm milk with sugar, Olivia fell asleep and soon detached from her body. She opened her eyes and smiled upon seeing Lolla by her bedside.

– Long time no see you! Olivia ran and hugged her spirit friend. Lola hugged her back.

– It's been a while. I'm very happy with your change.

– My uncles helped me. Today, I had a conversation with Uncle Eugenio that greatly changed my view of the relationship I have with my mother.

– Your spirit wished to reincarnate as Arlete's daughter.

– Olivia nodded and had a flash of a past memory. Her parents had died in an accident, and she had been raised by her aunt. Hence, her affinity with Alzira.

– Scenes came quickly: Olivia as a beautiful, outgoing girl. She discovered that her mother had gotten pregnant by another man before getting married, and worse, she hadn't died in the accident.

– Arlete returned after many years and was rejected by her daughter. Olivia didn't want to know about her, but Alzira tried to mediate and make everyone live well and in harmony. Olivia didn't accept and moved to another city. Arlete went after her, and Olivia decided to leave the country.

– She moved to Venice, Italy. There, she met a handsome man named Frederico...

– Lolla touched her forehead, and the memories ceased. Olivia opened and closed her eyes several times.

– What happened? It seems like I entered into a trance.

– You had access to scenes from your last life on Earth.

– Now I know why I felt so much repugnance towards my mother. She wanted my money and tried to take the house where Aunt Alzira and I lived.

– Arlete had suffered a lot. The steamer in which she was traveling with her husband sank and she almost drowned. Arlete was rescued, but she lost her memory. She wandered back and forth until she regained her memory. Insecure and middle-aged, she wanted you to support her at all costs. She tried to forge documents and remove you from the house where you had lived.

– Arlete was desperate. She was afraid of dying on the street, like a beggar, as had happened in another life.

– I understand a lot now, but before you touched my forehead, I saw a handsome young man. I felt warmth throughout my body and opened my eyes.

– At the right moment, you will remember more details about this young man. Soon, you will meet again.

– Olivia felt a flutter in her stomach. She didn't know why she felt both love and fear of him. Lolla put her arm around her neck.

– Don't worry, honey. The important thing now is that you are going to England and a new stage in your journey begins.

– I can't wait to go back to England. I miss it so much!

– You need to rest. From now on, you must be balanced and at peace with yourself. Don't forget that I'll always be by your side.

– But how will I remember? I know I'll wake up and forget our entire conversation.

– Your spirit will call me. Don't worry.

– Lola kissed her cheek and Olivia kissed her back. She returned to the bed and her double; that is, the part of the perispirit that was coarser and closer to the body, remained a few feet above her body. The girl closed her eyes and fell asleep again.

# Chapter 24

– Even going back a few years in history, Olair woke up and realized that he was no longer in the room. He seemed to be in another environment, heavier, more sinister and darker, very dark.

– He opened his eyes, partially remembering the conversation with Loila.

– I must have dreamed – he said to himself.

– He got up and began to feel around. He heard a voice in the darkness.

– So, buddy, do you like your new home?

– New home? Where am I?

– In hell, the Catholics would say – laughed the other. Olair could see nothing. He felt cold and thirsty.

– I want to drink something. Where is the water?

– I have no idea – the voice replied in the darkness.

– I'd love to get out of here.

– It's not that complicated. If there were light, maybe I could find the way and move forward.

– I'll give you some advice. Is there someone you feel angry with, a lot of anger?

– Yes – Olair replied, thinking of Gisele.

– Then think about that person. Take advantage of the darkness of the environment and mentally place that person in front of you now.

– Why?

– Do it and don't ask me. Obey! – the voice was firm.

– Olair nodded. He didn't have to close his eyes. The darkness was absolute. He thought of Gisele so strongly and so angrily that; he immediately found himself at her side. The change from a completely dark place to where she was, with some light, blinded Olair for a moment. He opened and closed his eyes many times, until his vision became accustomed to his surroundings.

– Gisele was getting ready when Olair appeared next to her. She applied lipstick, sprayed a very sweet and strong perfume on her neck and wrists, looked at the reflected image in the mirror, and blew a kiss.

– You look beautiful, girl! She left the bathroom and walked to the bedroom. Rodinei was lying on the bed. At first, he had thought of using Gisele to get the house and swindle Olair. Then he would get rid of her. He had no intention of marrying or starting a family. However, with Olair's death, he began to have real feelings for the fake blonde.

– He stretched on the bed and smiled.

– Come, my princess. It's time to sleep.

– Sleep? – She pouted. – I thought we were going to date.

– If you want. Well, you know I'm always ready. The thing is, today I worked a lot at the bar. We had a lot of customers.

– Sure. I learned to make codfish cakes. I'm not very fond of the kitchen, but I've known how to make these cakes since I was little. I learned it in Aquidauana, from a Portuguese friend of my mom.

– Come closer.

– Gisele nestled herself next to Rodinei.

– Why so much lipstick?

– To mark my man's body.

– She spoke and laughed. She spoke and giggled. Then she started kissing various parts of Rodinei's body.

– Olair looked at all that and felt an overwhelming rage.

– How can you love each other? I just died!

– Half an hour later, they were tired and very sleepy. Gisele felt thirsty.

– Want some water, my love?

– A little.

– I'll go to the kitchen and be right back.

– She got out of bed, put on flip-flops, and went to the kitchen, completely naked. Gisele might be a fake blonde, but she had a spectacular body. Olair followed her.

– Why did you do this to me, Gisele? I love you.

– She didn't even notice his presence. She grabbed a glass, opened the refrigerator and took out a pitcher of water, filled the glass, drank it and refilled it. Olair continued between anger and rejection:

- Why did you choose Rodinei over me? Why did they play this trick on me?

- Gisele remembered him and said aloud while putting the jug back in the fridge:

- Olair died a year ago, and it feels like he died centuries ago. I don't miss him. Not at all.

- Olair scratched his ear.

- Did I hear correctly? She said I died a year ago? But I died yesterday...

- Gisele continued to speak aloud:

- That scandal died late. He trusted me and he went down a tube. I trusted Rodinei and I did well. We're getting married and I'm going to help him more and more at the bar. We're going to have a family, something I never would have dreamed of with that dirty pig.

- She said and grimaced. Olair felt all his anger coming back with a vengeance. He felt an overwhelming hatred and let out such a shrill scream that the glass of one of the closet doors shattered. Gisele screamed and ran into the room.

- What happened? - Rodinei asked.

- The glass in the cupboard cracked.

- So what?

- I don't know, Rodinei. I felt a chill down my spine.

- He laughed.

– Do you really believe what the client told you the other day, that Olair's spirit must be wandering around the world, like a soul in pain?

– Gisele trembled with fear.

– I believe it. I was never religious, never attended church or worship. But I am afraid of the soul in pain.

– Olair went to a better place. The fool must be with his wife, holding hands, sitting on a white cloud.

– I don't know, Rodinei. It's been a year since he died, and I had some nightmares. In them, Olair always yelled at me and tried to suffocate me.

– You were impressed with how the old man kicked the bucket. He dropped dead right in front of us.

– Must be that.

– You'd better forget it. The man is dead and the house is ours. We're going to get married and have a beautiful family. I want lots of children. Gisele laughed out loud.

– Not so much, Rodi. Not so much.

– Olair was stunned. He couldn't believe that those two scoundrels could get along. They had done him wrong.

– A spirit approached him. Olair was startled.

– How did you get in? – he asked, scared.

– The spirit smiled. His teeth were yellowed and darkened by nicotine.

– I don't like Rodinei. The plague goat took my life. Allow me to introduce myself. My name is Evanildo – He extended his hand and Olair did the same.

– Pleasure. I'm Olair.

– Evanildo was short, but stout. His eyes were naturally red. They were scary, he wore loader's clothes and carried a fishmonger of pure action on his shoulder.

– I used to attend the catimbó.

– Olair looked puzzled, and Evanildo explained:

– *Catimbó* is a regional cult in the Northeast, where manifestations of spirits who lived mainly in that region of Brazil occur, and they are called *Catimbozeiro* Masters.

– I see.

– The guy continued:

– I was a good man. I cultivated herbs and helped the people. I met Rodinei when he brought his girlfriend, who was sick. My group healed her, and we fell in love. Rodinei felt betrayed and came to confront me. I tried to calm him down, but he killed me. The next day, he killed Maria das Dores. Then he fled to São Paulo.

– Where is Maria das Dores?

– Evanildo's eyes sparkled with emotion.

– She is fine. Accepted death and lives in Jurema.

– Where is this place? I've never heard of it. Where does she live?

– In Jurema.

– Evanildo laughed.

– It seems you don't understand anything about the spiritual world.

– Olair shook his head negatively.

– Were you at least Catholic?

– I was raised Catholic, but I never attended anything.

– But it helps to understand. The spiritual universe of the *Catimbó* follows the same pattern as Catholicism, whose beliefs in heaven, hell, and purgatory are quite widespread among the *Catimbó* people.

– Ah, I see...

– The difference is that for us there is also Jurema, where the masters of Jurema and their subordinates live. Jurema is made up of a set of villages, towns and states, with a rigid hierarchical organization, involving all the *catimbozeiro* entities, a hundred Jurema chiefs and enchanted, under the command of one or even three masters.

– Why don't you go live there, next to your beloved, Maria das Dores? – Olair asked, curious.

– Because after I died, I couldn't let go of my rage. Das Dores has tried to convince me to change my mind, but the anger is too great.

– But if you were a good man, why on earth are you now getting involved with revenge?

– And look who's talking? Aren't you here for the same reason?

– Olair was astonished.

– How do you know that?

– Evanildo laughed.

– By the colour of your aura. I can also perceive the thoughts of others. I feel that you want to get revenge on her

– he pointed to Gisele. – You were a religious man. I wasn't. That's why I don't understand your desire for revenge.

– Out of pure will. After Rodinei sheds a tear of remorse, I'll calm down. As for you...

– Evanildo stopped and nodded his head, waiting for a response from Olair.

– She and Rodinei messed with me. They took my home and my life. I can't let them be together and happy. They have to pay for what they did to me.

– I agree.

– What can we do? I've thrown myself at her, but she doesn't feel anything. It's like I can't reach them.

– We have more power than they do. I'll show you.

– Evanildo grabbed the fishwife and lifted her up with his arm. He uttered some strange words to Olair's knowledge.

– The environment began to fill with astral parasites. These "little creatures" from the swamps of the umbral started sticking to Rodinei's body. Immediately, he felt an itch.

– Gisele asked:

– Are you feeling okay?

– I don't know – Rodinei replied. – Suddenly, I started feeling an itch, a scratch all over my body, as if I were being bitten.

– Gisele looked closely.

– There's nothing on you.

– But it's itching.

– Wait, I'll get some alcohol from the kitchen.

– She got up and went to get the bottle. Olair stared at Evanildo in surprise:

– How do you have so much strength? – You can have it too. I can teach you some astral tricks. Then we'll end the lives of these two. What do you say?

– Olair reached out and nodded:

– Agreed!

# Chapter 25

- That early night, after reflecting on the conversation with her uncle, Valeria thought about the relationship she had with her son since his birth. There was, indeed, a natural aversion due to the fact that Frederico was Dario's son. Just thinking about her old boyfriend, Valeria felt unparalleled remorse.

- If I hadn't slept with Dario that morning... Oh, my God! How could I be so weak, so venal?

- This feeling of bitterness accompanied her for almost twenty years. Alongside this feeling, there was also a sense that Frederico had emotionally hurt her a lot.

- There is no reason for that – she tried to justify herself –. Federico never hurt me; he was always a good son.

- Valeria had no clear idea, but her spirit had suffered a lot at Federico's hands in other lives. There was a possession, a dominion he had exercised over her since time immemorial. From the Middle Ages onwards, their spirits, through successive incarnations, underwent major transformations. If before both were insatiable lovers and destroyed everything and everyone with their unhealthy passion, then they went through a period in which Federico exerted a very strong influence on Valeria's desires and longings.

– Life, always merciful, led them to experience situations of possession and detachment until they reached the current incarnation. Frederico finally learned to detach himself from her. Valeria developed a natural feeling of rejection, a result of the fear of being enslaved or dominated again by him.

– The relationship between them underwent more significant changes when Olivia began to reincarnate close to him. And with Olivia by his side, Frederico began to feel true love, that pure, unconditional love without possession or the need to enslave the object of his affection.

– Frederico finally learned that we reincarnate to change personality and not to perfect the essence, which is already perfect. He and Valeria discovered that personality is nothing more than the soul's clothing.

– In the face of this situation, Valeria still felt this natural rejection of Frederico. She accepted him as her son to awaken in herself the loving feelings that only motherhood can provide.

– I love my son. Why can't I get closer to him? Why?

– The question echoed through the room, and Valeria felt a warm tear stream down the corner of her eye. From that moment on, she began to soften the deeply rooted beliefs from other existences.

– She blew her nose with a handkerchief. He got up and went to the bathroom. She washed her face and looked at her reflection in the mirror. She looked tired.

– In fact, I'm starting to get old – she said aloud.

– She gave a little smile, left the bathroom, and spotted the bouquet of roses. She walked over to it, took the card from the roses, and dialled the number. A man's voice answered:

– Hello.

– Please... I would like to speak with Thomas.

– It's me

– Hello, Thomas – she greeted cordially. – It's me, Valeria.

– On the other end of the line, he shuddered and fidgeted in his chair.

– You called! – he exclaimed, happy.

– Yes. I couldn't resist the beautiful bouquet of red roses. They are beautiful. Thank you.

– You're welcome. I'm very happy you called.

– I've been very busy. I have a lot of work, many projects in progress...

– Thomas cut her off with kindness in his voice:

– Is there time in your schedule for us to have dinner together?

– Valeria swallowed dryly. She was taken by surprise.

– Sure... when?

– Can it be tonight?

– Tonight? – she asked, her voice expressing surprise.

– Yes. Tonight. I'm free tonight. How about you?

– Valeria pretended to check her schedule and replied:

– I'm free too. Can we make an appointment somewhere?

– I'll pick you up at your office.

– No! I need to get ready. I don't look good.

– You've always been beautiful.

– If you saw me at this exact moment, I'm sure you would change your mind.

– Thomas laughed. – You women! Alright. I'll pick you up at your place at eight-thirty.

– Agreed.

– They hung up the phone. Thomas felt a gentle warmth touch his chest. Valeria trembled with emotion. It had been years since she went out for a romantic date. She felt insecure.

– After twenty years...

– She spoke, and instinctively her fingers touched the pendant on her neck. Valeria closed her eyes and smiled:

– I am happy, and I won't let myself suffer.

– She got up, tidied her desk, took a vase and filled it with water. She arranged the roses in the vase, placing it on her desk. She grabbed her bag and went home.

– When she arrived at the Morumbi mansion, she parked her car in the garage and one of the maids came to greet her.

– Your son left and left you this letter – Valeria looked at the envelope

– Where is Frederico?

– He left tonight for London.

– Valeria got out of the car and slammed the door shut. She took the envelope from the maid's hand and rushed into the living room like a whirlwind. She found Americo smoking his pipe, wearing a nice robe and reading a book. He pushed down his glasses with his fingers and smiled:

– Good evening, daughter.

– She didn't even respond and followed up with another question:

– What is it that Federico travels without saying goodbye to me?

– What difference would it make? Why would he have to say goodbye to you?

– Because I'm his mother, for heaven's sake.

– America turned his head from side to side.

– You have the title of mother, nothing more. You never cared about your son. What's gotten into you? Are you feeling regret?

– No, it's just that... – Valeria didn't know what to say.

– Frederico left very sad. It broke my heart.

– I thought he was leaving the day after tomorrow.

– He moved up the flight.

– He could have at least let me know...

– Valeria, are you using drugs?

– She stood in front of her father, stunned.

– What a stupid question! I've never taken drugs.

– Then stop behaving like a clueless woman, unaware of things.

– I don't understand, Dad.

– You've never given a damn about your son. Why are you now upset about his trip to England?

– Before she could retort, Americo pointed to her hands:

– Federico left you a letter. By the way, that's the envelope you have in your hands.

– Valeria looked at the envelope and opened it. She sat down next to her father. She took out the paper and read:

– Mother,

– I don't even know if I can call you that... anyway, it's just a mere formality. I've decided not to delude myself and beg for your love. I grew up far from your presence, distant from your affection. I managed to survive, and now I'm a grown man. I don't blame you for the way you treated me all these years. Everyone gives what they have. I can't demand from you what you don't have to give me. I hope that when I return from England, in a few years, we can at least become friends. I don't know if I'll overcome the rejection you imposed on me all these years, but I promise I won't let you bring me down ever again. After all, I have my self-esteem, and I learned from Aunt Natalia: I won't let myself suffer. Never again.

– Kisses and see you later, Frederico

– Valeria finished reading and couldn't contain her emotion. She approached her father and hugged him tightly.

– Dad, I've never been a good mother. I feel like I've lost my son forever. He hates me.

– Hush! – asserted Americo. – Frederico doesn't hate you. He talked a lot with Natalia and Adamo before writing to you.

– Before coming here, I thought about my relationship with my son. I know that part of the distance between us was because he couldn't forgive me for getting pregnant with Dario.

– It happened and that's that. Wouldn't it be easier to move on and move on? If Federico was a troubled, aggressive, bad son, I would even agree with your position. However, this kid never gave you an ounce of work. He was always loving and sociable.

– I know, I know.

– Daughter – Americo's voice became serious – it's time to let go of these beliefs from past lives.

– I don't know how to start...

– The necessary wisdom to let them go comes from the soul, through the experience of accumulated experiences.

– I love my son. I just don't know how to give you my love. In fact, after all these years, with what I just read, I feel like I lost Federico forever.

– You're being dramatic. Frederico poured his heart out in a letter because there was no way to talk to you face to face. Regardless of what you feel. If you truly love your son, there will come a time when you'll know how to convey that feeling to him.

– I'm going to visit him.

– Don't do that for now. Let Frederico live this new stage of life on his own. I'm sure this season in England will do him a world of good.

– What do I do now?

– Radiate love for your son so that nothing bad happens to him. Think about Frederico with love. The rest, life takes care of.

– You're a great friend, Dad. I love you very much.

– I love you too.

– Well, I need to get up and get ready.

– Aren't you having dinner with me?

– Not tonight. I have a date.

– America's face contorted in a funny expression.

– Did I hear correctly? A date?

– That's right.

– I'm glad you're going out and having fun. Just work in the air – Valeria stood up and kissed her father on the forehead.

– Let me get ready. You always have to make a good impression on the first date!

– She smiled and went up to her room. She walked to the closet and chose a beautiful bottle-green dress. She picked out accessories: necklace, earrings, bracelets, purse, and shoes, and hurried to the bathroom. She took a refreshing shower and dressed. She applied a delicate perfume to her body, brushed her red hair back, and liked the image she saw in the mirror.

- Thomas was punctual and picked her up at the agreed-upon time.

- You look beautiful!

- Thank you.

- It seems like I was here yesterday, visiting you after that accident.

- That yesterday was twenty years ago, Thomas. - I know. I lost two decades of my life.

- He started the car and accelerated.

- Don't say that. I thought I had lost years of my life, and if it weren't for all these experiences that you and I have been through, maybe we wouldn't be here together.

- Really, or do you think so?

- Yes. My uncle Adamo always tells me that the joy of life comes down to the contentment of the soul doing what it wants to do, without the interference of the mind.

- Is your uncle a philosopher? - he asked, laughing.

- No. My uncle Adamo is one of the most incredible people I've ever met in my life. He and Natalia, who is his wife and my best friend, along with my father, are my pillars in this life.

- And your son is not included in the bill? - Valeria blushed. Her mind was used to blocking out her son. She bit her lip and said:

– Forgive me for being frank, but my relationship with Federico, my son, was never the best.

– I appreciate your honesty. It's similar to the relationship I have with my daughter, Alice.

– Do you and Marion have only one daughter?

– Thank God we had only one daughter. If it were up to Marion, we would never have children. She always said that pregnancy ruins the body.

– Why did she go through with the pregnancy, then?

– To secure the good part – he pointed to himself. – Marion got pregnant to force me to marry her.

– Nowadays, pregnancy doesn't secure a marriage.

– I'm a man of principles and even old-fashioned. I thought it was fair to marry her and start a family, try to build a home for our daughter. Unfortunately, things aren't as we imagine. Alice grew up feeling like an ugly duckling.

– I've seen photos of your daughter in magazines. Alice is a beautiful young lady.

– She lives insecurely. She hates being compared to the great star Marion Krystal.

– I'm sorry.

– You don't need to be sorry. I tried to be a good father, but my daughter always wanted to surpass her mother in everything. Is it as if the two of them lived in eternal competition? As for me – he shrugged – I was weak and should have followed my heart's desire.

– Marion is possessive. Would she let you go without causing trouble?

- Thomas laughed.

- I've been out of the picture for a long time. I paved the way for Marion to enter the American film market. Once she established herself as a big star, she pushed me aside. Now, she's dating a rich Russian film producer. He's going to turn her into a big star in Europe. Marion even thinks about changing her name again.

- She never changes - said Valeria. - Always the same. Always had immense vanity.

- But time passes, and age catches up. I don't know how Marion will cope with old age.

- They arrived at the restaurant. It was a trendy address and was crowded with cars and people at the entrance. Thomas stopped, got out, and handed the key to the valet. He walked around the front of the vehicle and opened the door for Valeria.

- Thank you very much. You're a gentleman.

- As I told you, I have principles. You can call me old-fashioned, but I still open the car door, send flowers... small gestures of affection that a woman deserves to receive every day.

- Valeria blushed and nodded. She didn't say anything. They entered the restaurant, and the maître, recognizing Thomas, greeted him with a broad smile.

- Mr. Tomás! It is a great pleasure to see you again. I'll take you to your table - Tomás pulled out the chair and Valeria sat down. Then she turned around and sat in the chair in front. The table was tastefully set and there was a candelabra with a lit candle, creating a romantic atmosphere in the room. Thomas ordered a red wine and they continued the conversation.

– You know, Valeria, I'm forty-five years old. I've built my nest egg, have a good life. I'm legally divorced. I'm a free man.

– And your daughter?

– Alice is turning twenty, and feeling suffocated by her mother's success, she decided to move to Australia, far away. My family has properties there, and Alice is well settled. She enrolled in a hospitality course in Sydney. She's dating an heir to a famous hotel group.

– So, you're truly free.

– And what about you?

– Me? What do you want to know?

– Everything – Thomas replied, with a beautiful smile. – Tell me about your life, your projects, your dreams.

– Valeria noticed Thomas' mature beauty. He was still handsome. His hair was turning gray, mint style. His whitish complexion gave him a virile air and a sweeping charm, his perfectly aligned white teeth appeared when he smiled. She was delighted. They placed the order, and when the plates arrived, Valeria continued to talk about her life. She told him about the pregnancy, talked about her relationship problems with her son and how she was currently trying to be a better person, in the sense of understanding herself better and loving her son in her own

– The conversation flowed pleasantly, and during coffee time, Thomas gently placed his hand on hers. Valeria blushed, and he leaned in.

– Do you want to be my girlfriend?

– Just like that, all of a sudden?

– And how long should it take? We are no longer those young people we were twenty years ago. We've gone through some major transformations in our lives and, if we like each other, why not give it a try? That's why I took the first step and sent you that bouquet of roses. I did what your Uncle Adamo told you. I stopped and reflected on my life, analysing what I wanted and what I no longer wanted. I'm sure I want to have a relationship with you – Thomas' voice was firm.

– I would love to, but I'm afraid.

– Afraid of what? That it won't work?

– Yes – said Valeria, apprehensive. – I've never been successful in matters of the heart.

– So what? We try. I'm sure that, if it depends on me, you will feel like the happiest woman in the world.

– She felt warmth enveloping her body. She shook her head and sipped the remainder of her wine.

– If that's the case...

– Thomas didn't let her finish. He pulled Valeria's hands forward, and their faces were very close. The kiss was inevitable. Both their hearts raced.

– We're off to a good start – she said, feeling her whole-body tremble.

– Let's leave here. I'll take you with me.

– To your place?

– No. After the divorce, I moved to a flat, right here in Jardins. Who knows, maybe we'll have our own home? At least I won't spend money hiring an architect!

– They both laughed. Thomas asked for the bill, paid, and they left. Handing the car over to the valet in the lobby of the flat, Thomas put his arm around Valeria's waist and whispered in her ear:

– We're going to have a beautiful night of love. I promise.

# Chapter 26

- It had been almost two years since Frederick had arrived in England. He had begun his studies at the university and diligently devoted himself to his studies. His life was limited to studying and studying. From time to time he wrote to Natalia and Adamo. Also, he wrote letters to Americo and sent greetings to Valeria through his uncles and grandfather. He had enjoyed a regional vacation for sightseeing in London.

- He was a handsome young man but very shy and quite reserved. Nevertheless, he had met and befriended two lovely English guys, Edward and Justin. Frederico had some difficulty making friends with girls, and his English friends decided to invite him to travel during the holiday. The journey of eighty kilometres to the capital took an hour and a half.

- Federico gladly accepted. He did nothing but study. When he arrived in London he was delighted. The boys took him to various tourist attractions in the city, including Buckingham Palace, Big Ben, the British Museum, St. Paul's Cathedral and the famous Harrods department store. They saw musicals in theatres located in the bustling Piccadilly Circus, frequented pubs, those typically English pubs.

- On an early Saturday morning, Frederico woke up in good spirits, and his friends invited him for a stroll through

Hyde Park, one of the largest parks in London. Afterward, they would walk through the bustling Portobello Road antique market. It was late winter, and the sun helped alleviate the cold, making the walk enjoyable.

- Frederico loved antiques and agreed to meet his friends near lunchtime. They had already chosen a cozy restaurant further south in Notting Hill.

- He bought his grandfather a fountain pen. Then he bought English china for his aunt. An old lighter for his uncle and a jewellery box for his mother. Federico thought of all the members of his family. He smiled at the memory of Valeria. As time passed, the feeling of rejection diminished and he began to understand the differences with his mother. He was becoming a man, and distance was being a great friend to reflect with total impartiality on his relationship with his mother.

- Federico learned, through letters exchanged with his aunt, that Valeria was dating Tomás, an old flame from the past. The young man smiled happily.

- "Mom has never had a serious relationship with anyone. Now it's time for her to be happy. I also hope to find someone and be happy," he reflected.

- The young man pondered and accidentally bumped into a girl's elbow. She was carrying a package that fell. She brought her hand to her mouth and nervously spoke in Portuguese:

- My God!

- She opened the package and whined:

– The vase I bought for Aunt Alzira shattered. Now what?

– Frederico bent down and helped the girl pick up the shards.

– Forgive me... A thousand times sorry.

– I'm glad you speak Portuguese. It's easier to understand my anger – Olivia said in a raised voice.

– I didn't mean to. I was lost in thought.

– It doesn't matter.

– Of course it matters. You must have bought this for someone special.

– It was a Murano vase for my aunt.

– Let's look for another one.

– I don't have money to buy another one. I spent a handful of pounds on this one – she pointed despondently at the shards.

– We'll find a similar vase. This market is large, and there's a lot to see.

– Olivia felt some revulsion when their hands touched. The boy seemed nice to her, but something inside her naturally repelled him. The young woman threw the pieces into a trash can and walked through the fair, picking up her pace. Federico followed her soon after. He followed Olivia and, when she stopped in front of a stall of Murano pieces, when it was time to choose and open her purse to pay, he saw that there was no money. The vendor replied in English:

– Even if I wanted to sell you the vase, I just sold it to this guy for a higher price – she pointed to Frederico.

– Olivia opened and closed her eyes.

– What's happening with you? Are you going to stalk and torment me?

– Frederico thanked the vendor in English and walked alongside Olivia.

– Take it.

– What is it?

– Your aunt's vase.

– I don't want it, thank you.

– I'll feel better if you accept the gift. I was the one who knocked the other one over.

– No, thank you.

– Olivia spoke nervously, and when she got into this agitated state, her eye twitched slightly inward. Frederico noticed and smiled:

– Are you always so nervous? A bit fiery?

– I have my way of being.

– I'm here in peace. Friend. Can it be?

– Okay. I'm Olivia.

– I'm Frederico.

– He extended his hand, and she didn't shake it.

– How much longer are you going to be upset with me?

– It's over.

– Olivia felt like she knew Federico from somewhere. She had sympathized with him, but something deep in her subconscious refused contact with the boy, it was as if she was taking some risk. She could not understand this feeling.

– I was supposed to have lunch with two friends from college. Can I cancel and have lunch with you? What do you think?

– I need to leave soon. In a month, I'm going back to Brazil.

– Why?

– Because my exchange program lasts for a year. Next month will be a year. I need to return to São Paulo and finish high school.

– How old are you?

– I'm seventeen. And you?


– I'm twenty-one. I also live in São Paulo.

– Are you here for work?

– No. I study economics at the University of Cambridge. I have a few more years of course.

– Do you plan to go to Brazil on vacation?

– I didn't plan to, but now that I've met you, who knows?

– You're cheeky, aren't you? – Olivia grumbled, "You don't know I'm dating anyone!

– Of course, you're not dating. If you were, you wouldn't even talk to me.

– You're right. I don't have a boyfriend.

– Haven't you met anyone in London?

– I have, but guys my age just want to party.

– So I'm already ahead because I'm older, I'm wise, I'm from a good family?

– Olivia laughed.

– You have a sense of humour. You seem shy, but you have a sweet way of speaking.

– I'm polite, I don't bite, and we live in the same city.

– Who knows, someday we'll meet there? When you finish your career, I'll be twenty years old.

– Will you wait for me?

– Wait for what?

– Federico was shy by nature, but when he saw Olivia he felt fearless, daring. He didn't even seem to be himself. There was a natural ease in his speech, as if he had known her for a long time. His empathy for her was instantaneous. Therefore, he was categorical in his response:

– Wait for me to be my girlfriend.

– You're a very bold, young man.

– And you're charming when you're angry. Your gaze wanders sideways.

– Olivia covered her face with her hands, embarrassed.

– Sorry. When I'm nervous, I get cross-eyed. I had surgery, but there's still a trace.

– Frederico took his hand to hers and gently placed them down.

– There's no need to be ashamed. I said it looks charming. I liked it.

– You're just saying that to make me feel good. I don't need your pity.

– I didn't say that because I feel sorry for you. I would never be so rude.

– She smiled awkwardly. She could tell the boy was sincere. They walked through the fair and arrived at the meeting place with their friends. Federico introduced them to Olivia and told them he would have lunch with her. He would meet friends at the hotel later.

– The two said goodbye to the guys and went to the station. They took the metro and got off at Piccadilly Circus. Frederico took her to a nice restaurant.

– The conversation flowed pleasantly, and Olivia still felt that discomfort in her chest.

– He's so handsome, so friendly and polite... He would make a wonderful lover. What makes me feel this tightness in my chest? – she wondered, thinking.

– Federico was delighted. He thought Olivia was a rare gem, a jewel. She was young, but well-spoken, eloquent and up to date with current events. When she was upset, she seemed a little cross-eyed, and Federico found this defect, shall we say, an added charm to the whole.

– In the late afternoon, they agreed to meet again the following weekend. When they said goodbye, their lips almost touched, and Frederico felt a new, different emotion that would disturb his sleep and concentration on studies for the entire following week.

- Olivia felt a thrill of pleasure. She liked the guy, but the discomfort still disturbed her.

- "One hour will pass," she told herself while walking towards the dormitory where she was staying.

- Frederick arrived in Cambridge and wrote a long letter to Natalia. On the lines, he wrote with passion. He told her that he had met a lovely young woman and, strange as it was, he was in love. It had been something like love at first sight. In the last lines he emphasized that he would continue studying and ask the girl to go to his aunt and grandfather's house. He wanted his family to meet Olivia no matter what.

- The guy sealed the letter with his tongue and was radiant. Friends teased him, saying he had turned into someone else. Once reserved and shy, he was now more confident and self-assured.

- Frederico counted the hours until the next weekend. They arranged to meet at a cafe near Trafalgar Square.

- Olivia wrote to her aunt and father. Although she was one step closer to a better understanding with her mother, she found it a little difficult to write directly to Arlete.

- She was happy, she had fulfilled her dream of studying in England and realized that, although she loved the arts, she was business inclined. She had worked part-time in a department store and realized she wanted to study business administration. Theatre was a thing of the past. Now she was ripe and ready for a new life.

- She had also commented on the meeting with Federico, but without much enthusiasm. Although she felt butterflies in her stomach when their lips almost met, there was that uneasiness that wouldn't leave her alone. Perhaps the comments about Federico were more of a fact in the letter than a passionate note.

– The week passed, and Frederico travelled to London. They spent the day together and had a great time. After leaving the Wax Museum, Frederico went straight to the point:

– Why do I feel you're so distant?

– I'm too young to have a lover and... – he interrupted her with kindness in his voice:

– I didn't ask you to date. I'm saying I feel you're distant. If I want to hold your hand, you repel me. Why?

– I don't know, Frederico. Fear.

– Fear of me?

– I think so, I don't know. It's something that bothers my chest – she pointed. – I swear I like you, but I feel a strange, odd thing, as if you're going to do something bad to me.

– I can't believe it. I've been so respectful, so gentlemanly.

– I know – Olivia was red. – I confess that you're a really nice guy. I like your company, but there's this strange thing. I can't explain.

– Perhaps I go to the pot too thirsty. You're leaving next week and it's not fair for you to go away and wait three years for me, even if I can visit you on my vacations.

– It's not that. I swear it's not.

– Frederico abandoned the protocol and planted a cinematic kiss on her. Olivia let herself be embraced, and in that moment, she felt no repulsion, no fear, nothing. On the contrary, she felt her chest expand and warm up. Her legs went weak, and she had to lean her body against the wall behind her. She was ecstatic.

– "Wow!"

– Did you like it?

– If I liked it? I loved it!

– He hugged her tenderly.

– I'm in love with you, Olivia.

– Don't you think it's all too fast, Federico? We hardly know each other. I'm going back to Brazil and who knows when we'll see each other again.

– I'll do everything possible to see you, believe me.

– I don't want to interfere with your studies. You're studying at a prestigious university; you can't lose focus.

– I won't lose focus; quite the opposite. Knowing that I have you by my side, even from a distance, supporting me, writing to me, answering my calls... Well, Olivia, I'll study with even more determination.

– Really?

– Of course, I am. Look, I promise I'll talk to your dad. At the end of the year, I'm going on vacation to Brazil and we'll announce that we're engaged.

– I'm leaving next week. It's better if we exchange addresses and keep in touch through letters, like good friends.

– No "good friends" talk. I want to be your boyfriend. I've never felt this – he pointed to his chest – for any girl.

– Neither have I, although I haven't met many boys..

– Be my girlfriend, will you?

– Only if you buy me a promise ring.

– Frederico exalted with happiness.

– I'll buy it! I'll buy it!

– Olivia laughed.

– Okay. My flight leaves on Saturday afternoon.

– I'll come on Friday. We can have dinner, and...

– I'll be back on Friday. We can have dinner and... – None of that. You have class and you're going to study. Saturday afternoon you take a train and meet me at the airport.

– Frederico embraced Olivia around the waist, and they twirled down the sidewalk. He kissed her several times on the cheek and lips.

– I love you! They said their goodbyes, and Frederico returned to Cambridge in a state of pure joy. He felt like the happiest man in the world.

– Olivia returned to the boarding house and, even if she didn't want to, it was impossible not to smile. She found a Spanish friend sharing her room.

– Hi, Mercedes. I'm so happy. I'm dating a Brazilian guy who studies at the University of Cambridge. He must be from a good family, and...

- Olivia stopped talking. Mercedes had tears in her eyes.

- What's wrong? Do you happen to know Frederico?

- The girl didn't respond and lowered her head sadly.

- It's not that.

- Then what is it? Let's celebrate! I'm leaving next week and I'm taking our friendship, a fluent Englishman and a boyfriend. Look at all the good things!

- Mercedes sniffed, and one of the teachers approached Olivia.

- Dear, we received a call from Brazil. Your father is unwell, and your family is asking you to return home immediately.

- Olivia covered her mouth.

- My dad?! What happened to him?

- Mercedes intervened, trying to choose her words carefully.

- Your father had a heart attack and was hospitalized. Your aunt called and asks you to return as soon as possible.

- I'll call her now. I need to know what really happened.

- It won't help. Your aunt and your mother are at the hospital. They said your uncle Eugenio has already talked to the school responsible for the exchange, and the ticket has been changed for tomorrow.

- The teacher said nothing. She hugged Olivia and cried. Alzira had called an hour earlier to inform that Osvaldo had suffered a sudden heart attack. They were waiting for Olivia to arrive for the funeral but asked not to tell her the truth.

- Olivia left on the next day's flight, with just enough time to sign the paperwork at the English school and stop by the agency Eugenio had recommended to pick up the return ticket. Although the school didn't say anything, Olivia felt that something very serious had happened to her father.

- She departed without even having the chance to inform Frederico. To make matters worse, the following Saturday, Frederico went to the airport with a small jewelry box in his suit pocket. Hours passed, and Olivia didn't show up.

- As he left Heathrow Airport, he encountered another classmate of Olivia. The Chinese girl struggled to express herself in English, and the only thing Frederico understood was:

- Olivia travels to Brazil on Monday.

- "She left without talking to me! She didn't want to be my girlfriend. She chose to leave and rejected me," he thought, as a tear rolled down his face.

- Frederico felt an unparalleled pain, much worse than the rejection he experienced with his mother. He felt like the worst of men. Olivia had made a fool out of him and didn't even say goodbye. It was the end.

- The young man took a taxi and wandered along the Thames River. He took the velvet box from his coat pocket and shook his head.

– "Why did you do this to me, Olivia? Why? I'll never love again. Never. Love only hurts and destroys. Olivia didn't like me, just like my mother doesn't like me. I was born to live alone. That's my destiny. To be alone."

– The young man was inconsolable. In a fit of anger, he threw the small box into the river. He wiped away his tears with the back of his hands and returned to Cambridge, feeling like the saddest man on the face of the Earth.

# Part III

The achievement of happiness

# Chapter 27

– Arlete smiled with satisfaction. The cafeteria's revenue had doubled since she took over the business from her sister and aunt.

– I'm good at this – she said proudly.

– So good that I'm thinking of handing over the entire business to you – added Alzira.

– No! – she protested. No way. It was you who started the business. You started with a small salon in São Bernardo and today you have a network of franchises.

– The thing is, now I want to focus on writing recipe books. It's an old dream, as you well know.

– Arlete sighed. – You're right. Ever since you were young, you've wanted to write a recipe book. The publisher's invitation came at the right time.

– I won't have time to manage the stores. Aunt Lurdes will be my assistant. There are recipes that only her mind has kept. There are many things I forgot.

– Arlete laughed. – Aunt Lurdes has an enviable memory. She'll reach eighty and be more lucid than the two of us combined.

- It's true. But I'm so happy for you! - Alzira was emotional.

- Why?

- Well, Arlete, you stopped working to take care of the house, your husband, and your daughter. The years passed, and you became a widow. Olivia is going to graduate as a business administrator. You emerged from a deep depression and now have become a businesswoman.

- Arlete gave a half-smile. - What could I do? When Osvaldo died, I felt the ground disappear beneath me. After twenty years of a relationship, I lost my partner. I entered into a profound sadness. I wished to die alongside him.

- And leave Olivia orphaned by both father and mother?

- I got the strength, I don't know from where. I thought about my life and my daughter. Obviously spiritual knowledge helped me a lot to overcome all this pain. I confess that I think of Osvaldo every day. The longing is immense, you have no idea.

- Imagine, - affirmed Alzira. - I love Eugenio above all, but if life decides that he goes first, I also realize that I will miss his company a lot. However, I have the belief that life is eternal, and this life is just a passage with a predetermined time. It makes my heart feel less heavy.

- That's what I feel today: a less heavy heart. I dreamed of Osvaldo the other day. He was well - energetic and working, welcoming newly departed victims of accidents.

- I also dreamt of him once.

– Really? What did you dream about? – Arlete was very curious.

– It seems it was that old dream, which I had had for years. Do you remember when I dreamt about a certain Malachi?

– I do. This nightmare has populated your mind for many years.

– After a while, I dreamt about that friend – Alzira pondered for a moment – her name was Lolla. It was she who clarified a series of events related to my past life. Malaquias had been her boyfriend – she pointed to Arlete – and then you met Osvaldo and fell madly in love with him.

– Arlete nodded, and Alzira continued:

– Osvaldo owned lands, and you both had a daughter. Sometime later, you decided to take a trip, and the ship was raided. You and Osvaldo died, and I took care of the girl. Needless to say, the girl was Olivia. After a few years, you reappeared, with no memory and wanting money from your daughter. She was frightened by your dementia and went away.

– I vaguely remember when you told me about this dream.

– Malachi appeared, your old boyfriend, who wanted to prove that the daughter was his to keep the land. I challenged him and he ran away. It seems to me that you tricked a couple of poor farmers and took their land. The last time I dreamed, Lola assured me that Malachi had been reincarnated as Olair, our father.

– If we had any unresolved connection from the past with our father, I believe we sorted it all out in this life. My happy marriage made me see my father from a different angle. A father can only give us what he has.

– I also understood why he treated us that way. And Mom contributed a lot to him having that stupid way of being.

– Mom never took a stand, never had an active voice. If she had shouted and challenged him at some point during the marriage, perhaps everything would have been different.

– Today, looking back – Alzira said –, I see that everything was fine. We had the father and mother we deserved; we had the life our spirit attracted by the stance over many lifetimes.

– Arlete nodded up and down.

– I know that if I had to stay on this planet, it's because my spirit needs to mature a series of ideas and concepts. Today, I am an independent woman, living on my salary, working, and feeling useful. I help my daughter...

– Speaking of daughters – Alzira added – your relationship with Olivia improved significantly after Osvaldo's death.

– No doubt about it. There were two alternatives: either our relationship would be ruined or we would become friends. The second alternative won. Olivia's feeling of rejection towards me was overcome with therapy sessions, understanding and respect between the two of us.

– And love – Alzira concluded.

- Without love, we wouldn't have achieved anything. Today, I feel that I love my daughter, and she loves me in her way. Olivia has become an independent woman and is my right hand in business.

- That's why I feel at ease leaving the shops in your hands and pursuing my new career as a cookbook writer.

- They hugged each other emotionally.

- Alzira, you are a dear sister, but you were and always will be my great friend. I owe much of my personal transformation to your friendship and Eugenio's affection.

- We love you both very much. I didn't have children, and I feel a bit like Olivia's mother. After Osvaldo's death, I felt that we became closer.

- We've formed a beautiful family. The affection that emanates and circulates among us is priceless. It's our love that helps me overcome the adversities of everyday life.

- Alzira lowered her voice:

- Thinking about dating again?

- No.

- Don't you miss having a companion? - she asked, curious. - After all, you haven't even reached fifty years old. There's plenty of life left to live.

- My share of life was burned with Osvaldo - Arlete said with kindness in her voice. - Osvaldo was the great love of my life. I have already experienced this love and I don't miss holding on to someone. As I believe that life continues after the death of the body, I know that I will meet Osvaldo again and our spirits will live together, as long as the feeling of love allows us to do so.

- You move me speaking like this. It's a beautiful declaration of love.

- Today, I don't feel like a sad woman. Quite the opposite. I feel happy and fulfilled. I loved and was loved for years. Osvaldo was a gift that life gave me. I have nothing to complain about.

- But there's one or another admirer who is infatuated with you. The other day, the bank manager called and thought I was you - Alzira commented. - He was all shy and when he realized I wasn't you, he was puzzled.

- I value myself; I know that I attract attention, but I don't miss anyone. I lived my marriage within the principles of love, respect, and fidelity. Now I want to work and find pleasure in small things. I want to read a book without being bothered, cook for my daughter, wait for her to get married one day and give me grandchildren...

- - After Olivia came back from England, she didn't go out with any boy. Why is your heart so closed?

- Hey, aren't you her friend, doesn't Olivia trust you with absolutely everything? - Arlete poked, jokingly.

- She tells me a lot, and she claims that everything she confides in me is also told to you. One day - Alzira put her finger to her chin - Olivia told me she fell in love with a guy in London.

- That's what she told me too. It's been so long ago! She's going to be twenty-five and she doesn't want to have anything to do with anyone.

– Do you think she still dreams about that guy?

– I don't know, Alzira. I don't get involved in that department. I respect my daughter as I respect you.

– Speaking of Olivia, where is she?

– At the university. They have to meet with a group of students to submit their thesis.

– We have many joys to come.

– I hope so – agreed Arlete. – I hope so.

– Olair sat on the curb. He was tired. He had been wandering the planet for so long that he had even lost count of how many years he had been disembodied. Evanildo came over and sat down next to him.

– A penny for your thoughts.

– Olair smiled.

– I'm tired. This revenge against Rodinei and Gisele has exhausted me.

– Are you going to give up now? We're almost achieving our goal.

– They already have a miserable life. Rodinei's bar was robbed; the thieves broke into the safe and took all the money he had. Rodinei didn't want to keep money in the bank. He had a trauma from that government that dipped into everyone's money.

– Evanildo ran the tip of the knife along his chin, thoughtful.

- And the goat lost all his money and one of the robbers shot Gisele. She became paralyzed. They have a very difficult life.

- What good does our revenge do? We stay on the lookout, imagining, devising a way to harm them. And yet, we learn that life gives to each person according to his or her deeds. You both reaped what you sowed. You and I are just spectators.

- We left them with a heavy feeling in their heads and discomfort. Nothing more.

- Why should I continue watching these two suffer? I don't even remember our differences anymore, man - Olair spoke with a slow voice.

- He was very tired. In these almost thirty years since he discarnated, he remained stuck in time. He staked out Rodinei's house and invented a diabolical plan to take revenge on him and Gisele. But, for some reason Olair couldn't explain, his heart told him that everything was right, and he was feeling in his own skin what he had done to Rodinei and Gisele in the past.

- Memories of the past life were coming in fragmented, sometimes truncated form. Olair was trying to implement a plan for revenge, but it didn't take off. It was only in the mind.

- Evanildo also tried and failed. Every time he thought of hurting the couple, he remembered his beloved, Das Dores. And that, from where Das Dores was, he sent energies of balance and well-being to his loved one Evanildo.

- He did not understand how he received these vibrations; however, the moment they approached his aura, he stopped putting into practice his innumerable projects of revenge.

- Until the robbery, the safe theft, and the shooting happened. This sad episode occurred almost ten years ago. At least, over time, the couple's situation softened the tough hearts of the tough guys. Olair looked at Rodinei and saw how he dedicated himself to his wife, confined to a wheelchair. It made him think about Josefa's illness and how much he had neglected his wife.

- Evanildo watched Rodinei's efforts and began to sympathize with his rival. But Rodinei and Gisele underwent significant transformations. Through pain, both changed their outlook on life.

- They started again from scratch. Luck was that he had the house, the same house that once belonged to Olair and that he had spuriously taken from him. Rodinei pawned the house, took money from *Caixa Econômica* and recovered from the robbery. The money from the bar was not much, but it was enough to pay expenses and the main thing: the settlement that served his wife.

- Yes, after some time, he and Gisele formalized their relationship. They married, and she became a less petty and less arrogant woman. Time made her lose the voluptuous shapes and the peachy skin on her face. She learned that the body is nothing more than an instrument to guide us in this world. Taking care of it is our responsibility, but excessive care and undue vanity hinder our spiritual growth.

- Gisele learned this in the saddest way possible. The bullet hit her spine, and she lost the use of her legs. She spent the day at the cash register of the bar, inside a small armored glass house.

– The love she had for Rodinei was genuine. And his love for her as well. They lived their lives like this. Olair chewed on a twig, spat on the ground, and commented:

– They've had so much trouble that I don't have the desire to seek revenge anymore. I wasted too much time in this world that is no longer mine.

– And your family? – Evanildo asked.

– I never had any affinity with my daughters. I threw them out of the house, tried to swindle them and keep the house for myself. And what was the point of all this? Nothing. I lost everything: house, family and I can't even imagine if they are still in this world.

– They're still alive and well – a voice behind him said.

– Olair was startled and jumped up. Evanildo did the same and stopped the fishmonger.

– Who are you?

– Don't you remember me, Olair? – Laila asked.

– He stared deep into her eyes, scratched his chin, and said:

– You came to talk to me a few years ago, didn't you?

– Lola nodded and repeated the same phrase she had said before:

– Your fleshly body died. Your spirit is still alive. Simple as that. The death of the body is not the end of life. Life never exhausts. It is eternal!

– Now I remember! Was it Josefa who sent you? Right.

– How is she?

– She's fine. She recovered from her illness. She learned to value herself more, took courses, participated in experiences and today she studies and works in a Colony near the planet.

– I'm glad she's doing well.

– Wouldn't you like to come with us?

– No. I have no affinity with Josefa. I don't want to go.

– And how long will you keep wandering in this world? Have you noticed your condition? Do you see how

– It's true. I haven't seen myself in ages. Am I really that worn out? – Olair wondered silently.

– Laila nodded.

– Come, Olair. Look at your image reflected in the mirror.

– Olair awkwardly approached and almost screamed in terror at the sight of his image. He was no longer that portly and to some extent handsome, rustic type of man from years before, with unkempt, upright, white hair. The skin was blackened and had several blemishes. The suit, or what might be called one, was a soiled garment, as if he were wearing a patch of rags. And he was thin, very thin.

– This can't be me – he said, disturbed.

– Of course it is.

– Maybe this mirror is bewitched – Evanildo suggested.

– It's not – Laila replied. – The mirror reflects the real state of your spirits. Want to see yourself?

– Evanildo shook his head.

– No way.

– Olair was devastated. He felt lost and aimless. Lola signalled and another spirit appeared in the form of a woman. She was a very beautiful woman, young, dark-skinned and dressed in *cangazo*. Her short, black, curly hair bounced over her shoulders. The eyes were two large, shiny black jabuticabas; the mouth was full and well defined.

– The woman approached, and Evanildo widened his eyes.

– Das Dores!

– It's me, my dear.

– Evanildo felt a lump in his throat. He cleared his throat.

– I see you! How nostalgic!

– I missed you so much, too. I miss your embrace.

– He shivered. It had been so long since he had seen Das Dores that he could hardly believe the scene.

– Das Dores...

– Come live with me. The time has come to let go of the desire for revenge. Why commit to sad situations in the future? Come with me, and let's plan our new life. We have much to learn and live. Give me your hand.

– Evanildo looked at his friend of many years, attempting a farewell.

- I think our friend here will stay alone. I can't stand being here anymore, stuck in this world.

- Olair shrugged.

- Go your way, my friend. Go with your partner to a life of dignity.

- Do you want to come with us? - Das Dores invited.

- Come with you?

- Yes. I feel that you will really like our city. And you don't need any documents. You can enter with me and live close to us.

- Olair's eyes shimmered with emotion. He looked at Laila.

- You're a free spirit. You can live wherever you want, as long as the chosen place is compatible with your energy.

- I feel so lonely that the only friend I have is Evanildo. I'd like to leave with them.

- Then go - replied Laila. - Venture into the new. Go take care of your spirit's health.

- Olair nodded and left with the couple. Laila smiled happily.

- Now I just need to have a little chat with Taviño and then with Olivia. Otherwise, everything is going as expected!

# Chapter 28

– Lolla approached a young man and touched his shoulder. Taviño jumped in surprise.

– What are you doing here? Again? – he asked.

– It's me again. I became the nanny of a disembodied rebel. What do I do? This kind of work has shown me what a spirit should not do when living in the world of erraticity.

– Why don't you leave me alone?

– Because I like you.

– Taviño felt his chest open.

– Why do you like me?

– Because I like, that's all. Liking is not explained – replied Lolla.

– No one has ever liked me.

– Maybe in this life.

– My father and mother never cared about me. Then I met Valeria. The little affection she gave me made me fall in love.

– That ended. You passed away and Valeria continued to live on the planet.

– Are you going to be trapped in this world for many more years? Isn't this tiredness enough, this life of going from nowhere to nowhere?

– What good does it do me to follow you? I don't remember acquaintances who appreciate me.

– Don't you remember Anita, your nanny?

– Taviño opened his mouth and smiled.

– How could I forget Anita? She was the only good thing my parents gave me. Anita took care of me, gave me love and affection. She wasn't part of the family, but she liked me as if I were her son.

– Anita passed away a few months ago. Wouldn't you like to visit her?

– Taviño felt tempted.

– I planned to use Marion to annoy Thomas and Valeria. I don't like seeing her with someone else.

– You don't like her because he fell in love with her. Valeria gave you a bit of affection, just like Anita.

– Anita was like a mother to me. Valeria... was a different feeling.

– If Valeria ignited this passion in you, another woman can do the same. What do you say?

– Really?

– Of course. You're a young guy. You still have a youthful spirit.

– Valeria is getting old – said Taviño, inconsolable. – I confess I don't like old women.

– Lolla laughed.

– Valeria is aging according to Earth's years. If you were still on the planet, you would be over fifty years old. – Really? All that?

– Yes. All that.

– Taviño scratched his head, thoughtful. Lolla took advantage of the moment and ventured:

– Leave Valeria aside. She's found love and is very happy. Why don't you come with me? I can guarantee that you will live with Anita. Then, as time goes by, maybe you'll become interested in someone else?

– Okay. I'm not one to be thrown away.

– You're not. But first you must leave this world. You have no connection to the planet for now. You need to take one more step for your growth, for the development of your spirit.

– If that's the case, I'll go. But before that, can I do something?

– What is it?

– Can I say goodbye to Valeria?

– Hum, hum.

– Taviño approached Valeria and gave her an affectionate kiss. Then he held out his hand to Lola and they disappeared into the room.

– Valeria felt a pleasant sense of well-being, and in her mind came the image of Taviño.

– My God! How many years! I hope you're doing well.

- Talking to yourself?

- Yes, dear - she stretched up and kissed Thomas on the lips.

- Who do you hope is doing well?

- Wow, I remembered a boyfriend I had when I was fifteen.

- Mmm, look at my jealousy! What a story to remember and cry about your childhood sweetheart?

- Valeria laughed.

- It's not a childhood boyfriend. Taviño was a boyfriend from adolescence.

- And where is this guy now?

- Oh, you can relax. Taviño died when I was fifteen. It's been a long time.

- Better that way.

- Look at you talking! - Valeria said and patted Thomas' shoulder.

- Let him stay on the other side, and we stay on this side. Well, one less competitor.

- What a competitor, nothing! Even if Taviño were alive, I only have eyes for you. I love you!

- Thomas opened his eyes and smiled, showing his white and perfect teeth. He requested:

- Say it again.

- I only have eyes for you. I love you.

– He jumped on top of Valeria and kissed her several times on the lips.

– I'm the happiest man in the world!

– Valeria disentangled herself from her partner and got out of bed.

– The happiest man in the world needs to go to work.

– I wanted to date you a little longer.

– Later. Now we have to get ready for another day. I have three clients, a project I'm leaving with white hair, and later we're having dinner at Dad's house.

– Has Frederico returned from vacation? I thought he would come back next month.

– Valeria nodded as she put on her bathrobe.

– I thought so too. It seems he received an invitation to give a lecture at the university. After becoming an advisor to the Minister of Economy, it's a lecture here, a class there.

– Frederico is a smart man. Who knows, he might climb higher in the federal government?

– All indications are that he will. I rejected this son and today I love him unconditionally.

– I'm glad you saw the good man you brought into the world.

– Nothing like a little therapy and spiritual treatment. Today I understand a lot. I learned to accept myself unconditionally and to love my son in the same unconditional way. We don't have a traditional mother-son relationship, but the important thing is that we love and respect each other.

– Then she went to the bathroom. Thomas lifted his body onto the bed, reached out and grabbed the remote control. He flipped through the channels until he reached the news channel. He followed the weather forecast, the report on Rio de Janeiro's preparations to host the Pan American Games and other news from the country and the world.

– Then he got up, opened the window and let in the sun. He smiled and stretched. He was on his way to the bathroom when he heard that famous little song in which the announcer interrupts the program to give breaking, and usually unpleasant, news to the population. The reporter was standing in front of a beautiful mansion on the outskirts of Los Angeles, in the United States:

– Confirmed. Actress Marion Krystal was found dead by one of her employees at her home here in Los Angeles. The 51-year-old actress, married to Russian producer Pavel Medved, the Bear, was away from the screen recovering from an accident that disfigured her beautiful face on the set of her latest film. The body of the actress will be veiled...

– Valeria emerged from the shower with a towel wrapped around her body and another towel drying her long reddish hair. She saw Tomás sitting on the bed, bleary-eyed watching TV. Before she could ask what had happened, she saw on the screen a picture of Marion and, next to it, the year of birth and death.

– Marion has died?

– Yes. She was found dead by one of the household staff.

– Could it have been a heart attack? After all, after that strange accident two years ago, Marion disappeared from the spotlight.

– I think it might have been. I'll call Alice. She may have more information.

– Thomas called his daughter. Alice now lived in the Caribbean with her husband and was not aware of her mother's death. Thomas hung up the phone.

– And? – Valeria inquired.

– Nothing. Alice didn't know about the death. They hadn't spoken for a long time. After Marion married the Russian producer, she forgot she had a daughter. She always put her career above everything.

– That's right. Marion always wanted to be a star.

– Yeah.

– Dear, do you want to go to the funeral?

– No. Marion and I were married for a while and had a daughter. After the years, she wanted nothing to do with Alice and pursued her career in Hollywood. She married the Russian producer. We don't even have any assets in common. Anything. I'd rather you go with me to a church. Let's light a candle for her soul.

– I agree with you. A candle and a prayer is the best thing Marion can receive at this time.

– Valeria and Thomas' heartfelt act helped a little to ease the drama Marion had gotten herself into. After all, what had happened to her all these years?

- After her marriage to Thomas and the birth of their only daughter, Marion invested in her international career. She considered Brazil a small country, light-years away from the professionalism that the American film industry offered. She separated from her husband and left Alice in the care of nannies and governesses. She met the Russian producer and, with him, made a name for herself in world cinema.

- Marion was not a bad actress, but she had an arrogant attitude, she was stupid with her fans and her beauty was no longer the same as in her youth. She refused to play the role of a mother or grandmother. She always wanted to play the roles of a sexually attractive woman: in one film she was the seductress who destroys homes; in another, she was the single, well-rounded executive who made guys go crazy for her. Audiences grew tired of the uniformity of roles and her popularity began to wane.

- Roles became scarce, and Pavel managed to get her a kind of "comeback." Marion agreed to play the role of a poor and widowed mother struggling to get her son into a good university.

- She underwent plastic surgery, liposuction, and dyed her hair. She shaved off about ten years and became truly beautiful again. It was supposed to be a triumphant return to the screen, and there were even whispers that she could win the long-awaited Oscar.

- During the start of filming, Marion demanded that her dressing room have two air conditioning units. The technicians informed her that the trailer was not suitable to be adapted to receive two air units. If she wanted to, she would have to use a smaller dressing room, or even share with other actresses, to make hers fit her requirements. As expected, she stamped her foot and demanded that both teams be set up immediately. This was done. Two days later, while preparing to film, one of the devices shorted out and the trailer caught fire. Marion tried to get out, but was trapped and suffered third-degree burns that damage the muscles and bones in her face.

- After three surgeries and knowing that her face would never be the same again, Marion swallowed a whole blister of tranquilizers. Her husband and the family doctor released a statement to the press that her death was due to a heart attack.

- Her death made headlines in major media outlets worldwide. Fans made pilgrimages to her mansion's gate and placed flowers and candles along the fence. Due to her disfigured face, the wake was held with the casket sealed, and she was buried in a cemetery near Los Angeles, famous for housing the remains of cinema, music, and television celebrities.

- To the world, Marion died of sadness and had a place in the sun. Her fans were sure she would shine eternally in heaven. They were wrong. Marion could fool the media and the fans. But she could not fool herself. As soon as the flesh body died, her perispirit opened her eyes and she could not move her arms or legs. She would like to speak, but the words wouldn't come out. She wanted to scream, kick and get up, but nothing. His perispirit remained attached to his body and, to his despair, he "attended" the wake and the burial. When the coffin was placed in the mausoleum, she panicked. The darkness was total. She heard other voices in the distance, calling for help. They were tormented spirits attached to the physical body, just like her.

– Days passed and Marion's flesh body began to enter a state of decomposition. At first, the unbearable smell made her nauseous. Then she got used to the putrid smell. The worst was yet to come. Marion felt her body rotting and maggots feeding on her dead flesh. It would still take a few years for her silver cord to be disconnected and for her to be picked up for help in the astral.

– Here in Brazil, in a small town in the interior, a lady watched the news and laughed. Trapped by the events of the past and on a pair of crutches, Laura swore:

– You tried to kill me. I hope you suffer and wait for me. When I pass away, I'll find you, demon.

– The scene of the accident, many years ago, came vividly to her mind, and Laura felt anger. A spirit approached her and whispered:

– Enough of so much anger. You reaped the results of your actions. For many lifetimes, you and Marion have accused and hurt each other. But, as we have eternity ahead, someday, obviously, you will change.

– Laura didn't feel the presence of the spirit. She muttered something and downed a glass of vodka. It would still take another life to cleanse the anger she harboured for Marion from her heart.

# Chapter 29

– Olivia was radiant. The corrective and definitive surgery on her eye was a tremendous success. There was no trace of strabismus anymore. She became more confident, and her self-esteem soared.

– A lover of the arts, she realized that she had a knack for business administration and managing the family's affairs. She joined forces with her mother, and together they expanded Alzira's cafeterias to all the capitals of the country through a franchising system.

– I'm so glad you gave up the desire to be an actress – sighed Arlete after checking the balance sheets sent by the franchisees.

– That phase has passed, Mom. I Continue to love the arts. I'm thinking of opening an art gallery.

– An art gallery?

– Yes – replied Olivia, smiling. – My artistic side has manifested through painting. It's challenging to secure sponsorship, so I've decided to exhibit my paintings in my gallery. This way, I'll contribute to the spread of culture in our city and give a chance to artists who can't get their works into already established galleries. As you can see, art continues to nourish my spirit.

– Arlete approached her.

– You've matured a lot in recent years.

– After Dad passed away, I realized I needed to be more grounded and help you.

– Arlete was about to speak, but Olivia interrupted.

– I used to think I could only have a connection with the arts if I were an actress. Then I realized that art manifests itself in various ways. I could be a musician, poet, actress... I decided to learn painting techniques, and it brings joy to my soul. In day-to-day life, I've noticed that I'm somewhat like you, Aunt Alzira, and Aunt Lurdes.

– Like how?

– We're natural entrepreneurs.

– Arlete smiled.

– That's true. I only realized this skill after Osvaldo died. Until then, I took care of him, you, and the house. Nothing more.

– Nothing more? Olivia asked, surprised. – You've always been organized, Mom. You managed the household budget, took care of the maid, never let anything be lacking at home. Dad and I never had to make a single purchase. The pantry was always full, food was always on the table, the house was always clean and fragrant. You learned through experience to be organized, and you transferred that acquired knowledge over the course of your marriage to the business. You became a successful businesswoman.

– You helped me a lot, too.

– I won't take away your merit. There have always been conflicts between us. Arlete felt awkward. She didn't know what to say. Olivia continued:

– Dad was the one who mediated between us. He diffused our fights, lightened the burden of our arguments. After he was gone, I started relying more on my conscience. If we started an argument, I immediately tried to imagine what Dad would do. If that didn't work, I went to my room and thought. I learned that I will never change your way of being, and I have to like you just the way you are. Loving, Mom, is feeling good for the other without conditions. In love, there's no "if": if you were more like this, more like that... You are who you are, and it's up to me to understand your way and choose to live with you or not. I chose to be by your side and strengthen our bonds of affection. Today, besides being your daughter, I am also your friend.

– A tear escaped from the corner of Arlete's eye. She hugged her daughter tightly.

– I've always loved you. Always. I think I had an authoritarian way and wanted you to be everything I couldn't be. I had a childhood and adolescence marked by violence and censorship. My father was a brute and only communicated with me and your aunt through the belt and slaps in the face. Unfortunately, my mother couldn't stand up to him and protect us. Alzira and I had to fend for ourselves.

– If you hadn't had the parents you had, maybe the strength of both of you would still be hidden behind some caprice. You two didn't have time to be spoiled. You had to learn the hard way to believe in your own strength. Look at you today: you became a woman loved by your husband in the years you were together, had the opportunity to learn a trade and succeed in your work, and you have me, who will always be by your side.

– No. You'll soon be dating and getting married.

– Can we go out and flirt together, what do you say?

– Is that a proposal to make to your mother? – Arlete was astonished. Olivia laughed.

– You're approaching fifty and you're independent. I guarantee there are plenty of men like this – she made a youthful gesture with her fingers – wanting to date you, Mom.

– I don't want that. I've already had my share of love with Osvaldo.

– You still have a lot to live. Wouldn't you like to find a companion for your old age?

– No way. I loved and still love your father. I believe in the continuity of life after death, and I know we will continue together. I don't miss it, and I have no desire to find a companion. I have acquaintances who became widows and remarried. I have nothing against it because I'm in favour of people being happy. They were unhappy and found in their new husbands' ideal companions for this new phase of life. I don't need and don't want that. I am happy and feel fulfilled with you, with my work, and with the company of my sister and my aunt. Eugenio is a great brother-in-law and fills the role of a man in the house. When I have a problem to solve at home, I call him. Besides, you'll get married and have children one day. I want to be a present grandmother!

– You speak with such conviction!

– But that's what I feel. You will get married.

– I don't know – observed Olivia.

– You need to go out more. You only care about work and painting your canvases. A twenty-six-year-old girl needs to have friends, go out, go to clubs. Isn't that what they say nowadays?

– Olivia laughed.

– It is, Mom. But I don't like clubs. I'm more of a homebody.

– And do you think a husband will fall from the sky?

– Why not? You and Dad didn't meet in an ordinary way?

– Arlete opened a huge smile.

– It was magical. I wasn't a flirt, and your father came to me. He rang the doorbell at home.

– The same happened with Aunt Alzira. She didn't find Uncle Eugenio like that, out of nowhere?

– True. Maybe we have that luck with our loves. The same can happen to you.

– That's why, Mom, I'm not in a hurry.

– Are you not in a hurry, or have you not forgotten that young man?

– Olivia avoided the subject.

– What young man?

– The one you met in England. Wasn't he Brazilian? Hasn't he come back?

– I don't know.

– Nowadays, we have the internet, we have social networks. It's so easy to find or reconnect with someone from the past.

– I only know his name, Mom. Frederico. I don't know his last name, marital status, nothing.

– Arlete winked at her daughter:

– Why don't you get in touch with your friends from the exchange program?

– This story is part of the past. The last thing I want now is to find a boyfriend. I'm going to talk to Aunt Alzira about the gallery project, and I'm also going to enroll in that postgraduate course.

– Why take a postgraduate course?

– Because I love knowledge, Mom. The more I learn, the more confident I feel to take as many steps as necessary for my growth, whether personal, emotional, or spiritual.

– You're talking differently today.

– Besides being well with myself, I also met with Célia.

– Arlete nodded up and down.

– Célia and Ariovaldo are two angels who appeared in our lives. Alzira and I will always be grateful to them.

– I was very happy that you and Aunt Alzira gave one of the cafeterias for them to manage.

– They deserve much more. For us, one more or one less store will not interfere with our prosperity gauge. Ariovaldo is an honest and competent man. I feel that this gesture of mine and Alzira's was a recognition of the help they have always given us over all these years.

– You are very generous, indeed. The more you give, the more life repays you, be it in health, money, or even family harmony. I miss Dad a lot, but we are a happy family.

– They hugged each other, and with a great sense of well-being, Olivia went to her room and fell asleep.

– She dreamed. She opened her eyes and saw herself next to Lolla.

– How I missed you! – Olivia said and hugged the friendly spirit.

– Lolla embraced her tenderly.

– I see that your progress is moving at a fast pace.

– At least I learned to judge less. I stopped being critical of myself and others. Today, I understand and accept my mother just the way she is. You know, Lolla, if my mother wanted to deprive herself of my friendship, I would distance myself from her without resentment or grudges.

– Arlete has always loved you. In a past life, you had a great disappointment with her. You believed that your mother had died in the same accident that killed your father. When you saw her, after many years, you couldn't believe that Arlete had stayed.

– Memory-impaired and lost in the world. Her low self-esteem contributed to her not accepting the facts as they were. She convinced herself that she had been abandoned by her mother and remained that way, even after passing away.

– Today, I realize that I was blind. I didn't want to see reality.

– Do you understand why you were born with a slight strabismus?

– Olivia nodded.

– Reincarnation is a balm for our spirit. Through it, we have the opportunity to face the same situations, with the same group of people with whom we had disappointments in the past. As we take a step further in expanding our consciousness, it becomes easier to untie the knots of past enmities and misunderstandings. Each incarnation clarifies our consciousness and enlightens our spirit.

– Today, I see my mother as a great friend. I think the remnants of the past have disappeared. My spirit has learned new skills, and now I manage the family business. My connection with the arts will continue through paintings.

– Your progress is spectacular, Olivia. I feel an unparalleled happiness in seeing you well. However...

– When you speak like that, it's because there's some surprise.

– Indeed. You reconciled with your mother. And what about the love from another life?

– You mean him?

– Hmm, hmm. You reunited, and you rejected him. Are you still traumatized?

– He killed me. Someone who kills has no love.

– Are you sure he killed you?

– After I died, I saw the scene.

- Did you see the scene, or did you see what you wanted to see?

- I don't understand, Lolla.

- We tend to see only what we believe. Sometimes the truth is right in front of us, but in the face of our illusions, we don't see it. Avoiding contact with the truth hurts the soul and delays the spirit's evolution process. Although we have all of eternity to develop our lucidity and intelligence, it doesn't hurt to have the courage to see the facts as they are, without the weight of feelings and without the veil of illusions.

- You speak as if I haven't seen the truth.

- So, let's see. Close your eyes.

- Olivia agreed. In moments, she saw the scene she so feared. She and Frederico were in love. They were passionately in love and were going to marry in a few months. However, another man, Frederico's jealous brother, had fallen in love with her. Faced with her refusal to date him, the man became desperate and pushed her. She lost her balance and fell into a canal. Unable to swim, she began to drown.

- Frederico was far away but saw the scene. He ran and tried to save his beloved. She reached out, but Frederico couldn't save her.

- Olivia opened her eyes, and a thin layer of sweat trickled down her forehead.

- Paco pushed her into the river. Frederico tried to save her, - said Lolla.

- The impression I had was that Frederico was pushing me down, - she said, stunned.

– You were dying. Your body naturally began to sink. Frederico tried to save your life.

– Olivia put her hands to her face, embarrassed.

– I cursed him for years in the Umbral. I believed that the forgiveness he asked for was because he regretted killing me.

– No. Frederico was asking you for forgiveness because he couldn't save you. You saw what you wanted to see.

– Poor guy! He tried to pull me out of those waters,

– and I accused him unjustly. We spent years exchanging unfounded accusations. Oh, Lolla, I feel so ashamed!

– The time has come for you two to meet again.

– Will we have a new chance?

– It depends on you. Life will bring you together. Whether you stay together or not is a matter of free will.

– What is that? – Olivia asked.

– Free will is making choices with lucidity.

– Lolla, what about the guy who threw me into the river?

– After that life, he was reborn and passed away young. Paco reincarnated as Dario and is Frederico's father.

– Olivia covered her mouth.

– Paco gave life to Frederico?

– Yes. After he passed away, Paco felt very

– bad seeing you and Frederico exchanging unjust accusations.

– He felt responsible and wanted to make amends from the bottom of his heart, at least to be forgiven by his brother. Bringing Frederico back to life was a balm for his spirit.

– Where is he now?

– Dario passed away many years ago. He provides assistance

– at a post near Earth, and his perispirit was affected by drug abuse.

– Oh!

– His lungs were damaged, and in a possible return to the planet, he will be born with respiratory system deficiencies.

– Could I see him?

– Not now, Olivia. First, you need to reunite with Frederico and end this adversity. If your reunion ends in a possible agreement, and you decide to live your lives together, Paco – or Dario – will have the chance to return as your son. Eliel, a long-time spiritual friend, will extend the invitation to Dario in a few years. If everything goes according to probabilities, Dario will return to the planet soon.

– Will I be his mother?

– It will be an interesting way to settle past differences. Your spirit has learned to deal with the feeling of rejection. Now is the time to put those teachings into practice. You are learning to direct free will, making increasingly better choices guided by cosmic morality.

– I don't know what my life on the planet would be like without your support. Eliel's help has also been crucial. I've dreamed of him many times in recent years.

– Lolla smiled.

– We are part of a group of disembodied and incarnated spirits who help each other, always in harmony with the greater good.

– When will I reunite with Frederico?

– It all depends.

– Depends on what, Lolla?

– On you embracing the truth and accepting it. If you feel in

– your heart that Frederico was helping you instead of hurting you, you can make a positive choice for the betterment of your spirit.

– I'll try. I swear.

– I trust you, Olivia. I'm sure you will act with clear ideas, without judgment.

– They hugged, and Lolla concluded:

– You need to return to your body. You will wake up soon and have another blessed day ahead.

– Can I ask you a question? – Olivia asked, feeling shy.

– Go ahead.

– How is my father?

– Osvaldo is doing well. It took him some time to accept the end of his last earthly experience. He was very attached to you and Arlete. He overcame the attachment, studied, and now works in the same group as Dario. Soon, I'll be able to arrange a meeting between him and your mother.

– Mom would be very happy. She complains that she doesn't dream about him.

– Because the time for their reunion hasn't come yet. If your mother had contact with Osvaldo a few years ago, she would have experienced a terrible emotional collapse. Imagine reuniting with the person you loved so much in life and being aware that you are temporarily separated? It takes a lot of emotional balance and spiritual knowledge to accept and understand the situation.

– You're right. But knowing that my father is well fills my heart with joy. Can you send him a hug and a kiss from me?

– Of course.

– Tell him, Lolla, that my mom and I love him very much.

– They said their goodbyes, and Olivia went back to sleep. The next day, she woke up excited and full of energy to face another day on Earth.

## Chapter 30

— Lurdes was already over seventy years old and remained very active. No one would say she was that old. She dyed her hair a dark blonde that enhanced her green eyes. Her skin remained silky, although she had never faced a surgeon's scalpel. Excited about her niece's success, she was always by Alzira's side on the cooking shows. It didn't take long for her to become Alzira's stage assistant and also gain national recognition. Lurdes exuded charisma and made a beautiful pair with her niece. The show became a leader in audience ratings from Monday to Friday mornings.

— A student from Olivia's postgraduate course discovered that she was the niece of the famous Alzira from the TV show. Olivia tried to be discreet and rarely spoke about her aunt or the success of the program. However, her classmates bombarded her with questions, and one of the professors invited her to give a brief talk about Alzira's success story.

— Olivia agreed, and the following week, there was another invitation: they wanted her to bring her aunt to give a lecture on business management.

— And how would I know what that is? Alzira retorted.

– It's just for you to go there and talk to the people about your success story, Olivia said.

– You said you've already done that. Why should I go there and repeat everything? Alzira replied.

– I present it from my point of view, Aunt Olivia said in a playful voice. – Today, you're a celebrity! My classmates and the mothers of my classmates love you. What's the harm in going there and talking just a little? Half an hour, at most.

– Take advantage of your uninhibited way of expressing yourself, Arlete added.

– I wasn't like this. I changed over the years, Alzira replied.

– That's exactly why, affirmed Lurdes. – Talking about your life and your past can help many other young people steer their careers.

– Really? – Alzira asked, unsure.

– Of course, Aunt! Tell the students about the exercise that Celia taught you to do years ago. Remember when you wanted to be a teacher, and she showed you that you should make sweets?

– That was so many years ago. I don't know if it's worth talking about...

– Olivia interrupted her with kindness in her voice.

– It's worth it. Many people study just because they study, without enthusiasm. They are not aware of what they want. Your life journey shows that success only happens for those who believe in and love what they do.

– Everyone does that.

– You're mistaken, Aunt. Many people follow other people's advice, forget to consult their hearts. Our society values appearances, and unfortunately, many do what they don't like and lose the joy of fulfilling their souls. Hence the sadness, depression, lack of enthusiasm...

– Alright, agreed Alzira. – I'll do it.

– They scheduled the lecture for the following week.

– Americo had a severe bout of rhinitis and, due to his advanced age, was hospitalized. Nothing serious, just two days in the hospital for various tests to reassure the doctors and the family.

– I'm fine, really. Just because I'm old, they treat me like a child?

– Calm down, Dad, reassured Valeria. – The rhinitis attack was very strong. You've been sneezing a lot, and your lungs can't work when they're so overloaded.

– I'm fine. I still have a life ahead of me.

– I know that.

– There's no need to be treated like a little baby. I enjoy working. I'm Frederico's right-hand man in our organizations.

– We know that too, Adamo added. – However, it's time to undergo a battery of tests again. If everything is normal, Natalia and I will take you for a season in Florence.

– I can't leave now. I have a lot of work.

– Work can wait, Natalia intervened. – If you had a wife, you'd have other plans in mind.

– I'm fine like this, alone.

- Everyone laughed. Valeria continued:

- I'll go with Natalia to the office, and we'll be back shortly after lunch. Adamo will keep you company.

- There's no need. I'm fine alone. I'm not sick.

- If you allow, Adamo said, I need to go to the travel agency to book our return ticket to Italy.

- Are you sure you want to leave?

- I am, Adamo nodded. Natalia and I have thought a lot, and we've come to the conclusion that we want to live in Florence.

- And the office? America asked. Are you leaving my daughter?

- Natalia laughed.

- I'm not leaving your daughter. Now we have the internet, computers... Technology is on our side. I'll manage the projects remotely. And every six months, we'll come back for a season. Do you agree? - Natalia asked, gracefully running her fingers on America's chin.

- He laughed and nodded.

- Alright. You have to follow your heart. Suddenly, he became sad.

- What's wrong, Dad?

- Nothing, Valeria. I was just thinking if my life would be different if I had persevered and pursued my girlfriend.

- This story is over fifty years old! - Adamo exclaimed. - Don't you think it's better to leave it for the next incarnation?

- If I could, I would start it all over again. Age is not a limiting factor for me, Americo replied energetically.

- Everyone agreed, and each went about their business. Americo was comfortably settled in the hospital room. A friendly nurse appeared and measured his blood pressure. Then another came and carefully drew blood from his veins. Americo enjoyed the attention and drifted off to sleep.

- Two hours later, he woke up, and with nothing else to do, he picked up the remote control from the bedside table and turned on the television. He flipped through channels, somewhat disinterested, until he settled on a random channel. A friendly woman in her fifties was hosting a cooking show.

- Americo smiled.

- I don't know how to fry an egg. I admire people who can cook. This woman knows a lot.

- He adjusted the pillows on the bed and raised his body. He stayed there, fascinated by Alzira's teachings. The way she spoke gave the impression that any human could make the same dishes, delicious ones, that she presented.

- At a certain moment in the show, Alzira called her assistant. Lurdes entered, and as the program had an audience, she was applauded and cheered. People loved her.

- Americo paid attention, and at a certain moment, his eyes narrowed.

- Is it who I'm thinking of? - he asked himself aloud.

- A nurse entered the room.

- Mr. Americo, the doctor will come to talk to you shortly. It seems everything is in order. You should be discharged this afternoon, and...

- She noticed that Americo wasn't paying her the slightest attention. She looked at him and then at the television.

- Do you like cooking?

- No. But I think I know this woman.

- Alzira? Her show is a huge success, Mr. Americo.

- He couldn't take his eyes off the screen. He asked:

- Who is the lady next to her?

- That's Lurdes. Known as Aunt Lurdes, the pastry chef.

- Do you know her last name?

- The nurse shook her head. Then she said:

- Oh! One of the nurses brought a celebrity magazine for us to read and pass the time. I think there's a note about Alzira and Aunt Lurdes.

- Could you find that magazine?

- Yes, sir.

- The nurse left, and Americo kept his eyes on the screen.

- It must be her! Aunt Lurdes!

- The young woman returned with the magazine in hand. She opened it to the page and showed it to Americo. Reading the full name and age, he had no doubts: he had rediscovered his youth's girlfriend.

– I need to be discharged today!

– The doctor is coming, and...

– Americo cut her off:

– Now! Go call the doctor now, my girl. I need to get out of here.

– The nurse nodded and went to call the doctor. Americo was trembling like a leaf in the wind.

– Lurdes! You're alive. Do you still remember me?

– The lecture Alzira gave at the university was a success. At the end, she received a standing ovation. Many students had the recipe book under their arms and lined up for her autograph.

– She agreed and told Olivia, – We'll take a while. Call your uncle's cell phone. Tell Eugenio that we'll be delayed.

– Sure, aunt. But I have to go to the courtyard. There's no signal inside the auditorium.

– Alzira started signing the books, and Olivia left. She went to the courtyard, raised her cell phone high with one hand, searching for a signal. Once the device showed a signal, she called Eugenio. After hanging up, she was greeted by a classmate.

– Olivia, your aunt was magnificent in her speech.

– Thank you, Ismael.

– What a life story! Alzira had a tough life, a rough childhood, and became a successful woman. She's an example to follow.

– I think so too.

– I would love to meet her. Can you introduce me to her later? My mom is a big fan and would love to have a signed book.

– Of course. Let's wait for people to leave. That way, you can chat with her a bit.

– Really?

– Of course, Ismael. You're one of the best friends I have.

– I really like you too.

– They hugged, and Ismael asked, – Have you seen the new economics professor?

– No. I was sad to hear that Professor Durval was sidelined due to illness.

– They say this one is good. He studied abroad. He has a Ph.D. in economics.

– For the price we pay for the course, it's only fair to have a competent professional teaching us. Especially in economics!

– He's friends with my dad – Ismael lowered his voice.

– We're hosting a dinner on Saturday. Want to come and meet him?

– I don't know...

– Olivia, you never go out, just work. You're not going to tell me you have work on Saturday night!

– She laughed.

– You're right. I'm becoming a workaholic.

– You need to take a break for leisure. You're coming to dinner with us on Saturday. That's final.

– Alright. I'll come.

– The week passed quickly, and Saturday arrived. In the late afternoon, after preparing some reports, Olivia closed her eyes and sighed. She was a bit tired of just working. But what could she do? She didn't like going out, avoided nightclubs, and turned down all of Ismael's invitations. She preferred watching TV or American series on video. She loved staying at home in the company of her mother.

– She arrived home, tossed her bag on the dresser, and sat on the sofa. She took off her shoes and started massaging her toes. Arlete entered the room and smiled.

– You're home early.

– I decided to stop earlier. It's Saturday, and Ismael is hosting a dinner.

– Are you going out? – Arlete asked, surprised. – Finally.

– Oh, mom. Stop it. I like staying at home.

– But staying at home won't bring a boyfriend.

– And who said I want a boyfriend?

– Arlete approached Olivia and kissed her forehead. She sat beside her.

– Dear daughter, we all want to experience love. We are born to live in groups, in society.

– I don't like going out at night. Those nightclubs play unbearable, irritating music. People drug themselves heavily. I don't blame anyone because everyone is responsible for their choices. But it's an environment that doesn't suit me. There, I said it. Go out with your friends.

– All my friends are married, mom. No one is left.

– At least you have Ismael's friendship.

– It's not the same. Maybe I'll end up like Aunt Lurdes, who gave up on love.

– I feel that your aunt closed herself off due to fear. If she allowed herself to love again, life would undoubtedly bring someone to her. After all, we attract our counterparts with the essence of our energy.

– You could attract someone into your life.

– No, I can't. I already had my love. Your father meant and still means a lot to me.

– Haven't you dreamed about him anymore? – Olivia asked, curious.

– No. Our separation was sad, and I miss Osvaldo to this day. However, I can't deny that, when I became a widow, I felt lost. Your father meant everything to me, and I was overly dependent on him. I asked for his opinion on everything. After some time, I accepted the situation and learned to appreciate my qualities, developing my own strength. That made me feel more capable. Death is irreversible, and accepting it reveals wisdom.

– I admire you a lot.

– Thank you, daughter. Besides, life only allows an encounter between the incarnate and the disincarnate when that meeting benefits both. I feel your father closely connected to us, even after so many years disincarnated. On the day Osvaldo's spirit is emotionally balanced, we can meet.

– Dad's death brought us closer.

– That's fate.

– Olivia took a deep breath and let out a pleasant sigh.

– The conversation is good, but I need to get ready. I have to be at Ismael's house at eight sharp.

– She spoke, stood up, and went upstairs. She took a warm and refreshing shower. Since there was no time to go to the hairdresser, Olivia brushed her long brown hair and made a graceful ponytail. She applied subtle makeup and wore a beautiful strapless emerald green dress, enhancing her neckline. She sprayed a delicate perfume on her neck and wrists. She put on a pair of high-heeled shoes and chose a small purse. She descended the stairs and grabbed the car keys.

– You look very beautiful – Arlete affirmed.

– Thank you, mom. Well, I don't have a set time to return.

– Don't forget to wear your seatbelt. Drive carefully. Don't answer your phone while driving, and...

– Olivia interrupted Arlete with a gentle voice:

– Less, mom. Less.

– She kissed her on the cheek and left. She got into the car, fastened her seatbelt, started the engine, and soon her car disappeared around the corner.

# Epilogue

Olivia arrived at Ismael's apartment at eight on the dot. It was a dinner for a few people – Ismael, his sister, and their parents, along with Olivia and the aforementioned professor. She was warmly welcomed by Ismael's parents.

– Welcome to our home, – Norma greeted.

– Thank you.

Ismael pulled her aside, and they sat on a sofa. Amelinha, Ismael's sister, a friendly eighteen-year-old, greeted Olivia and joined them.

– After dinner, we're going out dancing. Would you like to join us? – Amelinha asked.

– No, thank you. After dinner, I'm going home to rest.

– The night is beautiful. I even counted some stars in the sky.

– Really?

– Yes, Olivia. Ismael told me you're quite the homebody.

– I've outgrown the age for going to clubs. In your age, I used to go out a lot.

– How old are you?

– I'll turn thirty next month.

Amelinha covered her mouth.

– I can't believe it. You don't look your age. What creams do you use?

The three burst into laughter, and soon the missing guest arrived.

Olivia was sitting with her back turned and didn't notice when Norma gently touched her shoulder to make the introduction.

– Olivia, this is our friend, Professor Frederico Calini.

She lifted her face and froze. Over a decade had passed, yet Olivia was sure she was standing in front of Frederico. His hair was starting to turn silver at the temples, and he wore glasses. Otherwise, he remained the same as when she met him in Landres: handsome and elegant.

She tried to stand up but couldn't. Frederico approached and kissed her on the cheek.

– The years have passed, and you've become even more beautiful. How are you, Olivia?

– G-good – she stammered. – And you?

Ismael interrupted:

– I can't believe it! How do you two know each other?

– I met Frederico when I did an exchange program many years ago – Olivia replied.

– And I got stood up by this girl. Unforgettable – Frederico interjected.

Ismael sensed the tension between them and excused himself.

– I'll grab a drink and be right back.

Olivia stood up and smiled.

– At least you remember me. Not bad.

– Mind if we catch up in private? – Frederico invited.

Olivia nodded. Ismael brought a glass of wine for each of them and stepped away. Frederico raised his glass:

– Cheers!

– Cheers!

They sipped the red wine, and Frederico got straight to the point:

– I understand you were very young back then, but I was very saddened by your sudden disappearance.

– I completely understand your position. If I were in your place, I'd feel the same. I did try to find you, but I only knew your first name, nothing else.

Why did you reject me?

– I didn't reject you. – Olivia sighed.

– How not? You vanished and left me. No message, no warning, nothing.

Norma appeared and announced that dinner was served.

– We'll continue the conversation later – Frederico declared.

– Yes.

Dinner proceeded pleasantly. Norma and Bonifacio, Ismael's parents, were cultured and fun people. Frederico talked about how he managed to balance his executive career with teaching. Olivia spoke about the "famous" Aunt Alzira. At the end of dinner, Amelinha said goodbye to everyone to meet her friends at the club.

– It's one of the coolest clubs in the city. It has branches in other metropolises like Florianópolis, Ibiza, and New York – she said excitedly.

Despite the young woman's enthusiasm, the two declined the invitation.

Frederico approached Olivia:

Do you have plans?

– I do.

– Ah, what a shame.

– I have two movies to watch. But I can leave them for tomorrow.

He laughed.

I thought you might have someone.

– I don't.

– I'm also alone. Would you like to go to a bar to continue our conversation?

– I don't like bars, Frederico. Usually, the noise is too much, and we have to shout to talk.

– I know a bistro in the Gardens that stays open all night. It's a cozy place, and there's no noise. We can talk freely.

– Okay.

– Did you come by car? – he asked, considerate.

- I did.

- Leave your car and come in mine. Later, I'll take you to your place.

- You don't have to worry.

- I'm a modern man but with principles considered old-fashioned. I'll take you home, and tomorrow I'll pick you up to get your car.

Olivia said nothing. She was enchanted. They said goodbye to the family and left. Norma nudged her son:

- Do those two have something?

- Look, Mom, if they didn't, you can be sure they will! - exclaimed Ismael.

- They make such a beautiful couple - affirmed Bonifacio.

- I agree - replied Norma.

On the way to the bistro, Frederico and Olivia chatted about trivial things. They talked about the American bubble, the upcoming elections. Nothing too personal. They arrived at the small restaurant and went in.

Indeed, it was a cozy place, decorated in the Provencal French style. The furniture was patinated in white, and the decoration showed excellent taste. They sat at a table towards the back of the bistro. They ordered a sweet tart, sparkling water, and two coffees.

Once the waiter brought the desserts and coffee, Frederico repeated the phrase:

- You disappeared and abandoned me. No message, no warning, nothing.

- I was very upset. On that day of our outing, upon arriving at the dormitory, I was informed that my father had suffered a heart attack and was very ill.

- I kept waiting for our reunion and imagined many answers, hundreds of them. I confess I never imagined this answer.

At least you're telling the truth. I have nothing to hide.

And how is your father? Did he get better?

He died.

I'm sorry. I didn't imagine...

Olivia shrugged:

- When they called me in Landres to inform me, he was already dead. The family hid the truth from me so that I wouldn't lose my balance.

I'm sorry, truly. I imagine how tough it must have been for you.

It was. Shortly after my father's death, I finished high school and went to work. I helped my mother, and some time later, I enrolled in a business administration course.

You wanted to be an artist.

Olivia laughed.

- Who knows, maybe someday? I grounded myself and realized I had a vocation for administration. Today, I am a fulfilled and satisfied professional. As for being an artist, I take canvas painting classes. I dream of opening an art gallery and sponsoring unknown artists without resources.

Your soul is that of an artist; there's no denying it.

Frederico spoke, and their fingers touched. Both felt a small spark.

– Olivia, I have so much to tell you! I would love to see you again.

– Me too.

– Now that I understand your disappearance, everything I felt for you has come back even stronger.

She didn't reply.

You look beautiful!

I had corrective surgery, and I'm no longer cross-eyed.

I didn't mind. I found it a charming feature.

Well, you'll have to find another. This "charm" is no longer mine!

They laughed, and he delicately placed his hands on hers. He brought one to his lips and kissed it.

– Will you give me another chance?

– Let's start from scratch.

Frederico didn't answer. He tilted his head, and their lips touched. A lingering and delicate kiss.

Both felt their hearts beat irregularly.

– Do you want to be my woman?

– Wouldn't that be a girlfriend? – she asked, smiling.

– No. I met you more than ten years ago and never forgot you. I'm thirty-three years old. I don't have time for games.

– I'm not talking about games but about getting to know each other better. I need to know more about you, your life. I want to meet your family, and I want you to meet mine.

– We'll do all that as long as you don't drift away from me again.

They kissed again. From above, illuminated rose petals gently fell onto the couple's aura.

Next to them, the spirit of Lila smiled happily.

– Eliel, my friend. We achieved our goal.

– They reunited, and judging by the color of their auras, they have a long path of love and complicity ahead.

– Let's leave them alone and go.

– Yes – agreed the spirit. – Before that, shall we go to that place? I would like to ease Marion's pain.

Lila nodded. In the blink of an eye, they were in the city of Los Angeles, in the same cemetery where stars like Natalie Wood and Marilyn Monroe were buried. Eliel approached Marion's spirit, still attached to the mortal remains. She still didn't know where she was. She screamed for help, begged for assistance. Eliel let a tear escape from the corner of his eye. Lila touched his shoulder.

– Don't be like this, my friend. We know that other paths would have yielded better results.

– Marion's suicide was an act of rebellion. I understand that she wanted to escape from the situations that were suffocating her soul. I know that, with time, she will learn to cultivate true values.

– Let's pray for her.

They closed their eyes and held hands. They offered a heartfelt prayer, and for a few minutes, Marion stopped feeling pain. She calmed down and fell asleep.

Eliel thanked:

– Thank you, Lalla.

– Nonsense! Marion doesn't need judgment but compassion.

– Indeed – agreed Eliel. – God takes care of everything and everyone with perfection and love. Let's go.

– We will come back in a year – assured Lolla.

The reunion of Américo and Lurdes was touching. The two, well-advanced in age, decided to give love another chance after so many years.

– Let's get married and be happy, – said América.

– No, sir! – protested Lurdes. – I don't want to get married.

– How come? We're almost at the end of our lives! I don't have time for dating and engagement.

– If I get married, I'll be your wife.

– And that's what I want most: for you to become my wife.

– I don't want to be a wife. I want to continue being the independent Lurdes who is with you because she likes you. I don't need your money. Over the years, I matured. When we were dating, I was a naive girl full of dreams. I was raised to marry, have a husband, children, and take care of the house. That's not what happened.

- I've explained a thousand times that Amélia got pregnant and...

Lurdes gently interrupted him.

- I know that, and I understand. I'm not here to judge you. We're all responsible for our choices. I became a strong woman, discarded illusions, and started seeing life as it is. I became more confident and started liking myself more. When I retired, my nieces came to live with me, and life changed completely. We formed a close-knit family, filled with sincere bonds of affection. We started a business, thrived, and became well-off. I'm already over seventy years old, and all I want is a companion. I want to be by your side, América, because I like you, nothing more. No demands, no paperwork.

- People will make comments.

Lurdes shrugged.

- Let them. I'm past the age of caring about society's gossip. If you want to be with me, it'll be on these terms. We'll be free but faithful. But each of us will live in our own home. Spend three days in yours, and then you spend three days in mine.

- That's six days. The week has seven. One day is missing, - counted América.

- I need one day for myself. When a person lives alone, they develop habits over the years. I'll try to adapt to our new life as a couple, but it's crucial that I have one day for myself, taking care of my garden, my plants, reading a book, or doing nothing, just enjoying the moment. Many people have no idea how good it is to be your own friend. I'm too happy with myself.

– But...

Before he could continue, she concluded:

– No buts, not even half but. These are the conditions. If you want to rekindle our relationship, great. If you don't, it's not a problem. We spent fifty years apart. I can spend another fifty with myself!

– You're as feisty as pepper! What a woman!

– And for this reason and many others, the country's most prominent businessman wants to be with me.

They both laughed and kissed each other with love.

– I promise I'll be the most affectionate, romantic, and supportive "boyfriend" you could dream of in your entire life. I love you, Lurdes.

– I love you too, Américo.

In a soap opera–like atmosphere, Thomas pressed Valeria:

– Let's get married.

– Well, well. Aren't we already "married"? – she asked while combing her hair, ready to go to bed. We've been living together for years, but I want to get married for real. Let's do it like my father and Lurdes. No paperwork.

Their case is different.

Different how? Each of us has our own money. Each of us has our own house. The same goes for us. I'm with you because I love you, nothing more. Why a certificate? Are we going to have a child at this stage of the game?

Thomas laughed.

- Of course not. Let's leave that task to Alice and Frederico. I want to have a marriage certificate, wear a ring on the left hand, throw a little party...

- Oh, my God! A man almost sixty years old dreaming like a young boy.

- And am I not your young boy? Go on, say it.

Valeria shook her head. She got up and lay down on the bed. She embraced Thomas.

- You're my young boy.

- Say it again.

- You're my love, my everything. Now, make me an irresistible marriage proposal. Maybe I'll consider your proposal.

- Well, I was thinking... Frederico and Olivia are getting married in three months, right?

- Right.

- So, we could take advantage and have a joint wedding. One big celebration. Mother and son getting married on the same day! What do you think?

Valeria smiled cheerfully.

- You know, that sounds like a very interesting idea. Let's first talk to Frederico, and then...

Thomas put his finger to her lips.

- Silly girl. I've already arranged everything with Frederico. My stepson loved the idea. Your future daughter-in-law also approved. Natalia has already ordered the invitations, and Adamo will gift you the dress. It will be an intimate reception, for a few friends, at your father's mansion in Morumbi.

– Does that mean the whole family was conspiring behind my back?

– Oh, and the honeymoon is a gift from your stepmother, Lurdes.

– You got me! I can't refuse.

Thomas hugged her and kissed her several times on the face and lips.

– We're getting married! We're getting married!

The wedding of mother and son was featured in the media. Valeria and Thomas went to enjoy their honeymoon in Europe, preferring the charm of Paris. Olivia and Frederico headed to the paradisiacal archipelago of Fernando de Noronha.

The couple was amazed by the beauty of the location. They went diving, enjoyed the dolphins, and explored the beaches in general. They descended from the boat, took off their sandals, and ran along the sand.

Baía do Sancho is one of the most beautiful beaches in Brazil. Isolated, covered with native vegetation, white sand, and emerald-green sea, it is a place of rare beauty.

Olivia gazed at the horizon and said:

Life is beautiful.

– I agree.

– I want to showcase the beauty of life through works of art. I was thrilled to learn that your mother will sponsor my art gallery. You don't know how fulfilled my soul feels. I also want to organize traveling exhibitions, bringing art to distant places with limited access to culture. I'm excited.

Frederico listened to his wife and smiled. Olivia's happiness radiated from every pore. He turned her towards him and looked into her eyes:

Are you happy?

I am.

Do you have any idea how much I love you? – Frederico asked, while adjusting Olivia's hair, whose strands danced to the rhythm of the wind.

– Many times, back in London, when you approached, I was torn. A part of me wanted to embrace you, and another part naturally repelled you. Thank God that feeling has passed, and I only feel love when I'm with you.

– I'm glad you feel that way. I would never do anything to disappoint you or make you sad. There are many people on the planet, and there are many kindred souls. I am fortunate to have found, or rediscovered – he smiled – you.

Olivia said nothing. She hugged him tightly. They stayed like that for a good while, embraced and quiet, feeling their hearts beat serenely.

– Shall we take a walk? – she invited me. – It'll be dark soon.

– Let's, my dear – Frederico replied.

Both felt light-hearted, a sense of total harmony with the spiritual piano. Now, they truly accepted and understood that all these life experiences had been beneficial and necessary for them to take the next step towards achieving happiness.

Frederico extended his arm to Olivia, and their hands intertwined. He turned his face, and their lips drew near. They kissed with love and smiled. They continued walking along the beach as the sun bid farewell. They were in love and happy.

### *To whom I dedicate my words:*

For over forty years, I have been in contact with Spiritism, and my life has positively transformed as I found myself facing the eternity of the spirit and the magnitude of existence. The books I psychographed enriched me with values, and I know that many readers have awakened to spirituality through these novels.

Through these works, you and I have automatically built a great bond, invisible to human eyes but strong and powerful in the eyes of the spirit. Even though we are physically distant, we are connected by these ties that strengthen our spirits, united in the same objective of progress and harmony with good, always!

I hope that, upon reading our stories, you can become aware of your degree of responsibility in life and activate the inner key to live better with yourself and others, making the world a much more interesting and enjoyable place.

Marco Aurelio and I wish that you continue to tread your path of goodness and that your life becomes increasingly full of happiness, success, and peace. Feel free to write to me and share the feelings our books have awakened in you.

I understand that some people prefer anonymity or wish to contact me discreetly, without using social media. For this reason, write to the email: leitoresdomarcelo@gmail.com. This way, we can establish contact.

With affection,

*Marcelo Cezar*

## Zibia Gasparetto's Greatest success stories

With more than 20 million titles sold, the author has contributed to the strengthening of spiritualist literature in the publishing market and to the popularization of spirituality. Learn more of the author's successes.

## Romances Dictated by the Spirit Lucius

The Life Force

The Truth of each one

Life knows what it does

She trusted in life

Between Love and War

Esmeralda

Thorns of Time

Eternal Bonds

Nothing is by Chance

Nobody is Nobody's

God's Advocate

Tomorrow Belongs to God

Love Won

Unexpected Encounter

On the Edge of Destiny

The Sly One

The Morro of Illusions

Where is Teresa?

Through the Doors of the Heart

When Life chooses

When the Hour Comes

When it is necessary to return

Opening for Life

Not afraid to live

Only love can do it

We Are All Innocent

Everything has its price

It was all worth it

A real love

Overcoming the past

**Other success stories by André Luiz Ruiz and Lucius**

The Love Never Forgets You Trilogy

The Strength of Kindness

Under the Hands of Mercy

Saying Goodbye to Earth

At the End of the Last Hour

Sculpting Your Destiny

There are Flowers on the Stones

The Crags are made of Sand

**Books of Eliana Machado Coelho and Schellida**

Hearts without Destiny

The Shine of Truth

The Right to be Happy

The Return

In the Silence of Passions

Strength to Begin Again

The Certainty of Victory

The Conquest of Peace

Lessons Life Offers

Stronger than Ever

No Rules for Loving

A Diary in Time

A Reason to Live

Eliana Machado Coelho and Schellida, Romances that captivate, teach, move and

can change your life!

# Romances of Arandi Gomes Texeira and The Count J.W. Rochester

Lancaster County

The Power of Love

The Trial

Cleopatra's Bracelet

The Reincarnation of a Queen

You Are Gods

**Books of Marcelo Cezar and Marco Aurelio**

Love is for the Strong

The Last Chance

Nothing is as it Seems

Forever With Me

Only God Knows

You Make Tomorrow

A Breath of Tenderness

# Books of Vera Kryzhanovskaia and JW Rochester

The Revenge of the Jew

The Nun of the Marriages

The Sorcerer's Daughter

The Flower of the Swamp

The Divine Wrath

The Legend of the Castle of Montignoso

The Death of the Planet

The Night of Saint Bartholomew

The Revenge of the Jew

Blessed are the poor in spirit

Cobra Capella

Dolores

Trilogy of the Kingdom of Shadows

From Heaven to Earth

Episodes from the Life of Tiberius

Infernal Spell

Herculanum

On the Frontier

Naema, the Witch

In the Castle of Scotland (Trilogy 2)

New Era

The Elixir of Long Life
The Pharaoh Mernephtah
The Lawgivers
The Magicians
The Terrible Phantom
Paradise without Adam
Romance of a Queen
Czech Luminaries
Hidden Narratives
The Nun of the Marriages

## Books of Elisa Masselli

There is always a reason
Nothing goes unanswered
Life is made of decisions
The Mission of each one
Something more is needed
The Past does not matter
Destiny in his hands
God was with him
When the past does not pass
Just beginning

## Books of Vera Lúcia Marinzeck de Carvalhoç and Patricia

Violets in the Window
Living in the Spirit World
The Writer's House
Flight of the Seagull

## Vera Lúcia Marinzeck de Carvalho and Antônio Carlos

Love your Enemies
Slave Bernardino
the Rock of Lovers
Rosa, the third fatality
Captives and Freed

**Books of Mónica de Castro y Leonel**

In spite of everything

Love is not to be trifled with

Face to Face with the Truth

Of My Whole Being

I wish

The Price of Being Different

Twins

Giselle, The Inquisitor's Mistress

Greta

Till Life Do You Part

Impulses of the Heart

Jurema of the Jungle

The Actress

The Force of Destiny

Memories that the Wind Brings

Secrets of the Soul

Feeling in One's Own Skin

World Spiritist Institute

www.ingramcontent.com/pod-product-compliance
Lightning Source LLC
LaVergne TN
LVHW041739060526
838201LV00046B/857